CANCERLAND

CANCERLAND

A MEDICAL MEMOIR

DAVID SCADDEN, M.D.,

PROFESSOR OF MEDICINE,
HARVARD UNIVERSITY

WITH MICHAEL D'ANTONIO

THOMAS DUNNE BOOKS
ST. MARTIN'S PRESS
NEW YORK

AUTHOR'S NOTE: THIS IS A TRUE STORY, THOUGH
SOME NAMES AND DETAILS HAVE BEEN CHANGED.

THOMAS DUNNE BOOKS.
An imprint of St. Martin's Press.

CANCERLAND. Copyright © 2018 by David Scadden
and Michael D'Antonio. All rights reserved. Printed
in the United States of America. For information,
address St. Martin's Press, 175 Fifth Avenue, New
York, N.Y. 10010.

www.thomasdunnebooks.com
www.stmartins.com

The Library of Congress Cataloging-in-Publication
Data is available upon request.

ISBN 978-1-250-09275-5 (hardcover)
ISBN 978-1-250-09277-9 (ebook)

Our books may be purchased in bulk for promotional,
educational, or business use. Please contact your local
bookseller or the Macmillan Corporate and Premium
Sales Department at 1-800-221-7945, extension 5442, or
by email at MacmillanSpecialMarkets@macmillan.com.

First Edition: July 2018

10 9 8 7 6 5 4 3 2 1

FOR KATHRYN, MARGARET, ELIZABETH, AND NED

CONTENTS

THERE ARE ONLY TWO LASTING BEQUESTS WE CAN
HOPE TO GIVE OUR CHILDREN. ONE OF THESE IS
ROOTS, THE OTHER, WINGS.

—JOHANN WOLFGANG VON GOETHE

CANCERLAND

INTRODUCTION

Mundt just disappeared. Mrs. Sullivan was spoken of in hushed tones before she, too, disappeared. Mrs. Macchi just slipped into the darkness of her home and never reappeared. They all moved from the living to the cancer-stricken, and my knowledge of them as a child was that cancer equaled irredeemable loss, unspoken of, incomprehensible and deeply sad. I suspect that experience was shared broadly fifty years ago and may be still. But it is wrong, or at least incomplete. Cancer no longer hoods hope, no longer is a mysterious vengeance of higher powers and slowly is becoming the thing that changes people's lives, but something they can speak of in past tense. This book is some effort to map how much has changed in the nearly four decades of this oncologist's experience and why. How ideas and serendipity evolve into medical advances at least as viewed by someone who has had a seat in the theater of change.

The book came about because Michael D'Antonio and I were speaking of how much of what happens in science remains unknown to people outside of it. Science is a way of thinking about and discovering the basis for things we know through our experience. We know them, but don't know what causes them or how to change them. Science gives us a glimpse of what underlies or is the cause of what we experience by perturbing some element of the composite. By so doing, it defines what causes the composite to be what it is. That inherently gives some power to then change what is. Science, at least life science, opens the possibility of not just knowing what is but shaping it. Moving from understanding to shaping is inefficient and made all the more so when it involves people rather than experimental models in a laboratory. The maddening slowness of medical advance cannot be willed away or engineered out of the process. There are simply too many uncertainties. Michael and I thought that by opening the door on the process of medical advance, particularly in cancer, it might bring light and hope and perhaps some inspired action to accelerate the change we all so desperately need.

The experience of most when encountering cancer is to step into a foreign land, Cancerland. It is populated by unknown concepts, new imperatives for daily living, and people who seem too technical and remote to be real. However, every doctor, nurse, and technician you meet will have a deep and personal experience with some form of this disease. This is often true for the receptionist who checks your name on the roster of appointments and the phlebotomist who draws your blood. In fact, on some level, we all have a personal connection to cancer because it is so common that it must be regarded as not an aberrant event but part of the human condition.

Roughly half of us will be diagnosed with cancer, and one in five Americans will die from it. Cancer is, as it has always been, such an immutable fact of life that in many families, stories of cancer are passed from generation to generation in hushed and fearful tones. Typically, the tale is told with metaphors that summon images of war. Patients are brave "fighters." Treatment is a "battle" against an "enemy," and death is greeted as a "defeat."

Considering cancer's fearsome effects and the difficult challenge it presents to patients, caregivers, and science, the martial metaphors come easily and can be truly apt. This was especially true in the past, when cancer was so little understood that people often imagined it as an invader from some foreign place. Among the ancients, cancer was believed to be caused by, among other things, evil spirits and the influence of wicked men. This was true even in the 1950s, in the leafy, comfortable, middle-class suburb of Wyckoff, New Jersey, where I grew up among some deeply religious people who felt that certain kinds of illnesses reflected badly on the sufferer. Cancer was, in their view, a product of moral failure or spiritual crisis. Others feared that cancer was an infectious disease, like the flu, and that you could catch it via exposure to someone who had it. This belief instilled shame in people who were diagnosed with cancer and fear in those who knew them. The result was isolation that deepened the suffering of all.

In my Wyckoff years, I knew three people who developed cancer and died. One was the mother of my friend Johnny Sullivan. She was diagnosed after the birth of Johnny's brother Paul. As she grew sicker, Mrs. Sullivan withdrew from view. After she died, her passing wasn't discussed, although we kids observed that Mr. Sullivan had taken charge of everything that went on in the family. He was father, mother, and grieving husband, all at once.

Second in my childhood experience with cancer was a woman who lived next door to our house on tree-lined Carlton Road, Mrs. Macchi. She had lung cancer. I was allowed—encouraged, actually—to visit her. The idea was that this visit would somehow brighten her day. Her house was extremely quiet, with the shades drawn, and she was so gaunt that I was terrified by her appearance. She was very grateful that we came to see her, but I was so afraid, I was speechless.

The experience reinforced a lesson that my parents taught by example throughout their lives. They always believed that if you could be of some help to someone, you had an obligation to act. They did this themselves in many ways. What stands out is my mother assembling packages for families in Eastern Europe (the Iron Curtain still hung) and helping find jobs for those who got through. My father hired jobless men transitioning from Puerto Rico, but it nearly broke him when he saw those same people looting his store in Paterson, New Jersey, during the race riots of the 1960s. However, I never saw my parents turn away from or cast anything but a sympathetic eye toward a person in need. My maternal grandparents were generous in the same way. They helped to literally build their community's church with hammers and saws, lumber and nails. At their home they kept spare rooms for people in need. When a family arrived this part of the house would be named for them, becoming, for example, "the Smiths' place" and then "the Joneses' place." They were of very modest means, but they believed in action on behalf of others. They were nurturing people of exceptional warmth. My grandmother baked and regularly turned our kitchen into a small factory for tins of cookies and doughnuts to give away. My baseball glove shared the same storage room with the tins, to which I account my being chosen early in pickup games. My grandfather, a photographer, let me stand by his side in the basement darkroom and experiment with the magic of making black-and-white prints. The combination of chemistry and art impressed me deeply, making clear that creativity and science were partners, not separate realms.

The third case of cancer in my childhood experience involved a boy in my second-grade class. His last name was Mundt, and if he went by any other name, I don't recall it today. One day, Mundt just didn't come to class. He never came back. No one seemed to know where he went, and it was made clear that we shouldn't talk about him. Only later did I learn he had died of leukemia.

Mrs. Sullivan, our neighbor, and my classmate Mundt were, in their illnesses, reminders of our mortality, our scientific ignorance, and the limits of medicine. Some people did survive cancer in the 1950s, thanks to either surgery, radiation therapy, chemotherapy, or a combination of these treatments. However, most who were diagnosed with cancer of the breast, lung, colon, or liver—fairly common types—were dead within a year or two. People with acute leukemia, like Mundt, had almost no chance of living for even six months after diagnosis.

What we call leukemia is actually a number of diseases, each affecting the blood and lymphatic system. The two chronic forms of the disease can linger in the body for long periods of time, causing only vague symptoms, including fatigue and night sweats. The two acute leukemias are characterized by more profound fatigue, bone and joint pain, and fever. Seen through the lenses of a microscope, the blood of a leukemia patient exhibits an excess of white cells. (The name of the disease is derived from two Greek words: *leukos*, which means "white," and *haima*, for "blood.") Today, we know the leukemia picture is more complicated. For example, in the type that typically afflicts children, acute lymphoblastic leukemia, the real problem is the wildfire production of lymphoblasts, which are precursors to the mature, infection-fighting white blood cells called lymphocytes. This overproduction of immature cells depresses the creation of mature infection-fighting cells and oxygen-carrying red cells. Under these conditions, patients are extremely vulnerable to infection, bleeding, and organ failure.

Had he been born and diagnosed ten years later, Mundt and his parents could have hoped for a different outcome. In the 1960s, newly refined chemotherapy protocols produced remissions, and by the end of the decade, actual cures were being reported in childhood leukemia. In 1970, the first gene associated with cancer was identified, and in 1971, the so-called War on Cancer was announced by that most embattled of presidents, Richard Nixon. The president held a rare public signing ceremony for the bill and spoke of the effort to find "*a* cure" that would end a scourge that killed more Americans each year than died during all the combat of World War II. Nixon added:

> We would not want to raise false hopes by simply the signing of an act, but we can say this: That for those who have cancer

and who are looking for success in this field, they at least can have the assurance that everything that can be done by government, everything that can be done by voluntary agencies in this great, powerful, rich country, now will be done and that will give some hope, and we hope those hopes will not be disappointed.

After he finished his formal remarks, Nixon picked up a pen and signed his first name on the bill. He then turned and handed the pen to Benno Schmidt Sr., whom he had appointed to oversee the cancer initiative. "Benno," said the president, "you get the Richard." Nixon signed his last name with a second pen, which he then gave to A. Hamblin Letton, M.D., of the American Cancer Society. With this flourish, the act became law, and just as a ribbon-cutting might signal that a new highway is open for traffic, the president seemed to put the country on the path to a great achievement. He certainly hoped this was the case, as he said, "I hope that in the years ahead that we may look back on this day and this action as being the most significant action taken during this administration."

I read about the big new cancer research program when I was in high school. Like everyone else, I hoped that this effort would yield yet another great leap forward for science and technology, like NASA's Project Apollo, which had put men on the moon in a little more than eight years' time. I had been the kid in my neighborhood who launched rockets in the backyard and tracked down creatures from a local creek for what now seem horribly cruel experiments. The rockets often turned unwittingly into bombs, I still bear the scars from one, but fortunately, my knowledge of amphibian anatomy was not due to combining these interests. But science seemed equivalent to discovery, and if I could hear men declaring a "giant leap for mankind" from the moon, surely the war on cancer could be won.

When I wasn't outside, I was likely under duress helping my

father work on one project or another around our home. My father, who was also named David, was a self-taught mechanical wizard. He could repair just about anything, from a washing machine transmission to a balky heating system. His only formal training had been in the navy, in which he enlisted after the Japanese raid on Pearl Harbor, where he was sent soon after he became a seaman. He was bright, diligent, and good at fixing navigation systems, so he was sent a letter offering him a spot in Officer Candidate School. However, when it came time for him to report, he decided that he didn't want to spend the war at a desk on a protected base so removed from the fighting and the real business of winning a war. He tucked the letter into his pocket and dove into the ocean for a swim. The letter shredded, and he remained an enlisted man who would take the risk and the adventure of working at sea.

During his wartime service, my dad went from ship to ship, an itinerant navigation system specialist. His narrowest escape came when he was aboard a lightly armed destroyer tender, and a nearby ship—which was loaded with munitions—exploded. The explosion sent bombs and rockets flying into dozens of nearby ships, killing hundreds of men, including one in every three of his shipmates. Although ankle deep in blood, my father survived without a scratch. He rarely spoke of this, but it affected him deeply, giving him a great gratitude for just being alive. To me, he embodied virtues of what came to be known as the Greatest Generation, being far more interested in doing things than in talking about them or in wishing for what he didn't have.

After the war, my father came home to Connecticut, met my mother during a summer vacation in Massachusetts, and followed her to New Jersey, where he found work fixing office machines. He eventually bought out his employer, becoming a small business owner. There really wasn't anything he couldn't repair. One of my proudest moments in childhood came when I actually found the fix for some broken item we were both hunched over in the basement. He smiled as I explained it. He didn't say anything, but that visual hug was one of the most affirming moments of my young life.

My father's passion for figuring out how stuff worked made it easy for him to say yes when I asked for a chemistry set. He went one step further, setting up a little lab space for me in the basement of our family home. Here it helped to live in Wyckoff, where the nearby Fisher Scientific Corporation operated a sizable factory. My mother, who supported my interests and tolerated the strange odors produced by my experiments, sometimes took me to visit the company, where some of the workers showed me around, answered my questions, and let me take home beakers, test tubes, and pipettes that they were about to throw away.

The encouragement I received from my mother and father played a major role in my eventual choice of a life in science and medicine. One other major influence in those early years was Salvatore Baldino, who was our family physician. Dr. Baldino was the kind of general internist who wasn't afraid to treat people other general practice doctors might refer to specialists. He treated me for allergies that caused asthma, administering injections of the very substances that caused me to cough and wheeze.

As scientists discovered at the start of the twentieth century, by experimenting with serums made from pollen, the human immune system could be trained to stop overreacting to the microscopic substances in the environment that cause periodic illness like hay fever and a similar malady called "rose colds." (The breakthrough work was done by Leonard Noon and John Freeman, in Britain, who experimented with serum made from the pollen of timothy, which produces a long, feathery flower head.) As patients receive gradually increasing concentrations of serum, typically on a weekly basis, they become less sensitive to the substance and their immune responses become more normal. Spring comes, grasses, trees, and flowers bloom, but the sneezing and sniffling fail to appear.

Once I got accustomed to the routine, I rode my bike to Dr. Baldino's office and devoured the newsmagazines while I waited for my appointment. My appointments were always at the end of the day, which meant we could chat after the injections were finished. Dr. Baldino was genuinely interested in me as a person. When he asked, "How are you?" I knew he wanted a complete answer and not just a report on my symptoms. He wanted to know about my family life, how things were going in school, and what I was doing in my free time. He was, in other words, a role model as a physician. And fortunately for me, the communication went both ways. If I asked about my treatment or something else related to medicine, he shared what he knew and described the areas that remained a mystery and needed more study. This gave me a sense of science as an ongoing project, something exciting that was continually reaching new frontiers.

In the 1960s and early 1970s, scientists were regarded as explorers, less heralded than but on par with the astronauts. It seemed that life was being transformed by what legions of engineers and mathematicians contributed. I was awestruck by what I saw in science exhibits at the 1964 World's Fair; by hearing my parents speak of the fear of polio when they were children that I did not have to think twice about and simply had to stand in line at our town hall for my shot or sugar cube; by watching a man actually set foot on the celestial body of the moon; and what—a test tube baby? Certainly President Nixon understood this truth as he tried to make solving the many riddles of cancer central to his legacy or, at the very least, part of his bid for reelection. He followed his declaration of war with a proclamation making March "Cancer Control Month," and prior to the election, First Lady Pat Nixon was honored at a gala held by the American Cancer Society. The event, covered by the press, gave her husband's campaign a boost.

If anyone found it strange that the White House referenced "cancer control" as if it were something to be managed, like crabgrass or mosquitoes, no mention was made of it in the press. Of course, this was a time when many people felt science and technology were advancing so rapidly that almost anything, from the atom to the Nile River, could somehow be mastered. President Kennedy had summoned an army of engineers who spent billions of dollars and got us to the moon in roughly eight years. Why wouldn't people imagine that cancer, which seemed like one disease manifested in myriad ways, would be vulnerable to a similar effort? Even in medicine, where the Salk and Sabin polio vaccines were recent developments, Americans were accustomed to grand achievements.

It seemed that the country was excited by the prospect of a victory in the war against cancer, with news outlets focusing a great deal of attention on developments occurring after the Nixon announcement. Thanks to articles like "Hope in Chemicals Declared," which ran in *The New York Times*, many people came to expect miracles in short order. During the summer after Nixon's announcement, a press release noting the promise of research into a certain chemical compound led to wide press speculation about a drug found to be "100 percent effective against cancer in animals." No such drug actually existed, but medical centers were deluged with telephone calls about it. Cancer patients and their families trekked to Oak Ridge, Tennessee, and literally begged to get this compound from a doctor who was mentioned in the press.

Episodes similar to the one in Oak Ridge would arise with regularity as journalists and the public tried to understand reports on various streams of cancer research. A good example is the term *carcinogen*, which seeped into the vernacular, but in the struggle to navigate the science, it was easy to get lost. Most forms of radiation and many chemicals are known to cause cancer and are therefore regarded as carcinogens. The compounds in tobacco smoke may be the most well-established carcinogens, and antismoking campaigns have, predictably, helped reduce lung cancer in men almost every year since 1975.

However, exposure to a carcinogen, even tobacco smoke, does not guarantee that someone will develop cancer. The number of exposures matters in this dynamic, as do factors like a person's genetic makeup and the strength of his or her immune system. These complicating factors allow for both reasonable doubts and mischief-making by those who might profit from pointing out the fact that cause and effect is extremely hard to establish when you get down to individual cases. How could the general public square the fact that smoking caused cancer with the competing fact that most people who smoked died of something else? Certainly the tobacco companies made much of this disconnect. The industry-sponsored pseudoscientific research distorted the public's understanding of the health effects of its products and hid research findings connecting smoking to cancer and other illnesses. This disinformation campaign would become the model for future efforts to obscure scientific agreement on many other issues, including climate change. Practitioners of this dark art would prevail.

In the case of cancer, more confusion would arise as other compounds were linked to various forms of cancer in laboratory animals, and then skeptics pointed out that almost anything would make a lab rat sick if the exposure was great enough. The best-known example of this phenomenon involved the artificial sweetener cyclamate, which was banned as the result of animal studies that were subsequently refuted by more thoroughgoing research. In the mid-1970s, with researchers producing a torrent of new work, *Newsweek* posed the question "What Causes Cancer?" on its cover. The answer included a host of things, including medications, food, and many chemicals in our environment. Smoking was left out.

If all the competing reports on the causes of cancer weren't enough to make people throw up their hands in exasperation, then the ballyhoo that accompanied claims about various cures would be. Worst of all was the disappointment that came as hopes were dashed by those who, for various reasons, promoted, sold, and administered ineffective, unproven, and sometimes dangerous "treatments" to people with cancer. Here the one-word symbol would be a substance called Laetrile, which was derived from apricot pits and used, originally, as a meat preservative.

Highly toxic (one of its compounds was cyanide), Laetrile had been tried as a cancer treatment in the Soviet Union. In 1972, a U.S. lab reported that it had inhibited secondary tumors in mice that already had cancer. Laetrile did nothing against the existing disease, and this hopeful finding was later proved to be in error. Nevertheless, news reports were enough to spark a huge controversy. Promoters, among them an orthodontist and a professional wrestler, skirted the law to give Laetrile to people with cancer. Their supporters, who believed that a conspiracy was afoot to deprive them of the chemical, lobbied successfully to make this treatment legal in more than two dozen states. A national poll found that despite the overwhelming opposition of physicians and scientists, a huge majority of Americans favored legalizing Laetrile as a cancer treatment.

No reliable study ever found Laetrile to be effective against any human disease. Thousands of people who were injected with it suffered needlessly before the fad petered out. A *New York Times* editorial published at the time suggested that unrealistic expectations raised by "the Government's War on cancer" had set the conditions for both the controversy and a "bitter divorce between the public and physicians." As the legislators who legalized Laetrile against the overwhelming science demonstrated, trust in medicine had reached a low point. The paper also warned that "because of the continuing intractability of cancer, Laetrile will doubtless be resurrected in a new form" in the future.

The challenge of understanding cancer, including its intractability, was highly compelling to idealistic young people who noted the attention it was receiving across the social spectrum, from the White House to the press to the families desperate for treatment. I was among them. Although I had headed off to college certain I would study the humanities, my experience in a handful of science classes rekindled my interest in medicine as practiced by Dr. Baldino: a fusion between science and humanism. Raised to believe I had a responsibility to serve others, I imagined working as a small-town physician would be a dream, and so I applied to medical school. There I discovered both the limitations of what medicine could offer to patients and, despite how much I had to learn, how little was really known about the workings of the body. The revolutionary ability to understand the body and diseases at the level of molecules, molecular biology, was just beginning. Figuring out how things work at a fundamental level, such as individual molecules and cells, was just electrifying. I didn't think I had the ability to contribute at that level, but it was clear medicine would be transformed by it, and I wanted to be a part of making it happen.

I knocked on the door of Adel Mahmoud, a fabulous physician and scientist, and an inspiring teacher. He was working on how a dreaded parasite, Schistosoma mansoni, could outwit the immune system and cause the devastating liver diseases he had seen growing up in Egypt. He welcomed my clumsy presence in his lab. I spent whatever hours I could steal from my classes and rotations in his lab mostly making a mess but loving the chance to connect with solving a real problem. Nothing was more compelling than discovering for the sake of relieving misery. It drives me to this day. I added nothing to the lab's effort, I am sure, but it gave me a passion for trying to figure things out. Trying to understand a process to gain some dominion over it so that, just maybe, it could be tamed to help people I knew needed it.

I left medical school for the postgraduate training program I thought was the most rigorously committed to using science for patient care in the country, the Brigham and Women's Hospital at Harvard Medical School. It was tough, demanding, and unbelievably rewarding. Nothing was accepted on the basis of "because that is the way we do things." People, from interns to the most senior faculty, were expected to defend their decisions based on either scientific study or logical deduction from what science could offer. It is now called evidence-based medicine and is a commonplace, but the Brigham stood out then as it does today for baking that into the culture and into every patient care discussion.

One day, I got a call from my parents. My mother had advanced cancer. I was an intern and pretty frayed by the every-other- or every-third-night-on-call schedule. Thirty-six hours on, twelve off would now be considered torture. I was struggling to keep up with the patients under my care and still tie my shoes. My family was a cushion of comfort and stability I knew I could rely on. That was now gone. Not even the bright light of my mother was without jeopardy. I couldn't take time off, but a friend told me of the hospital toll-free line so I could check in often. That nearly got me fired: it turns out toll-free was anything but. I finally got my mother to have surgery at the Brigham. It was wrenching to be there as family and intern, but at least I could stay close to what was unfolding.

The paucity of options for my mother made my decision about training for me. I had to go into cancer care. But as I read more and got involved more, it seemed that clinical oncology research was largely focused on mixing and matching different combinations of poisons. There was a paucity of science beyond pharmacology. Hematology and the study of blood cancers were, in contrast, increasingly driven by the emerging field of molecular biology. Indeed, hematologists had almost invented what we now call precision medicine in blood banking and transplantation, where lab analysis of specific blood features could indicate compatibility or danger. In cancer, blood cancers were being recognized as distinctive because of specific genetic abnormalities. It seemed that figuring things out was closest to having an impact on people through the study of the blood, so I chose both hematology and oncology as my subspecialties within internal medicine.

The choice of specialties was also affected by a sense that when confronting cancer, people are their neediest and their most authentic selves. It is a time when connection to others is intense, but real and simple kindness resonates long. The darkness of the diagnosis dissolves veneers while putting deep values in sharp relief. For patients, their loved ones, and my fellow caregivers, cancer largely sweeps away what distracts us so much of the time and reveals the very essence of what it means to be human. In this state, we are revealed, and in the vast majority of cases, what can be seen is inspiring.

Given the options of science and medicine, I chose both. The decision led me to a forty-year devotion to the problem of cancer as it presents itself in our lives, in our laboratories, and, given its wider implications, in its social context. In this time, I have marveled at astounding advances in our understanding and felt intensely grateful to be working in this era of discovery. I have also been required, by experience, to accept that today's promise is often tomorrow's disappointment and that the processes that produce health and illness are incredibly complex. A telling example can be drawn from my own area of research. Where once we thought it was enough to know that our bone marrow is responsible for the production of blood cells, we now appreciate that the marrow and the adjoining cells engage in a complex dance that enables cell production. The niche that makes up this specialized environment wasn't widely recognized until about 1980, and we are still learning about how it works.

The complexity of different body systems helps to explain why laboratory advances and even experimental successes with animals do not necessarily translate into therapies for people with cancer. But we should not be discouraged by the fact that seeming leaps forward turn out to be smaller steps toward understanding. All the science that has gone before has brought us to a place where, as we develop more sophisticated understanding of disease, we can begin to imagine more sophisticated methods of treatment.

Today's research efforts bring together more teams comprising different kinds of scientists, including chemists, cell biologists, physicists, and engineers, than were ever seen in laboratories of old. Today, we even include experts in so-called big data analytics and information technology on our teams because these disciplines help us to understand profoundly complex systems and manage knowledge.

The current state of science and medicine finds us tantalized by possibilities. Cancer therapies that rely on engineered viruses and immune cells improved in the laboratory have been successful in small trials. Research has produced vaccines that can prevent certain kinds of malignancies, such as cervical cancer and liver cancer, by creating immunity against so-called oncoviruses, including human papillomavirus and the hepatitis B virus. Others, which have been approved to treat metastatic prostate cancer and melanoma, appear to be effective against active disease. The genetic variety found in cancers suggests that we may never find a silver-bullet vaccine to stop all malignancies. However, rapid advances in the technology that sequences genes offer hope that custom-made immunotherapies could be within reach.

More promise is coming from work on stem cells, including some of the projects in my own lab, and from investigations into the naturally occurring immune processes that keep mutations from developing into cancer. These and other developments, including technologies that allow for more precise surgery, radiation therapy, and chemotherapy agents, have yielded big headlines in the press. When a program such as *60 Minutes* tells viewers about brain cancer cured with attenuated polio viruses, as it did in 2015, excitement ripples through entire communities of people concerned with cancer.

Everyone hopes that we have arrived at a point where effective, less-toxic treatments and even cures for a host of cancers are at hand. Huge industries are emerging to support research into the treatments of the future, and the people who run clinical centers stress that they offer the very latest—*custom-tailored treatment* is the term of art—to patients who come seeking care. No one wants to miss out, and as a consequence, we are beginning to see a flood of advertising by hospitals and companies that make medical technologies. In New York City, you can even tune your radio to hear weekly hour-long broadcasts by a radiation oncologist who pitches his treatments as an effective therapy for patients who have been told by other doctors that they have no options.

With so much talk about potential breakthroughs and so much publicity touting options for care, a bubble of expectation is ever present. The pressure of this bubble is felt by every person who has an interest in cancer, which means all of us. We live in a time when molecular science is moving at an extraordinary pace, revealing the innermost secrets of how the body works, and our discoveries are giving us good reason to hope. The people, places, and ideas that energize these hopes are exciting to behold. However, we must balance our hope with understanding, lest we become diverted from the course that will serve us best.

ONE

DAWN OF THE BIOLOGICAL AGE

It says something that at many medical schools, a student's first contact with a patient involves a cadaver in an anatomy lab. For most medical students, the dissection of a human body, one often shared with a partner or two, is a rite of passage that reveals the physical, emotional, and spiritual reality of medicine while shielding them from the more challenging task of facing a living, breathing human being in an examination room. As much as people talk about the challenge of this process, it is far more difficult to work with a patient who can feel the impact of what a physician may say or do.

It also says something about my medical education, at Case Western Reserve University, that my first encounter with a patient was with a woman expecting a child. All students were introduced to an expectant mother with whom they were to interact and visit in medical settings and on house calls during their education. It was an incredibly powerful affirmation of what medicine is about and spoke legions about what the school valued and why I went there. Although respect and empathy are the expected norm in all cases, the cadaver model impresses a doctor in training with the facts of anatomy and, let's face it, death. The Case approach, which sent entering med students to visit women at home, take their vital signs, and guide them through the process of obtaining prenatal care, emphasized life.

My first patient, a woman Yvonne Anderson,* lived in a tough neighborhood off Euclid Avenue in downtown Cleveland. She was single and younger than I was, but when we met, *I* was the nervous one. I was twenty-three years old and feeling acutely the extent to which I *didn't* know medicine. But Yvonne sensed that she and I were learning the ropes of the medical system together and at least I might help by being inside it—something she certainly didn't feel as an African American first-time mother. Maybe I could at least help Yvonne navigate the system and get the best care for herself and her soon-to-arrive baby.

When I made my first home visit to Yvonne's, it was an epiphany. I knew medicine would stretch my mind about science. I didn't know how much it would open my eyes to cultures, the stuff for which there was no section of books in the medical library. I was about as white bread as anyone could be and walked down Yvonne's street for that first visit with my heart in my throat (medical term). All antennae were activated, as the neighborhood was not one I would have walked down even when in Paterson or New York. Shades were drawn on every window in every house, including hers. The doorbell didn't work, and the lack of response from my knock had me ready to spin around and head for cover. Then the door opened, and Yvonne gave me a stern look and walked me through dark rooms to the kitchen, where I would be expected to perform before her skeptical mother. One ceiling bulb, four mismatched chairs, and a table were the setting for the interrogation. Short-cropped answers from them, too-long, overcomplicated verbiage storms from me, and then we actually had a conversation. I was so relieved when a first laugh seemed to signal détente. By the end, Yvonne was making it clear that it was the two of us who would work together and win over the mom, who knew she would end up taking care of everything anyway. She made clear she knew more about

*Name changed to protect patient's privacy.

pregnancy and childbirth than I did, and I didn't mind getting a real-world education from her. It worked out, and I did indeed learn a ton from the Andersons. They taught me that medicine always exists in a human context. That context impacts what people hear. White and black, side by side, hearing the same words from the obstetrician—we often had different interpretations. I wasn't naive enough to think this wouldn't happen, but I never expected how extensive it would be and how it could really affect the quality of care and health itself. There was so much suspicion about doctors' motives and so little ability to pay for the nonprescription part of medical care that it was eye-opening. It was also hard to know without seeing up close the impact of the stress from poverty and the anxieties that come with living in an area that was so rife with crime that everyone kept the shades drawn to confuse would-be burglars. (It took me a while to figure out that safety was the reason that the Johnson home was so dark. In a crime-ridden neighborhood it was best to keep your business, and your posessions, out of view.) My thinking and my way of communicating with patients were forever changed by my experience with Yvonne.

In 1976, when I arrived at Case, much of Cleveland lived with the pressures that Yvonne and her family dealt with every day. Labor issues and foreign competition in steel, cars, and other industries had destroyed so many jobs in the city that it was steadily losing population. In two years, Cleveland would become the first big city to default on its debt since the Great Depression. Then there was the environment. The air and water in Cleveland were notoriously polluted. In 1969, an oil slick on the Cuyahoga River caught fire. A river on fire! First-year medical students were given T-shirts with that image stating, CLEVELAND: YOU'VE GOT TO BE TOUGH. But it was a fabulous place to learn about medicine and people's lives and how the two collided. My friends and I all volunteered in the funky Cleveland Free Clinic in the evenings, getting a rich supplement to our cultural education. I felt I could navigate things better for my patients when

Yvonne delivered her healthy daughter, Annette, and went to the pediatrician visits. I was going to class to learn about the body, but it was in the clinical experiences that I learned how to help people.

It was extraordinary to be first connected to hospital medicine through a birth. The word *awestruck* aptly captures what it was like to be a clueless medical student in the delivery suite, serving half as physician, half as patient advocate. Fortunately, not much was expected, because I was wobbly kneed through the whole experience. In the presence of a miracle, doing more than standing with mouth agape was beyond me. By the end of medical school, I had delivered more than a dozen babies, including twins, and done minor procedures postdelivery. Participating in the joy with parents at a delivery and understanding the remarkable state of pregnancy drew me to the field. But the need and the impact of emerging science were less evident to me in obstetrics, and I eventually turned away.

I was somehow compelled by basic scientific research, especially in the area of molecular biology. No one with even the slightest interest could have missed the fact that by the 1970s we had entered a revolutionary period. Great advances were being made toward understanding the chemical secrets of life itself, and with each new discovery, we were getting closer to designing more rational treatments that would save lives and ease suffering. These advances created their own big questions for politicians, religious leaders, government regulators, and everyday citizens. The city of Cambridge, Massachusetts, had already banned recombinant DNA research by my first year of medical school. All of society would be engaged in issues prompted by the promise and peril of the biology revolution. I could imagine nothing more compelling.

But as exciting as the scientific moment seemed, I wasn't completely confident in my abilities to participate. In undergraduate classes, I loved organic chemistry, which is the course almost everyone considers the make-or-break subject for people who hope to go into medical school. But organic chemistry is like mathematics, a language. You learn certain fundamental rules for how things relate and you can put them together in creative ways. That nature has done so to make the building blocks of life—proteins, RNA, DNA, lipids, and sugars—captures the imagination. Add the spark of being able to modify things by the same rules, and the language of chemistry starts to become song. But I was just a student, inspired but not equipped to really make the music. I assumed that was only for those born with a determination to be and do chemistry in capital letters. It has a complexity and diversity that can seem almost infinite and was, at the time, opaque and mystifying to me.

The connection to chemistry came back in a wave in the first class in medical school.

That first course, in a subject given the vague title of Metabolism, was supposed to give us a firm grounding in the ways that cells—the fundamental unit of life—create, store, and use energy derived from nutrients to assemble and maintain cells. It was remarkable to me how the reactions and principles of organic chemistry turned into the very basis for life. It was also remarkable how complex it all rapidly became. For a few of my fellow students, who had studied a great deal of science as undergraduates (I was an English major), the subject was so easy that they sat and read the morning *New York Times* while grunts like me struggled to understand the lectures. I didn't know whether I was not as bright as my classmates or there was something unusually hard about this course, but I truly struggled with it. Also, I felt uncomfortable just saying, "I'm stuck; help me." For all I knew, I was the only one feeling so lost.

Unlike at some other schools, where competition was overt and the general attitude was "survive it if you can," we were encouraged to think of each other as colleagues who learned together. In that very first course, I discovered classmates like Bruce Walker—one of my closest friends to this day—who were eager to both give and receive help. Away from the lecture halls, we often met in groups to review lectures that were sometimes filled with daunting medical and scientific details. Together, we solidified our understanding of the material but also considered how it all might relate to the responsibilities we would assume when we started caring for people whose well-being and even continued existence would depend on us.

Even though we were first-year students, far from becoming actual doctors, most of us were late-1960s idealists who wanted to use our talents and opportunities to help others. The people I knew didn't seem to focus on money or status, and they voiced strong advocacy for doing the right thing for patients. There was an implicit suspicion of the commercial side of medicine. Those I knew took very seriously the commitment to making the world better, to literally alleviate suffering. The anxiety most often spoken was that we might go into the world and make a serious, even fatal mistake with a patient because we missed something crucial in med school. With this in mind, we got together in the evenings and on weekends and tutored each other. Since classes were six days a week, the big break was when the dean of admissions would invite us over on a Sunday afternoon for croquet, cookies, and beer—a spectacular break even when your ball ended up deep in the poison ivy. For a few of us, the itch to get away was too great, and we took a weekend bicycling in Vermont rather than studying biostatistics. To a person, we learned to regret that gap in our knowledge made worse by the solid drenching of Green Mountain rain.

The tradition of student tutoring was well established at Case and kept all but the most ill-focused from falling behind. Once we got into the clinical time of our schooling, the third and fourth year of medical school, we were split into smaller and smaller groups, but the sense that doctoring meant continuous learning and teaching and learning again was preserved. People started distinguishing themselves by clinical specialties and areas of research. In the late 1970s, medicine was becoming more specialized as new disciplines arrived with their own requirements for training, testing, licensure, and standards for practice. Medical oncology was not a formal specialty until 1972, and many physicians eschewed any kind of subspecialty board testing and certification until it became imperative for participating in the era of managed care, the 1980s. This was not an entirely new idea. Physicians in ancient Egypt, believing each part of the body to be a separate entity, specialized along the lines of anatomy. In the modern era, some specialties like radiology emerged out of new technologies. However, the push for specialization came from those who believed that both clinical care and science would improve as minds were focused more intently on limited areas of interest and the amount of information in each burgeoned. Specialty information required specialty-specific knowledge that was tested by specialty-specific exams. This has led to an ever-heavier burden of credentials that physicians maintain, to the point of now-evident subspecialist revolt. But for medical students, it represented mostly a spectrum of information and activities that allowed them to sort themselves into comfortable spots across the spectrum. It also became evident that each specialty seemed to have a culture and an accepted set of behaviors. Personality-type matching with specialties was oddly predictable. The brooding self-reflectors never made the OR home, and the ex-athlete or ex-military rarely found the intangibles of psychiatry appealing.

I was inspired by all the advances being made in biology and genetic technologies, which were sending waves of excitement through this former English major, if not the medical world more broadly. This work promised to make comprehensible the opaque world of cancer and perhaps the immune system. Cancers of the blood, which reside in the realms of both hematology and oncology, were most compelling for study because you could see the disease evolve at the level of the cell by simple blood samples. What the patient was experiencing was sometimes vague, but the blood was more eloquent, revealing whether fatigue represented poor sleep or regrowing leukemia cells. Other so-called solid tumors were rarely so evident, requiring scans and x-rays and ultimately biopsies. To me, the proximity of patient symptoms to cells in the blood was very compelling. It seemed that the basis for the disease had to be closer to comprehension if you could actually visualize what was going on by blood samples. It was also apparent that cells of the blood were what protected us from invaders of all types: viruses, bacteria, fungi, and maybe cancer. Studying the blood seemed to me like a way to ride the rocket of new discoveries in molecular biology and have them meaningfully turn into therapies I could give to patients.

But before I could get aboard, I had to understand the landscape of the relevant science, which was changing faster than the seasons.

Most scientists recognize the creation of the first model of a DNA molecule, by James Watson and Francis Crick, as the breakthrough that began the era of molecular biology. (As *The New York Times* noted on its front page, their so-called double helix image brought us "near the secret of life.") At the time when their work was published, the British Crick and the American Watson were little known outside their specialty. A bookish man, Crick would say his one hobby was "conversation." A child prodigy who had appeared on the *Quiz Kids* radio show—sponsored by Alka-Seltzer—Watson had been briefly famous but then immersed himself in academia. He and Crick did their work at the University of Cambridge in a one-story, metal-roofed building affectionately called the Hut. However, there was nothing modest about their achievement, and as James Watson famously noted, Francis Crick was never in a "modest mood." They announced their discovery to much fanfare and arguably too little attribution to those with whom they had worked, notably Rosalind Franklin.

The double helix established how cell division transmitted genetic content in a way that preserved the information encoded in DNA. It made clear the mechanics of inheritance by showing that DNA has two strands, with one being simply a reverse complement of the other. They defined the rules for how making new DNA strands from existing ones could lead to perfect copies. They unveiled what had baffled thinkers since before science was a discipline. Thanks to the work completed inside the Hut, biology had reached an inflection point comparable to the advance made when physicists split the atom in the New Mexico desert in 1945. Watson and Crick energized biological science and made real the possibility of altering DNA and thereby cells and organisms. Biology would no longer be just describing the things that are, but a dynamic experimental field that could define how we function and what governs how we change in development and disease. The puzzles inside of puzzles that represent life science looked like they might have had hard rules governing them—more like chemistry or physics than traditional field biology. That meant unleashing not just discovery but creativity: methods to change biology, perhaps to develop new therapies for biologic disease.

As the world absorbed the news about the double helix, Alick Isaacs was investigating influenza viruses at the National Institute for Medical Research in London, sixty-five miles south of Cambridge. He was motivated in large part by the not-so-distant Spanish flu pandemic of 1918–19, which had killed an estimated fifty million people. In 1957, as a less deadly Asian flu blazed across the world, he was invited to tea by a Swiss virologist named Jean Lindenmann, who had come to the institute for a one-year fellowship. Lindenmann and Isaacs were two very different men. Isaacs was a quintessential Scot and prone to serious bouts of depression. Lindenmann had been raised in Zurich by cosmopolitan parents and was known for an ironic sense of humor. Both men were medical doctors and research scientists, and they shared a fascination with the way that people infected with one strain of a virus seemed to develop immunity against related ones. They were determined to discover how this occurred.

Good research of course depends on carefully designed experiments. Isaacs and Lindenmann devised a classic. First they grew cells from the membranes of chicken eggs in a nutrient solution. Then they added one kind of virus to the cells and, as the virus flourished, added another type. The cells resisted this second virus. Isaacs and Lindenmann then removed all the cells and the viruses, leaving only the culture in which they had been grown. When they added fresh membrane cells to the nutrient mixture and hit them with a third type of virus, something remarkable happened—the new cells resisted that infection. Something produced by that first batch of cells, left behind when they were removed, had interfered with the infectious powers of the viruses. They called this substance, which was a protein, interferon.

Isaacs and Lindenmann were not alone in their scientific interest. At roughly the same time, others working in Tokyo and Boston had also noticed that some process was stopping viral growth in certain circumstances—and they, too, identified the key protein. Taken together, this work showed that interferon functions as both a virus blocker and a signal sender, communicating to nearby cells that an invader is present. The signal stimulates the listening cells to produce their own interferon, which then stops the virus as it arrives. All this communication, going on at the cellular level, was a stunning revelation for those seeking ways to intervene on the body's behalf against viral threats that cause infectious disease in the short term and cancer later in life. (Viruses are now believed to be a factor in as many as 20 percent of malignancies. Among the ones we now know contribute to the risk of cancer are the Epstein-Barr virus, human papillomaviruses, the hepatitis B and hepatitis C viruses, human herpesvirus 8, HIV, and a related human T lymphotropic virus, HTLV-1.)

Unfortunately, in the years after it was discovered, the only known method of producing human interferon involved processing vast amounts of blood. A single one-hundred-milligram dose of natural interferon required sixty-five thousand pints. The only source was the lab of Finnish researcher Kari Cantell, who had arranged to obtain every ounce of blood donated by the Finnish people so that he could harvest the protein. The expense and technical challenges in producing interferon meant that it was used in very few medical trials. Nevertheless, small studies suggested that it could slow the development of some forms of cancer.

In the 1960s and 1970s, pharmaceutical companies, foundations, and government agencies poured more than $100 million—roughly $1 billion in 2017 dollars—into interferon research. This work established that cells produce many different types of interferon. Among the most important is the interferon made by T lymphocytes, which are essential to the body's infection-fighting abilities. These T cells are produced in the human thymus, which was long considered a vestigial organ of no real importance.

The history of the thymus and science underscores the challenge in understanding the human body. As recently as 1960, many physicians considered this little mass of tissue to be inconsequential. Some thought it was implicated in sudden infant death syndrome (SIDS), and even though the connection was never proven, they "treated" infants with radiation, damaging the thymus, with the belief that they were preventing SIDS. Then in 1961, an Australian immunologist named Jacques Miller found he could all but disable the immune system of mice by removing the thymus. His experiment and follow-on work showed that through the production of T cells, the gland contributed greatly to immunity. (Much more about these cells in a later chapter.) This understanding opened the possibility that the body could be rallied, perhaps with T cell–stimulating treatment, to better fight disease on its own.

The science that identified interferon and then the creation and action of T cells revived interest in the idea that infectious agents, such as viruses, were implicated in the cancer process. This possibility had been raised in 1910, when a cancer in chickens was linked to a virus by a scientist named Francis Peyton Rous, who worked at the Rockefeller Institute in New York. Any "cause" for cancer offered a chance to investigate the mechanism of disease and explore the possibility of treatments based on the body's ways of protecting itself. At the start of the twentieth century, Peyton Rous prompted a big search for human cancers caused by infectious agents, but years and then decades passed with no new discoveries. The chicken-virus-cancer link came to be regarded as an anomaly.

Anomalies die quiet deaths in science, except when they are confirmed. In the case of the cancer-causing infection, the confirmation finally came from an unlikely source—an Irish missionary physician named Denis Parsons Burkitt, who spent most of his life working in Uganda. (When he arrived, he became only the second surgeon in the entire country.) An unassuming man who had lost an eye in a childhood accident, Burkitt had almost failed at college and later said he had prayed his way through his chemistry courses. He said he considered his work "God's call" and insisted that he received much in return for his labor. "I gave a spoonful and got back a shovelful," was how he put it. As a scientist, Burkitt was fascinated by the types of disease maps epidemiologists use to show how illnesses arise in people across a community or region.

In the 1950s and early 1960s, Burkitt and his colleagues traveled thousands of miles to pinpoint the locations of children who developed a type of lymphoma rarely seen elsewhere in the world. (He joked that three doctors visiting hospitals across the continent "enjoyed the safest-ever safari in Africa.") The common factors in the cases Burkitt studied turned out to be a history of malaria, which weakened the immune system, and infection with the virus that came to be known as the Epstein-Barr. The malaria was spread by a certain type of mosquito, which is common in the region Burkitt studied. The virus, which most commonly causes mononucleosis, is so ubiquitous that 50 percent of all children contract it by age five. After infection, it remains in the body, where it is almost always kept at bay by the immune system. It contributes to cancer only when other factors, like a weakening of the immune system, are present.

What was eventually called Burkitt's lymphoma was characterized by extremely fast-growing tumors, typically found first in the lymph nodes of the neck or jaw, leading to a rapidly worsening illness, organ failure, and death. Under the microscope, lymph node biopsies exhibit a distinctive pattern that came to be called the "starry sky." The "sky" is composed of large, densely packed tumor cells. The "stars" are made of debris left behind by the white blood cells that attempt to fight off the cancer. Although he became famous for his work on this malignancy, Burkitt would go on to do other important work. He helped establish the link between dietary fiber and the prevention of colon cancer and devised methods for producing cheap artificial limbs to help amputees in poor countries. But his most important legacy, in addition to the lives he saved, was his lymphoma research.

Although Burkitt, Isaacs, Lindenmann, and Miller had achieved real milestones, science was far from a true understanding of the causes of most cancers, let alone treatments that could be termed "cures." Nevertheless, people hungered for answers to the questions that naturally arise in the case of cancer, especially "How did I get it?" and "How do I get rid of it?" Too often, the press, attuned to the power of the topic, seized upon reports published in serious journals and simplified them in ways that surely exasperated physicians. In 1962, *Life* magazine famously announced, on a cover that also featured a big photo of Marilyn Monroe, "New Evidence That Cancer May Be Infectious." *Life* was a staple of doctors' waiting rooms all across America. (I would bet that issue landed in Dr. Baldino's office in Wyckoff.) By using the word *may*, the editors preempted critics who knew that the headline was sensationalistic. This left it to doctors to explain that no, cancer wasn't contagious in the way people might imagine (as in transmitted person to person) and that patients needn't be quarantined.

In addition to alarming patients and the general public, the idea that cancer was infectious spurred a big government investment in research intended to discover more cancer-causing viruses or bacteria. Looking back on this time, it is surprising to see such a focused effort. Scientific progress doesn't usually follow the kind of straight-line route that can be directed from some central authority. More typically, research in one area gets unexpected aid from a breakthrough in another. Thus, more than a decade would pass, and enthusiasm would wane, before it became possible to see how we might actually create—or engineer—new models of life that would help us study and intervene in the cancer process.

In 1969, a team at Harvard led by Jonathan Beckwith became the first to isolate a specific gene among the three thousand or so in a type of bacteria called *Escherichia coli*. Soon came the gene-splicing experiments of biochemist Paul Berg of Stanford, who combined the DNA of two separate types of viruses to create a novel, engineered DNA molecule. (This process was called recombinant DNA methodology.) Berg, who had earned his doctorate at Case, had immersed himself in basic cancer research starting in 1952 and plunged into a lifelong investigation of biology at its most basic levels. He was followed by Fred Sanger, who devised a method for rapidly producing an image of long stretches of DNA. These discoveries and others excited scientists but sent shivers through the ranks of theologians, who wondered if humanity would usurp a role previously played only by God.

This concern, that scientists would abuse the power of the new biological science, echoed the fears raised when physicists unlocked the atom in the 1940s. Science and technology had reached a point where people could imagine them producing catastrophes that might affect millions of people and, perhaps, humanity itself. The public's anxiety, which was reflected in science fiction movies and apocalyptic novels like *On the Beach*, had been appreciated by Beckwith's group. When their achievement was announced, a member of the team, medical student Lawrence Eron, said, "The only reason the news was released to the press was to emphasize its negative aspects." Eron hoped that society would engage in a serious conversation about genetic engineering's potential to shape human populations for ill, as well as for good.

The discussion got going in earnest in 1974 when a group of biologists, including James Watson, declared they would suspend certain kinds of research out of fear that they would create something dangerous in their labs. (Watson had, along with Crick, received the Nobel Prize in 1962.) In a letter published in the American journal *Science*, and a British one called *Nature*, this group said it was concerned that gene splicing could produce drug-resistant microorganisms or cancer-causing viruses. "There is serious concern," wrote the scientists, "that some of these artificial DNA molecules could prove biologically hazardous."

Noting that much of the gene-splicing work being done involved *E. coli*, which is found inside every human being and throughout our environment, they said that any unwanted creations based on this bacterium could quickly spread. To avoid this possibility, they asked colleagues to suspend aspects of their work too. In addition to Watson, the signers included David Baltimore of MIT and Paul Berg.

A year later, Berg chaired a landmark meeting at a conference center on the Pacific coast called Asilomar, where migrating monarch butterflies flitted among the Monterey pines. The context for this gathering included the political crisis of the Watergate burglary scandal, which had forced a U.S. president to resign for the first time in history. Combined with the hugely unpopular war in Vietnam, Watergate had left many Americans feeling disillusioned and skeptical of those in authority who held the public trust. Opinion polls showed a steep decline in the public's trust in all sorts of institutions and authorities. Science and medicine weren't helped by revelations, in 1972, of a federally funded experiment called the Tuskegee Study, which denied treatment to African American men with syphilis so that the disease could be studied. The fact that government and science had collaborated in the abuse of the men in the study frightened people as they contemplated technologies that had the potential to produce both great benefits and vastly more harm than anything mankind had ever before created. Berg was among them.

The scientists and physicians at Asilomar were joined by lawyers and journalists, who advised them on everything from liability issues to communications. For some of the scientists, who never considered the issue, the fact that laboratories were also work sites covered under labor, health, and safety laws was a disturbing revelation. Few had ever considered the risks they were courting as they worked on what would be, for all intents and purposes, new forms of life. Others, including Norton Zinder of Rockefeller University, were already concerned that many in this new field—*his* field—lacked the experience in microbiology to keep themselves, their colleagues, and the public safe. Working first in small groups and then in one large body, the conference attendees eventually established six categories of genetic experiments, which they ranked according to hazard, and indicated how they should be regulated. On one end of the scale were experiments involving organisms that freely exchanged genes in nature and were already quite variable in the existing environment. On the other end were projects that posed such a high risk of creating new pathogens that they shouldn't be conducted at all.

Asilomar, as the gathering came to be known, produced standards that showed that science was listening to public concerns and eager to hold itself accountable. For those engaged in work deemed most dangerous, the group recommended a "high containment" strategy that required air locks for lab entries and filtering of any air leaving the space where experiments would be done. Anyone entering these labs would have to first shower and don protective gear. Upon exiting, they would have to leave these clothes in a secure area and shower a second time. The cost of upgrading labs to meet the standards would be high. Berg's own facility had just undergone upgrades costing tens of thousands of dollars (big money in the 1960s), and more would be required if he wanted to pursue the kinds of studies he was contemplating.

For skeptics, the results of Asilomar suggested that scientists were beginning to understand why thoughtful laypeople might be afraid of technologies that enabled the creation of entirely new life-forms. For those in government and politics, the guidelines produced at the conference served as a template for codes that would eventually have the force of law. In fact, as Asilomar ended, the National Institutes of Health embarked on a four-year process intended to turn the guidelines into enforceable regulations.

The slow pace of this work was supposed to reassure people that it was being done with care and consideration for a wide diversity of opinion. Of course, some were frustrated with the uncertainty caused by the delay. James Watson, who had so publicly signaled his worries about gene splicing, changed his mind. "Specifically, I was a nut," he said as he retracted his support for the moratorium on certain experiments. "There is no evidence at all that recombinant DNA poses the slightest danger."

Watson spoke with the great authority that comes with a Nobel Prize, but his tone—impatient, if not imperious—was a red flag to anyone who viewed the powerful with some skepticism. In the 1970s, both modern progressives and old-fashioned traditionalists could be discovered among the wary, who found something unsettling in the claims of powerful people, be they scientists, political leaders, corporate chiefs, or bureaucrats. No badge of status was enough to reassure some people, especially those who feared that an overconfident, overempowered elite could be dangerous.

The fear and anxiety many people felt about science and technology came into full focus in 1978 in Harvard University's home city of Cambridge, Massachusetts, when Mayor Alfred Vellucci convened public hearings to review the public health implications of DNA research. (Cambridge is also home to the Massachusetts Institute of Technology, so the prospect of this work taking place within the city limits was quite real.) Vellucci, a silver-haired man who was born in 1915, had long feuded with the university over mundane matters like parking and rowdy students. He had often appealed to Cambridge voters by bashing the university and, consequently, earned the ridicule of the student-run satirical magazine called the *Harvard Lampoon*. At one point in this long-running town/gown dispute, after *Lampoon* editors mocked Italian Americans by claiming the Irish discovered the New World, Vellucci proposed turning the office building where the magazine kept its offices into a public restroom. He also suggested calling the area around the place Yale Square. And he planted a tree in the sidewalk in front of the place to spoil the view from inside. (Over the years, the tree would suffer much abuse, including shorn limbs and poisoning.)

At the city council hearing, where Vellucci appeared in coat and tie, he asked witnesses from the Harvard faculty to refrain from using "your alphabet," by which he meant scientific jargon, because "most of the people in this world are laypeople, we don't understand your alphabet."

The very first person to testify, cell biologist Mark Ptashne of Harvard, struggled with the mayor's request, sprinkling references to "P1 and P2 laboratories" into his argument. (P1 and P2 labs conducted extremely low-risk work.) When he spoke of the gene-splicing work proposed for Cambridge, he said that "unlike other real risks involved in experimentation, the risks in this case are purely hypothetical." Ptashne, who was thirty-six, appeared in shirtsleeves and wore long hair and sideburns. He didn't help his case in the minds of skeptics when he noted that "millions of [*E. coli*] bacteria cells carrying foreign DNA" had already been "constructed" and that "so far as we know, none of these cells containing foreign DNA has proved itself hazardous."

Brilliant as he was, Ptashne was no match for the mayor in the political forum of a city council meeting. After the Harvard professor made his statement, Vellucci read off a long list of questions, which he suggested Ptashne write down. (He did.) First the mayor asked for a "100 percent certain guarantee that there is no possible risk" in any experiments envisioned by Harvard scientists. Then he moved on to a series of questions intended to alarm the crowd:

"Do I have *E. coli* inside my body right now?"

"Does everyone in this room have *E. coli* inside their bodies?"

"Is it true that in the history of science, mistakes have been known to happen?"

"Question: Do scientists ever exercise poor judgment?"

"Do they ever have accidents?"

"Do you possess enough foresight and wisdom to decide which direction that humankind should take?"

Before Vellucci was finished, he had warned of monsters created in laboratories and stirred up others on the council, who continued the attack. Council member David Clem complained that "there are already more forms of life in Harvard Square than this country can stand" and then asked Ptashne, "What the hell do you think you are going to do if you do produce" a dangerous organism?

Ptashne was exasperated by the questions and would later call the proceedings "an unbelievable joke." But the Cambridge community of scientists was not monolithic. David Nathan, a physician and biologist at Boston Children's Hospital, encouraged the politicians to complete their work on safeguarding the public because he was raising children in the city of Cambridge and didn't see any need for unnecessary risk-taking. The mayor and council ultimately banned recombinant DNA work inside the city limits for nearly a year. In this time, they wrote and approved a number of biological safety ordinances and created a review board to consider all planned recombinant DNA research. Among the members of the board were a Catholic nun, engineers, a physician, and a professor of environmental planning.

Despite the mayor's inflammatory rhetoric and fears among the faculty that the city might shut down research, something positive grew out of the Cambridge process. The city got ahead of other communities and figured out a way to accommodate science. In a few years, Harvard faculty and commercial research firms would make the city a hub for biotechnology—which would, in turn, become a driver for business growth. In an era when brainpower was quickly replacing heavy industry as a source of economic growth and development, cities, states, and nations that had found a way to regulate science without too much interference had enormous advantages.

When the new technologies were considered in political forums and at public meetings, nonscientists got a chance to question the experts and learn things that made them feel less wary and worried. Unfortunately, very few Americans lived in communities where scientists conducting recombinant DNA research were invited to answer their questions. The consequences of this gap between public understanding and the facts allowed all sorts of mischief to occur. One of the strangest episodes came a year after the Cambridge hearing, with the publication of a book, labeled nonfiction, that purported to tell the story of an eccentric millionaire who had brought scientists to a private island where they had produced his clone—a little boy—who was happily maturing inside a laboratory enclave.

In His Image: The Cloning of a Man was written by a journalist named David Rorvik, who had contributed articles to *The New York Times* and other publications. Rorvik knew enough science to make the tale plausible, and he was an excellent storyteller who provoked all the fears and ethical controversies you might imagine would follow a "credible" report on the first human clone. (He said the boy was fourteen months old, that he had seen him, and that he was "alive, healthy, and loved.")

After he was interviewed by Tom Brokaw on the NBC network's *Today* show, where he refused to divulge the name of the man who was cloned, Rorvik's book flew to the top of bestseller lists across the country. Publishers around the world clamored for the rights to publish translations. With rising sales came rising controversy, including a complaint from a British scientist who objected to his name appearing in the book. A court in London would eventually find in the scientist's favor and declare the book a hoax. But in the meantime, *In His Image* created such a stir that a congressional committee conducted a Capitol Hill hearing on the matter.

David Rorvik declined to testify before Congress, saying he was too busy on his international book tour. However, the experts who did speak to the Subcommittee on Health and the Environment of the House Committee on Interstate and Foreign Commerce explained that since no one had ever produced a clone of any mammal, the idea that a wealthy man had built a secret lab, staffed it with the best scientists, and cloned himself was ludicrous. However, they did speak encouragingly of new technologies and genetic research that could produce important insights into and even treatments for some illnesses, including cancer. This work was also likely to reveal important insights into the aging process. Robert G. McKinnell of the University of Minnesota noted experiments involving repeated transplantation of cells from a developing animal embryo to test theories about aging. (McKinnell would publish widely in cell biology and contribute to a textbook called *The Biological Basis of Cancer.*)

Aging and cancer were linked in the minds of cell biologists because both involve the mechanisms that govern cell growth and survival. In aging, the cells of all animals eventually succumb to the process called senescence as they gradually lose the ability to replicate and then cause inflammation. Reduced replication may thwart developing cancer cells, but inflammation pushes in the other di-

rection. Combined with a reduced repertoire of immune competence, imbalances in the usual cell harmony emerge. This is marked
by poor coordination in the immune system's response to everything
from viruses to genetic mutations. The change helps to explain not
only the increased diagnosis of cancer in older people but their
greater susceptibility to infectious diseases. Senior citizens who get
the flu are more likely to develop pneumonia because they can't fight
off the influenza virus as quickly as can the young.

Senescence is relevant to cancer because malignancies somehow
escape its limits on growth. They multiply in an out-of-control fashion that defies the usual mechanisms of aging. As they evade the
body's defenses and replicate willy-nilly, cancer cells inexorably
overwhelm and replace normal ones and eventually, like mutinous
sailors, gain control of organ systems and the body itself. This is true
even for very old people, whose cancers may divide and multiply as
if they had drunk from the fountain of youth. Terrifying as it is,
cancer's dynamism suggests that it may have taken a page from and
corrupted cellular secrets about development, longevity, and even
regeneration. What if the chemical signaling that spurs normal development could reveal abnormalities in cancer and conversely, lessons from cancer could be manipulated to deliver new, healthy cells
to rejuvenate aged hearts or livers? Could this mirror be turned
into therapies that help people with cancer or with injuries and
wounds?

Just as scientists studied the body's delinquents—cancer cells—
in the context of those that behaved well, they looked to the defender
of the body—the immune system—to suggest ways to stop malignancies. By the time I enrolled at Case, biologists understood that between normal cell division and the effects of radiation and other
carcinogens, complex living creatures faced innumerable opportunities to develop cancer every day. Seen in this light, the most important question we could ask about cancer was: Why don't we see more
of it than we do? And the logical next question was: Can we mimic

how the body controls cancer to help, or even cure, people with the disease?

Two years after the press and Congress went a little crazy over the human cloning hoax, a comparably loud press response greeted news of the first genetically engineered drugs, including human insulin, growth hormone, and synthetic interferon, which was made by a Swiss company called Biogen, which had among its founders a Harvard scientist named Walter Gilbert. A brilliant man with wide-ranging interests, Gilbert was Jewish and from Boston, while his mentor was a Pakistani-born Muslim named Mohammad Abdus Salam. Abdus Salam was a giant of nuclear physics who left his homeland to protest religious discrimination. Like Gilbert, he was wide-ranging in his interests, with an expansive imagination and an open mind.

Gilbert's interferon breakthrough was announced on January 17, 1980. The next day, the stock of the Schering-Plough Corporation, which owned 16 percent of Biogen, surged in value. Investors were no doubt encouraged by a study published in the Soviet Union that noted that a weak interferon spray had protected a small group of test subjects against exposure to cold viruses. Other research centers were exploring interferon in cancer treatment. If interferon could fight everything from the common cold to malignancies, then the sky was the limit for the companies that could produce it and those who backed them.

Although basic science advanced so quickly that it was hard to keep up with the headlines, excitement around this work was impossible to ignore. Everyone, including cancer patients, seemed to believe that cures were right around the corner and that if they just lived long enough, some new treatment would save them. In reality, though, patients were being treated with the same basic interventions—surgery, radiation, and toxic chemotherapy—that had been available for decades. These drugs, which were effective against some cancers, including those of the blood (leukemias) and lymphatic systems (lymphomas), almost always produced terrible side effects, including hair loss, nausea and vomiting, and profound exhaustion. It was not uncommon for people to say that living while undergoing treatment was not much better than death.

I saw the benefits and limitations of all these treatments on the mornings when I went from room to room, and patient to patient, to draw blood for the tests that doctors had ordered. I was good with a needle, which people appreciated, and this work paid me a much-needed income as a student. It also gave me the chance to improve my bedside manner. Many of the patients were sleeping when I entered their rooms, and they invariably struggled to recognize where they were when they awoke. I was always a little bit sorry about disturbing them and about starting their day with the pain of a needle stick, small as it might be. I learned to discern who among them wanted to chat and who preferred that I perform my duties quickly and leave. As I grew more confident, I took a little pride in the fact that I was better than most at drawing blood from children, and even infants, whose small veins and big fears made this work especially challenging.

As I made my rounds with my needles and tourniquets and glass tubes with stoppers, I came to appreciate the ways that a touch, or a word, benefited patients who were dealing with challenging conditions. And sometimes the best I could do was not touch someone. I learned this lesson with patients who had sickle-cell anemia and often experienced so much pain that they couldn't bear to be touched. After one intense encounter that reached the point where I was afraid a suffering man was going to punch me out, I started telling these patients in the first moments of an appointment that I knew they were in terrible pain and that they might be hoping that we would just let them get into bed, give them as much pain medication as they wanted, close the door, and turn out the lights. I then explained that I could not do that, but that I would do whatever I could to help them once we got through an exam, which I would do as gently as possible.

I valued this caring element of medicine because one of the things that became quite evident in medical school was that we really didn't know very much at all about how the body worked, and kindness was sometimes the most powerful treatment at our disposal. Of course, great advances had been made since the age of bloodletting and phrenology, but still, we lacked good medicines to treat a whole host of conditions. We couldn't answer most of the questions that people asked about why they got sick and whether they were going to get well. Medicine's limitations became crystal clear to me when I studied immunology, which was an area of great interest to cancer specialists, who dreamed that drugs like interferon might harness the immune response against cancer. When you look at how the body monitors for infections and cellular injuries, develops immunity, fights off infection, or repairs damage, it seems like magic.

Case was the kind of place where med students were permitted and even encouraged to knock on doors and ask questions. I went to see George Bernier, a professor of hematology and oncology, who was one of the leading hematologists/oncologists in the country. He stopped what he was doing and just listened as I rattled off a whole bunch of questions.

How does the body know to recruit immune cells to a particular site? You get an infection. Suddenly all the infection-fighting cells that are otherwise circulating in the blood find their way out of the blood vessels, into the precise spot where you have an infection.

How does the immune system know when to switch on and switch off?

How do you shut off the immune response so that you don't cause collateral damage?

Why do some bodies manage to repair cell damage and others do not?

Why do medicines help some people but fail in others with the same disease?

To each of these questions, Bernier responded with roughly the same answer, which was "These are things we just don't know."

Here was a truly great doctor, someone who would soon be named chief of oncology at Case, and he was saying that he didn't understand the very basic operation of the immune system. He didn't know why treatments worked in some patients and not in others. And he couldn't explain how the immune system recognized a threat to the body, responded to it, and then turned off its response when the crisis passed.

To his credit, Bernier wasn't defensive about how much he didn't know, and he wasn't annoyed by all my questions. When I found other students who shared the same curiosity about the immune system, we formed a group and essentially designed our own course of study. We read everything we could get our hands on, met from time to time to discuss what we learned, and met with Bernier himself. Only later, when I learned about how other medical schools worked, did I appreciate our professor's generosity. He made us feel as if we, the students, were the most important people in the school and that whenever we sought to learn more, we had a right to study and eventually own that material. There was also something special about the students in that small group and my class. We spoke very openly about our experiences as both students and doctors in training.

Sometimes the different roles we played—in my case, blood-drawer, student, caregiver—combined to teach us lessons that were more profound and lasting than we could have had if we'd remained in the library. One instance of this dynamic arose when I met a young man named Carl. He was just a few years older than I was and had suddenly been overcome by exhaustion. His appetite had disappeared, and he had lost some weight. He was plagued by night sweats and had a constant low-grade fever. He had also developed a lump in his neck.

Carl was a bright, friendly guy who was more puzzled by his symptoms than worried. He hoped he had some sort of infection, like the flu, and that it was just taking its time leaving his body. I knew just enough to be more concerned than he was. After talking with him and doing the necessary legwork of admitting him to the hospital, I went to the lab and made slides so I could examine under the microscope the cells taken from his blood. Following the standard protocol, I added stains called hematoxylin, which is violet in color, and eosin, which is rosy red. (Eos was the Greek goddess of dawn.) I put the slide into the clips beneath the lens, switched on the light underneath the slide, put my thumb and forefinger on the wheel that adjusted the focus, and bent over the eyepiece.

TWO

SEEING CANCER

Viewed through a microscope at low power, the stained cells from my patient Carl's blood had far too many cells stained blue, the cells of the immune system. The cells were sometimes clustered, making deep purple collections. Since they were lighted from below, they glowed in a way that made them almost seem beautiful, like African violets. But there was nothing but horror in those blooms. Carl had Burkitt's lymphoma, a diagnosis made definitively on the lymph node biopsy that followed that revealed the classic starry-sky appearance associated with this dreadful disease.

In the moment I recognized that I was seeing something malignant, something truly awful, through that microscope, I experienced several different emotions. I was excited to see, in a slide I had prepared, immediate clinical evidence of a disease that had previously existed, for me, only in the pages of a textbook. I think every new doctor must feel this little rush as he or she realizes that the material learned during years of grinding study is useful and directly relevant. But of course the diagnosis was a terrible thing for my patient, and I immediately began to feel overwhelmed by what I had unearthed, an unholy foe for him that would threaten all he knew and loved of life.

In the late 1970s, there was very little hope to be offered adults who were diagnosed with Burkitt's lymphoma. Children were sometimes cured by two chemotherapy agents—methotrexate and cyclophosphamide—which were effective against some leukemias and were being tried against other cancers. But in those rare instances when Burkitt's was seen in an American adult, the prognosis was bad. One of the faster-growing types of cancer, Burkitt's typically spread throughout the body, creating tumors in almost any organ system. In adults with advanced disease, it caused death due to organ failure in a matter of months or even weeks. Thus, Carl's slide was a view of his destiny, and it was terrible to imagine.

The diagnosis and prognosis came as a horrifying shock to Carl. He had never suffered from any serious illness and was expecting to lead a long and productive life. It was extremely unsettling to me too. I was a doctor in training who was eager to treat and even cure people with serious diseases. But there I was, face-to-face with someone who was very much like me—young, optimistic, hopeful—and he was being confronted with an undeniable and yet unacceptable truth. He had developed an incurable, fast-growing cancer that was going to end his life at a time when he felt like it was just beginning.

Life is never long enough, but if we are alert, we can develop an appreciation for it, and with this appreciation we may accept it as a limited gift. Indeed, the natural life span, which for Carl would have been about seventy years, gives us the chance to really know ourselves, love others, and experience the world. Few people in their twenties or thirties acquire much of the wisdom that comes with age. For this reason, and many others, they find it almost impossible to understand that their time is running out very quickly. Carl quite naturally entered a state of psychological denial. He could hear what we were telling him, and he knew he was in a crisis. But he considered the warm, intelligent people who were his caregivers and all the resources at one of the most advanced hospitals in the most advanced country in the world, and struggled to comprehend that we couldn't save him.

As we developed a relationship, I came to know that Carl had a keen sense of humor. He was also a baseball fan. One of his favorite books was *Eight Men Out*, which told the story of the Black Sox cheating scandal. When I saw him, he often repeated the phrase "Say it ain't so, Joe!" For a while, he would repeat the line, which has long been attributed to a little boy who begged the ballplayer "Shoeless" Joe Jackson to refute the charge that he had cheated. Legend has it that Shoeless Joe never did say, "It wasn't so." Neither did I.

The best we could do for my Carl was chemotherapy that barely touched his tumor and then palliative care, which meant making him as pain-free as possible. We also tried to comfort him emotionally, but we were limited in this regard too. Nothing that could be said would change the fact that this young man was being cheated out of a full life. He remained in the hospital and died in a matter of weeks.

Although I knew what was coming, I was not prepared for Carl's death, and it filled me with sadness. Some clinicians may try to develop what's called "professional distance," which they imagine will help them cope with traumatic situations, but I doubt that such a thing really exists. Medicine is an intimate enterprise in which every interaction is an emotional experience. The idea of distance connotes a sense of remove that is more likely a kind of denial and would require denying the humanity of the person who is your patient. This distance makes it harder to enjoy the happier aspects of just being with a patient who brings his or her own sense of humor, irony, or grace to a clinical moment. It also deprives us of the clarity that comes with the pain of someone's suffering or death. If being numb is what a doctor seeks, he or she has surely chosen the wrong profession.

In the bustle of life, it is very easy to overlook the blessing of a well-functioning body and the gift that is each ordinary day. When you work with people who cannot take these things for granted but who often meet their pain with clear-eyed determination and even humor, you are reminded that most of what we worry about every day is neither profound nor worthy of much attention. In medicine, real care often comes down to staying open to what patients like Carl are experiencing and teaching us even in death. Stubborn adherence to some standard that says we must be calm and emotionally removed can easily make patients and their loved ones feel as if we don't appreciate the gravity of what's happening before their eyes. Nothing is more profound than death, and any attempt to act professionally in some artificial way will be felt as alienating and disrespectful. This type of denial also deprives doctors of the genuine experience that helps us move through grief. It is the loss that is denied, and not addressed, that erodes our ability to recover and move forward.

The pain that I experienced when Carl died included a hard lesson in the limits of science and medicine. We may have discovered the double helix and begun to practice genetic engineering, but we were still unable to save people from most forms of malignancy. Indeed, most of the tools we have are sadly inadequate, often barbarically crude. Unsatisfied with the limitations of what I could offer patients as a doctor, I recognized that if I wanted to really make a difference in ways beyond comforting the person in front of me, I needed to do science as well as medicine, and I devoted more time to studying the basic mechanisms of cancer. I joined a group of students who met regularly with research scientists who were happy to add to our formal medical education. One of these professors, Adel Mahmoud, was a brilliant physician and biologist with a generous spirit. He was a small man who made a big impact as he gestured with his hands and spoke in a great rush of words whenever he was excited by a scientific concept, which was quite often.

Mahmoud had been educated in Cairo and London and was deeply interested in infectious diseases and vaccines. His main interest at the time was schistosomiasis, a disease caused by a parasitic worm—also called a blood fluke—that affected an estimated two hundred million people in the developing world. Sometimes referred to as "snail fever" because each parasitic worm spends part of its life inside a water snail, schistosomiasis causes organ failure and death. It was, and is, endemic in Mahmoud's home country of Egypt. It is also so common and has been for so long that ancient sources referred to the bloody urine of males, a common symptom, as a sign of maturity comparable to menstruation.

In modern times, the construction of Egypt's Aswan High Dam flooded thousands of square miles and created vast new habitats for the snail. Rising rates of schistosomiasis brought death and suffering, which inspired Mahmoud's work. In 1972, he published his first paper on the disease, which addressed the mechanism it triggered to cause anemia. Mahmoud then systematically attacked aspects of the disease ranging from its life cycle to its epidemiology. (The dam and the way of life in Egypt were key in this regard.) Mahmoud probed the worm for vulnerabilities in its various stages and development and places of residence. He conducted research on basic concerns, such as the best way to count the number of tiny worm eggs in a urine sample, to the mutation of the parasite in diabetic mice. Along the way, he became keenly interested in the fact that in some cases, the human immune system defeated the parasite, which suggested a pathway to a vaccine. A safe vaccine would, of course, engage the body's immune system to defend against the parasite and make postinfection treatment, with its side effects and unpredictable results, unnecessary.

Viewed from the distance of a few decades, I can see Mahmoud's work demonstrated how a huge problem could be broken into pieces for research. He was, by the time we met, a master scientific navigator who turned the disease he studied into a world of its own, completely worthy of exploration. In our first encounter, I asked him some very basic questions about the immune system's inability to reliably defeat schistosomiasis—how could it not recognize and destroy a worm?—and he wasn't content to just talk. He invited me to join his lab and contribute to the search for answers.

At the moment he made the offer, I wasn't at all confident that I could develop the skills, including the habits of mind, that scientists possess. I thought that serious research was done by men and women who were so extraordinary that I shouldn't even imagine joining them. But I accepted Mahmoud's offer and took my place at a lab table amid the type of glassware that I had once clinked around with in my parents' basement. If I didn't yet have the scientific reflexes to be a real investigator, Mahmoud was willing to let me start developing them.

My first assignment involved putting immune cell lymphocytes, the body's defenders, together with the tiny schistosome worms. Once they had a chance to do battle, I used a microscope to do an assessment, counting the parasites that remained, as well as the immune cells. Ideally, this labor would be one step forward in the effort to discover what might be enabling the immune response, and in time, this knowledge might be the key to a vaccine.

In the lab, I could see, in real time, that after first contact, the immune cells made good progress against the flukes. However, at some point, the tide turned. As Mahmoud told me, "The worm is capable of altering itself in a way that some survive." As this response occurred, the immune cells also adapted. As the weeks passed, my fluke counts varied, with the invader prevailing at some points and the defenders succeeding at others. In this case, the metaphor that suggests the body is the arena where battles are waged seemed especially apt. This work was simple, but it wasn't an academic exercise designed to produce a predictable result. Mahmoud saw no reason to engage medical students in busywork, so even though it required more from him, he assigned us real work. The work was quite thrilling to me, because I could see cell biology at work through the lens of the microscope. I never accomplished the goal of capturing that moment when the immune cells vanquished the parasite. Technology hadn't advanced far enough to make this possible. But the work had value nevertheless, and it opened my eyes to the possibilities of medicine based on immunology. It also set me on the road to becoming a scientist. These positives took the sting out of being left off the list of authors when the study I contributed to was published. Like every young doctor or scientist, I craved that kind of recognition, but Mahmoud gave me so much more that I couldn't imagine complaining about such a small disappointment.

The hope I felt doing science in Mahmoud's lab helped to balance much of what I saw in my clinical education where we doctors in training encountered patients at every stage of care, from admission through treatment and then in recovery. Much of what I witnessed in the various university-affiliated hospitals (included were a public hospital and a Veterans Administration facility) shocked me. It wasn't that the level of care was substandard. In fact, for the time, it was quite high. What was shocking was the trauma I saw inflicted on patients' bodies despite all the medicines, advanced techniques, and precautions. Nowhere was this more evident than it was in the operating room.

Modern surgery can be traced to the famous ether dome at Massachusetts General Hospital, where, in 1846, a dentist named William Morton used the gas to render unconscious a man named Edward Gilbert Abbott. (Earlier experiments with the gas had involved healthy volunteers who inhaled it and then stumbled around laughing. These demonstrations were dubbed "frolics" and were considered a form of amusement for participants and witnesses alike.)

The ether dome, which still stands, is a space as austere as an old New England church. Observers gaze down from rows of wooden seats that rise steeply from the operating room floor and are separated from each other by curving wooden barriers, which are painted white. Abbott, who was strapped to a chair, was given enough gas to make him completely unresponsive. A Harvard Medical School professor named John Collins Warren then removed a tumor from Abbott's neck. Warren's assistants, who were accustomed to holding patients still as they were cut, probed, and stitched, watched in wonder.

Dr. Warren, who was perhaps the most respected surgeon in the country, worked quickly and without saying a word. He knew that anesthesia was so revolutionary that skeptics might think it was a scam. Eager to quell the skeptics, Warren broke his silence as he finished the operation and declared, "Gentlemen, this is no humbug." Abbott, upon awakening, said he felt that his neck had been scratched.

When it worked, and it usually did, anesthesia made surgery a less painful and chaotic process, but it remained a gruesome affair, especially for the uninitiated. Except for truly minor procedures, surgery involves the kind of cutting, bloodletting, and (sometimes) breaking of bones that you might imagine occurs in a butcher shop. Although it is done with infinitely more care, surgery on human beings exposes us as animals quite similar to others, with our skin and layers of fat, muscle, and organs. Some of the odors that emanate from the body, like the metallic scent of blood or the smoky/meaty aroma from cauterization, are easy to imagine. Infected body parts and organs can be so putrid that the people in the OR sometimes put oil of wintergreen on their masks so they can continue to work. In my early training, I may have been most upset by amputations done on patients who had Buerger's disease. Almost always caused by smoking, this illness blocks blood supply to the extremities, causing pain, and gangrene, which often leads to the loss of fingers, toes, hands, or feet. The journalist John McBeth wrote about his struggle with this disease and the amputation of his right leg in a book chapter he called "Year of the Leg."

Although generally less dramatic than leg amputations, cancer surgeries of the late 1970s were done without most of the less-invasive techniques used today. Big incisions were required to expose tumors, which varied greatly in size and appearance. Some small lung cancers, for example, look like tiny heads of broccoli sprouting hairlike microvilli. In a smoker with advanced disease, the lung itself may be blackened by tobacco tars and the cancer could be a diffuse white mass. Brain cancers are often shaped by the surrounding structures and wind up looking like little pyramids, dumbbells, plums, or kidney beans.

The surgeries performed to remove malignancies were often quite complicated procedures. Great care was taken to remove as much cancerous tissue as possible without causing too much collateral damage. This was extremely difficult to do in this era before modern imaging technology and computer-assisted resection. Teams of physicians and nurses worked on patients who could be under general anesthesia for many hours. With less-reliable technology than we have today, manual experience was critical for the members of these teams.

The drama and stress of the operating room help explain why you find certain personality types beneath the surgical masks. As one study presented at a medical education conference in 2013 indicated, surgeons tend to be energetic, aggressive extroverts. They are less agreeable than other doctors, but more conscientious. These traits tend to become more pronounced over time. An old surgeon is likely to be among the most self-confident but also the most careful doctors in the hospital. He or she would also be, in professional terms, a direct descendant of William Stewart Halsted.

A clinician who was also a scientist, Halsted was the most influential American surgeon of the early twentieth century. He rose to fame after performing two emergency lifesaving procedures on family members. In the first, he removed his mother's gallbladder in an operation done on her kitchen table. In the second, he used his own blood to transfuse his sister, who was hemorrhaging after giving birth. Halsted created the first formal training programs for surgeons, invented sterile rubber gloves for use in the operating room, and applied the scientific method to research into anesthetics. Here he met his match in the newly developed medicine called cocaine, which he tested on himself. A paper written under the grip of addiction was so garbled it almost ruined him. However, he recovered both his health and his standing in the medical community and saved countless lives with dramatic operations. None was more dramatic than the radical mastectomy surgery he devised for breast cancer patients.

Halsted, who was an imposing figure with piercing blue eyes and a forceful personality, is widely regarded as the most important surgeon in U.S. history. His methods greatly reduced the risk, suffering, and mortality rates associated with most operations. This success made him a kind of demigod in American medicine, and he used his clout to influence practice across the country. In the case of his radical mastectomy, Halsted proselytized for his aggressive operation with messianic zeal. In his view, only the removal of the entire breast, as well as adjoining muscle and lymph nodes, could possibly save a patient with any trace of a malignancy. It became the standard and remained so even after a so-called modified radical mastectomy was devised in the 1940s.

As late as 1972, Halsted's radical mastectomy was still the surgeon's treatment of choice, with the largest percentage of patients undergoing this kind of procedure. Many patients also favored it, believing that the most dramatic intervention gave them the best shot at long-term survival. But as data accumulated, including some generated by studies that enlisted courageous patients in comparison trials, doctors began to see that there was often no real advantage to the Halsted operation. Almost two-thirds of women who got a radical mastectomy died within five years, a result that had been unchanged since the 1930s. Press reports on these numbers often mentioned First Lady Betty Ford, who had undergone a radical mastectomy, as an example of someone who may not have required it. One book on this subject noted that most of the doctors who performed radical mastectomies were not actually cancer specialists and may not have kept up with the research. When I took care of women who'd had radical mastectomies, I saw why they might question the treatment. The operation was more than disfiguring. It was absolutely devastating to the bodies of women who were left with little more than heavily scarred skin stretched over their ribs. No wonder some of them had their doubts about the procedure and whether taking so much flesh was really necessary or worth the loss of a part of themselves so visible and emotionally freighted.

Mrs. Ford's candor about her experience with mastectomy, at a time when many people still hid the fact that they had breast cancer, helped move society toward more open conversations about diagnosis and treatment of a disease that caused thirty-three thousand deaths per year. Science was also yielding information at a quickening pace. In 1974, researchers at the M.D. Anderson Hospital in Houston published a study showing a genetic component in breast cancer risk, and in 1975 came news that an early-detection program was extremely effective at finding signs of the disease at a stage when it could be treated most effectively.

By 1977, patients and activists were leading a growing effort to bring cancer treatment out of the shadows and to encourage more thoughtful treatments. Women were so willing to talk about breast cancer that twenty of them staged a protest inside the Saks Fifth Avenue department store in New York when managers refused to hire a woman who had recently had a mastectomy. The protesters, among them members of a postmastectomy support group, picketed the store and ceremoniously destroyed their Saks credit cards. Protesters like the ones at Saks and self-help support groups that advocated for patient autonomy irritated physicians who still clung to the doctor-as-God identity that had become common in the profession. To be fair, a great many patients *wanted* their doctors to be gods, because they found comfort in the idea that someone more knowledgeable was in charge. This is why Lewis Thomas described a physician's confidence as a source of "faith and hope," which my experience suggests has real value to patients and their families, who are reassured by the feeling that their shamans have a connection with some force beyond their own. At the same time, however, physicians know the limitations of medicine and that complications are common and so varied that even the simplest interventions can backfire. Even the simplest of "good" medicines, like penicillin, can have a lethal side in the wrong or, in penicillin's case, allergic person.

As a doctor in training, I occasionally thought about the Wizard of Oz pulling levers behind a curtain as I sought to be a source of assurance for patients. Sometimes I was simply borrowing the confidence of senior doctors, who had seen so many similar cases that I had confidence in their judgments. Nevertheless, the fear that I was a fraud persisted, and many of my medical school classmates harbored similar feelings.

My fears about being an impostor ebbed a bit as I was mentored by the top clinicians, including Richard Graham, who always seemed to strike the right balance, reassuring patients without promising miracles. Unlike other senior doctors, Graham adapted well to challenges that came with patients who had begun to read media articles about their illnesses and came armed with both questions and opinions. More and more people wanted to have a greater say in their care. For women dealing with breast cancer, the issue was also linked to the larger issue of gender equality. A great many felt that the largely male medical profession had too much say over their bodies, and they were eager for more of a voice in how they were treated.

Patients who did their own research often discovered options for care that they had never known existed. In the case of breast cancer, a surgeon at Cleveland Clinic, which was affiliated with Case, began performing an operation called a lumpectomy in the late 1960s. This technique involved removing the tumor and just a bit of nearby tissue, while leaving most of the muscles intact. The surgeon, George Crile Jr., was from a royal family of medicine.

His father, George Washington Crile, who is credited with pioneering blood transfusion in the United States, became famous as a field surgeon in the First World War. He was so respected in military circles that a World War II Liberty ship was named for him.

Heir to a great name in medicine, the junior Crile was so prominent that he could command a hearing for his ideas, but even he took a risk as he stood against Halsted orthodoxy. His critics said his success came because his patients were cherry-picked in a way that guaranteed Crile success. At one American Cancer Society meeting, a surgeon angrily complained that "women are coming in waving the articles [about lumpectomy] in their hands." This was precisely the point, in Crile's mind. He considered many radical surgeries unnecessary and thought women should have more options.

Some cancer surgeries were followed by radiation therapy, which aimed to kill additional tumor cells by damaging their DNA. Radiation was first used to destroy cancer cells in 1896, a year after Wilhelm Röntgen discovered x-rays. In the 1930s, the famous radium watch dial painters' case showed that radiation also caused cancer. Medicine is full of such paradoxes, so the radiation-cancer dynamic wasn't shocking to physicians. However, it did complicate the public perception of a treatment that was the only option for certain brain cancers and commonly used against leukemias and lymphomas.

As I saw in the hospitals affiliated with Case, radiation therapy came with side effects, including exhaustion, nausea, and sometimes pain. However, these were generally not as severe as the side effects caused by chemotherapy, which was also given to people suffering from a whole range of cancers. Developed and tested in the decades after the Second World War, chemotherapy drugs were basically poisons. They were medicines if they killed more cancer cells than normal cells, but they always caused lots of collateral damage. Their effectiveness had been shown first in children with leukemia. Success was later seen in testicular cancer and lymphoma, offering drug-induced cures when previously only surgery ("A chance to cut is a chance to cure") was able to claim curative effects. That led to a heady optimism and application of drugs singly and in combination against a range of cancers. Many—like lung, liver, and pancreatic cancer—were largely insensitive, but advances were made in colon and breast. Inevitably, these cell toxins acted blindly, killing healthy cells along with cancerous ones and damaging vital organs as well as tumors. Cells that divided rapidly, like those in bone marrow, the mouth, and the gut, were generally more vulnerable.

The focus of early chemotherapy drugs was to poison rapidly dividing cells, since that seemed a hallmark of a malignancy (a presumption since shown to often be incorrect). The result was to halt production of the normal cells that rapidly turn over in the body. Cells for virtually every tissue barrier against the outside world—such as hair, nails, and the tissues of the skin, mouth and airway, and intestines—are replenished at very high rates every minute of every day. When a poison is introduced that stops cell division, the consequences are predictable: mouth ulcers, hair loss, diarrhea, and infections. Low-level infections occur almost uniformly as the intestinal barrier is compromised and there is limited surveillance from immune cells to clear the invading bacteria. That causes the general misery of fatigue, fever, and loss of appetite we associate with infections. Further, the poisons affect sensory cells and often lead to severe nausea for which there was little potent antidote until the late 1980s. In my days as a resident, I saw hundreds of people suffering from these symptoms. Nurses and doctors tried to make them comfortable, but there was little we could do. The struggle could be heartbreaking to watch. Often lying still, except when they had to vomit, people knew they were somewhere near the precipice of death from the drugs that were supposed to help them. In rare cases, chemo *would* kill by damaging the heart, lungs, or kidneys, or making it impossible for the body to fight a serious infection.

The devilish thing about chemotherapy was that the cure rate was often improved by giving more of the drugs. This meant that even as they recognized the misery they were causing, doctors felt enormous pressure to give more of the drugs as soon as they felt a patient was recovered enough to stand it. In some ways, a physician would demonstrate his or her courage and commitment by giving more medicine than another might give. In order to be seen as good or admirable, patients were then encouraged to endure as much suffering as they could. Thus, a strange kind of challenge would arise as physicians sought to give as much chemo as possible and patients who were desperate for a cure, and to be seen as both good and courageous, accepted extraordinary amounts of suffering.

I saw many families debate how much a patient could stand, arguing about chemotherapy among themselves and with doctors. Often, when a spouse or parent begged for the treatment to stop, he would be overruled by the frail and exhausted patient, who was both afraid of dying and afraid of letting down the people he loved. Giving up was unacceptable to him, even if he spent much of the time he gained from the therapy feeling sick, weak, and half-alive. No one failed to recognize that chemotherapy had much in common with bloodletting, trepanation (drilling holes in the skull), and other "therapies" that were inflicted upon patients before medicine recognized they were useless. The difference was that chemotherapy had shown itself to help some people live longer and actually cured some cancers.

In the late 1970s, when I became involved in caring for patients, traditional chemotherapy was still on the upstroke of optimism for cancers broadly. The most strident advocates of aggressive treatment agreed with scientist and physician E. Donnall "Don" Thomas, who was quoted as saying, "Sometimes you have to burn down the barn to get rid of the rats."

A Texan who was educated at Harvard Medical School in the 1940s, Thomas was the son of a country doctor who had arrived on the frontier in a covered wagon. His first studies were done in a lab established for him in Boston by the chemotherapy pioneer Sidney Farber. In the mid-1950s, he went to work at a small hospital in Cooperstown, New York, where the inclement weather kept him inside working at his experiments.

As Thomas recognized, those who would burn down the house faced the inevitable challenge of rebuilding. In the case of cancer treatment, rebuilding the body depended on rescuing the bone marrow, which produces all the blood and immune cells: red cells for delivering oxygen, platelets for blood clotting, monocytes and neutrophils for clearing up debris and bacterial and fungal invaders, and T and B lymphocytes that more specifically respond to and kill pathogens either directly or through antibody production. Bone marrow is the mother source of all these cells and depends on stem cells to replenish them. When the bone marrow is destroyed, life is nasty, brutish, and short, with death from infection or bleeding occurring in a matter of weeks.

Although the science was still in its infancy, by the mid-1950s, it was known that infusions of bone marrow cells could "rescue" the immune systems of mice that had been blasted with so much radiation that all their bone marrow was destroyed. The experiment that produced this evidence was devised by R. T. Prehn and Joan M. Main, who worked at a public health hospital in Seattle. They destroyed the immune systems in mice, revived them with infusions of marrow cells, and then tested their immune function by grafting on a piece of skin from the marrow donor. The grafts took, proving that their tiny patients had received, along with marrow cells, the immune functions of the donor mice.

Thomas's early work was funded by the federal Atomic Energy Commission, which oversaw America's nuclear power stations, atomic research, and nuclear weapons production at places like the Hanford Reservation in Washington State and the Oak Ridge National Laboratory in Tennessee. In these places and others, extremely dangerous materials produced in nuclear reactors were processed to create weapons-grade plutonium and isotopes for both medical treatments and research. AEC officials worried about workers who might be exposed in accidents and die from the destruction of their marrow.

When doctors and researchers tried to imagine how to treat victims of massive radiation exposure whose bone marrow would be destroyed, they kept circling back to the idea of using healthy marrow cells to replenish the body. However, when this was tried with human beings, they were defeated by incompatibility of the immune systems. Either the recipient's residual immune system would attack and kill the donor cells or a more common phenomenon called graft versus host disease (GvHD) would occur, where the immune cells in the donated bone marrow would recognize the host as foreign and attack it. However, it was theoretically possible that marrow that closely matched the recipient's would not develop this reaction. In 1957, Thomas removed healthy marrow cells from one identical twin and infused it in another to treat leukemia.

Thomas's bone marrow research was done against the backdrop of a fierce debate among those who considered chemotherapy and radiation pathways to cures and those who did not. Oncologists who used these methods had to act with an almost ruthless attitude and sometimes pushed patients beyond what they could endure. Treatments would seem to succeed, but patients died of side effects. Critics questioned the morality of offering people with weeks or months to live such intense treatment, even with the aid of bone marrow transplants. But gradually, immunologic research permitted the screening of blood donors to find matches for cancer patients in need of marrow. A big breakthrough in this area came with the discovery, in 1958, of a human leukocyte antigen (HLA) system, which identifies foreign cells that do not belong to the body. (Much of the credit for this work goes to French immunologist Jean Dassaett, who began this work in the hematology lab at Boston Children's Hospital.) Driven by a complex of genes, the system tends to be similar in siblings. This is why Thomas's twin-to-twin transplant worked.

As often happens in science and medicine, Thomas couldn't be fully aware of the process he was manipulating. Better understanding would depend on others who would identify the many varieties of cells in the marrow and their functions. Included were stem cells in the red matter of the bones, which produce blood lymphatic cells, including those that fight infection. The idea of blood stem cells had been established at least as far back as 1908, when Artur Pappenheim provided his "unified theory of hematopoiesis" (*hematopoiesis* is the production of blood cells). However, in 1961, Canadians Ernest McCulloch and James Till first experimentally defined that such cells—stem cells—existed. Their work was a major breakthrough and paved the way for the whole field of stem cell biology.

Till and McCulloch were working in the context of the Cold War, a time when the horrors of nuclear weapons were known and countries were desperate to find ways to protect their citizens. It had long been known that the body can replenish lost blood, which is the main reason many ancient peoples developed the notion that blood is the body's life force. Genghis Khan's warriors were reputed to have multiple horses each so that they could bleed a horse they had just ridden for food and count on the horse replenishing its blood by foraging. This is said to have allowed them to cross the great steppes of Asia, where food for humans was scarce but abundant grasslands fed the horses. What was witnessed in World War II was that people could replenish their blood even after having their bone marrow largely destroyed by exposure to radiation. Some of those exposed to the explosions in Hiroshima and Nagasaki who had profoundly low blood counts and bone marrows that were largely devoid of cells recovered and did so robustly, achieving normal blood counts. That provided at least circumstantial evidence that there might be blood stem cells that could replete the blood. Countries like the United States, Canada, the United Kingdom, and Russia pushed to research the possibilities of stem cells as a radiation antidote. They fostered interactions between biologists like McCulloch, a physician, and physicists like Till.

Till and McCulloch used mice as test subjects, using one group to stand in for victims of atomic bomb radiation and another for marrow donation. The experiment worked, showing the cells drawn from marrow could be given intravenously and start to make blood sufficiently to allow an otherwise lethally irradiated animal to survive. When their study revealed nodules on mouse spleens, they dissected them to find colonies of donor stem cells, which they found were capable of producing a variety of different blood cells and renewing themselves, as transplanting another irradiated mouse made evident. These two traits—self-renewal and the ability to create different types of cells—were the cardinal attributes of stem cells. Till and McCulloch had shown that they indeed did exist and had profound abilities in rescuing animals from lethal radiation injury.

The kind of basic science done by McCulloch and Till informed the experiments in treatment carried out by Don Thomas. After moving to the Fred Hutchinson Cancer Research Center in Seattle, Thomas built a thriving lab and tried to tease apart the relationship between cancer and the immune system. He would later describe the effort he made as a matter of having "one out of thirty patients who lived [for] a year." Others considered the twenty-nine who did not survive and judged the work a failure. Thomas thought of the fact that all thirty were expected to die of their cancer in a matter of weeks and decided that one living was "highly significant." He lived the maxim that statistics were just a tool and "if you throw a hundred balls in the air and only ninety-nine come down, it might not be statistically significant, but it is damned interesting."

Working with his wife, Dottie, a college sweetheart whom he'd met when she hit him with a snowball, Thomas pursued bone marrow transplantation with a single-mindedness that bordered on obsession. Many, if not most, successful pioneers in science are able to muster this kind of determination, even in the face of repeated failures. The big problem for the individual, however, is that more often than not, the very big payoff never comes. A few colleagues may understand what you are doing and support your pursuit, but with each disappointment, self-doubt grows. The feeling is surely similar to that of an artist who completes one canvas after another without selling a single one. When the rewards are so elusive, how do you know whether you are engaged in something meaningful or caught up in folly?

Medical history is replete with stories of scientists who pursue an idea, sometimes for their entire lives, without definitive results. One of the greatest involved a young New York surgeon named William Coley, who entered practice in 1885 and was shaken by the death of his very first patient. The patient succumbed to bone cancer metastases even after Coley thought he had removed all her cancer by amputating her hand and much of her arm. As you might imagine, the operation was traumatic for the patient and, to some degree, for the doctor. The outcome tormented Coley, who began exploring hospital files on similar cases. He eventually came upon a report about a man with recurring bone cancer on his face who, after three surgeries, developed a raging streptococcus infection. After each fever spike, his remaining tumors shrank until they disappeared. Seven years after the man was discharged from the hospital, Coley found him in Manhattan's Lower East Side, where he was in excellent health. The only evidence of his illness was a large scar, which was the way Dr. Coley had identified him.

With more case studies, Coley came to believe that postoperative infections actually improved outcomes for cancer patients, and he theorized that the body's natural immune response helped rid the body of cancer. He tested his theory, which might also explain cases of spontaneous remission previously categorized as miracles, by trying to induce strep infections in people he operated on. The results included some responses and some deaths. Coley tried to make the process safer by using various dead bacteria that were eventually called Coley's toxins, and which caused fever but no deaths. The treatment was dismissed by many of his peers, some of whom called it quackery. However, others began to use infectious agents to treat diseases with some success. In 1927, Julius Wagner-Jauregg was awarded a Nobel Prize for using malaria to enlist fever to cure syphilis. Coley soldiered on with his research, and his treatment worked often enough to remain available to doctors who wanted to try it. However, when he died in 1936, his hypothesis was still unproven conjecture.

In the decades after Coley's death, great strides were made toward understanding the immune system, which defends us from the staggeringly plentiful microbes that surround us. Resident in and on us is a microbe burden that is thought to exceed the number of cells we have in our body tenfold. So every moment of life beyond the womb entails ongoing immune system combat with viruses, bacteria, and fungi that unchecked can readily overwhelm us. At risk of carrying the war analogy too far, the immune system maintains communications, develops weapons, identifies enemies, and moves against them with a variety of cells and proteins. This immune system also clears the cells lost by attrition and handles most of those abnormal enough to possess malignant potential. The whole thing is stunningly complex and filled with remarkable cell characters. Macrophage cells, for example, will devour and break down a hundred bacteria apiece. If they can't do the job of defeating an infection, they literally call for backup by emitting a protein that summons neutrophils, which are so fierce they are programmed to die within one to five days to prevent collateral damage to healthy cells. The process of threat assessment and communication can also enlist T cells and B cells in the campaign. When the conflict is over, memory and B cells retain information about the invader, which makes it possible for the body to repel future infections, generally without any signs of illness. This is immunity.

Awesomely powerful, adaptive, and effective, the immune system is so exquisite that it makes our intervention on the body's behalf, even with a complex of therapies, crude in comparison. It is so essential to survival that scientists like Don Thomas could only consider wiping it out if they were reasonably certain they could restore it. If Thomas experienced real doubts of his eventual success, he never voiced them to the men and women who worked in his lab. When they were asked about their boss, they described him as a man on a mission who responded to failure by saying, "Let's try again." Near the end of his life, a researcher named Beverly Torok-Storb said she once asked colleagues if they could share a funny anecdote about the man. No one could. "There are no funny stories about Don," she said. "None. He had a mission. There was nothing funny about it."

Although Thomas was remarkably even tempered, he was surely affected by the deaths he attended. Yes, the patients he treated were already desperately ill because of their disease, and no one promised anyone that that intense treatment followed by a transplant would work. But when the course ended with death, no amount of admiration for patients' courage erased their suffering or the grief of their loved ones. Thomas mourned the deaths but drew motivation from his successes. "Evidently it could be done," he would eventually recall. "We just have to find out how." The "how" would come to include refined techniques for harvesting, processing, preserving, and transplanting blood stem cells, as well as elaborate systems to safeguard patients from infection.

By 1979, the Fred Hutchinson Cancer Research Center was ready for a ten-year-old leukemia patient named Laura Graves, who traveled from her home in Colorado to Seattle to be treated. Although she did not have a sibling match for her marrow, the cancer center maintained a registry of staff blood donors, which included information on bone marrow compatibility. For the first time, a match was found in a registry. Laura Graves underwent an intense regimen of chemotherapy that destroyed her immune system. She then received the marrow harvested by needle from the donor's pelvis.

Laura recovered in a special room where caregivers were experienced with preventing infections. With their immune systems devastated, transplant recipients were so vulnerable to infection that they could die from microbes that are otherwise harmless. In one tragic case that illustrated the danger of infection, eleven transplant recipients would die at Roswell Park Cancer Institute in Buffalo when the delivery of air filters was delayed and an airborne fungus caused infections. Laura was protected in a hyperclean environment where she received medicines to stop infections as well as transfusions of blood and platelets. Laura recovered and left the hospital in good health with a functioning immune system. The cancer eventually returned and took Laura's life, but the successful transplant signaled the value of registries and procedures using unrelated donors and recipients.

The team at the Fred Hutchinson Cancer Research Center wasn't the only one working on the use of intense chemotherapy and rescue of the immune system with bone marrow transplants. Progress made by teams around the country contributed to the advances, as did the development of drugs that reduced the risk of GvHD. Further research on the harvesting and freezing of patients' own marrow, after the patients were treated into disease remission with anticancer drugs, would eventually make it possible for many more people to receive their own preserved marrow in autologous transplants. Their own stem cells were saved at a time when they were in a tenuous and inevitably short remission. Those cells could serve to bring back their immunity after the intense therapy that was strong enough to kill the patients and their cancer were it not for the stem cell "rescue."

Bone marrow transplantation offered treatment possibilities for other patients with immune disorders, including the kinds of illnesses that produced the phenomenon depicted in the 1976 movie *The Boy in the Plastic Bubble*. The film, which starred John Travolta, was based on the life of David Vetter, who was so vulnerable to infection because of a genetic abnormality that compromised his immune system that he lived inside a sterile plastic cocoon, breathing filtered air. David would eventually undergo a successful transplant, but the marrow donated by his sister contained the virus linked to Burkitt's lymphoma. He would die from it. But with rapid improvements in transplant techniques, other "bubble" boys and girls would receive marrow cells, develop robust immune systems, and be able to leave confinement and live normal lives. Fascination with children raised in medical isolation would fade to the point where many people were only aware of the phenomenon because of the film, and even then, there may have been confusion about whether the story was fact or fiction. Although the cure of bone marrow transplant dampened public curiosity about immunodeficiency, it did not end the drama around the treatment. Like cancer patients, children and adults who received transplants underwent chemotherapy to kill whatever functioning marrow cells or hostile immune cells they may have possessed. This was necessary to prepare the body to receive and nurture the new marrow cells.

By the end of my time at Case, victories like Laura Graves's transplant and setbacks like the tragedy at Roswell Park had led to a standard of care that greatly improved the odds of transplant success and, therefore, cures for immune diseases and blood-related cancers. I helped to care for patients who were overseen by senior Case faculty, including the aptly named Hillard Lazarus, who, like all transplant doctors, brought patients to the brink of death with chemotherapy and then restored them to life like the Lazarus of the Bible.

Despite many setbacks, successful transplants hinted at an intriguing future for oncology. Specialties like cardiology were high profile because of the number of people affected and the emerging impact of smoking-cessation campaigns and medicines that could reduce the known risk factors of hypertension and high cholesterol. These interventions slowed disease but couldn't be considered cures, while bone marrow transplant offered a fundamental reset. It could replace a defective blood system or enable intensive therapy to cure leukemia. That, for me, was very alluring. Make this high-drama process of transplantation safer and more patient friendly, and you might be able to build a new blood and immune system to affect all the disorders involving blood.

Likewise, it seemed that when people lacked a well-functioning immune system, they were likely to develop diseases that seemed to have few other connections. The immune system is implicated in diseases of the brain, the gut, the joints, the skin, and more. But understanding just how and why some organs are affected and not others remains a challenge. Sometimes things go haywire because of insufficient immune response, and sometimes the culprit is too much immune activity. In some people, a seemingly normal reaction to something as common as a physical or chemical insult can set off a cascade of events that produces disease. This is thought to occur particularly with viral infections. There the virus provokes a response of lymphocytes preprogrammed to recognize it with high specificity, but more cells can become involved, sometimes as bystanders caught up in the activation process or sometimes as cells with specificity for other targets that resemble part of the body. This spreading of an immune response can sometimes activate what is otherwise dormant, cells that attack the body itself. It is thought that type 1 diabetes or multiple sclerosis might be triggered by these kinds of overly aggressive immune processes. It is also thought that severe or chronic injury can provoke abnormal efforts of repair. For centuries, physicians have reported cases of cancers developing in places where people were burned or otherwise injured. The high frequency of liver cancer in parts of Asia correlates with places where viral hepatitis is more common and liver cancer occurs with increased frequency among those who have alcoholic cirrhosis of the liver. William Coley (yes, the same William Coley) treated a veterinarian who developed a tumor in the exact place where he was struck by the horn of a bull and developed swelling and inflammation. Coley treated him with his toxins, and the man went into remission. He lived for six years before dying of kidney disease. It can be debated as to whether the tumor was cancerous, as not all tumors are malignant. But it is clear that immune provocation can enhance anticancer effects. Indeed, a harmless cousin of the tuberculosis-causing mycobacterium called BCG is introduced into the bladder of people with low-grade bladder cancer and has been shown to reduce recurrence and progression.

Coley's veterinarian and these other illustrations point to the paradox of the immune system and frankly of many systems in the body. There is an equipoise that normally balances activating and suppressing activities and shifts that balance in response to particular challenges. Both the immune system and the clotting system of the blood have countervailing activities that manage to stay steady when we are well but can dramatically activate one part of the process or another when needed. A clot must form when we are cut, but it has to stop clotting and eventually resolve as we heal. The immune system is even more complex, with many players and many molecules within those players dictating how the multilayered response is orchestrated and resolves. In the 1980s, just identifying the participants beyond describing how they looked under the microscope was new. Still today, we are defining new cell subsets that make up the system, and our known repertoire of molecular participants is likely far from complete. Since we only partially know the roster, it is no wonder that we don't know much about how they play together. But this is slowly coming into focus. We are gaining tools for identifying and enumerating a wide range of cells, and we can now image how they move and grow and respond within tissues. We can do this over time in living animals, using special microscopes. It is starting to be possible to build predictive algorithms for how various components work together to achieve a beneficial result in the body. Of course, the hope is that this will yield more than just exciting biology and will eventually put tools in the hands of doctors so they can regulate the process in service of patients.

No cells are more essential to the life process than those that are created in the marrow. Hidden in the bones, the marrow produces cells that are circulated to every organ and tissue, where they perform functions that doctors like Don Thomas recognized, but in hazy detail constrained by the knowledge of the day. But their pioneering efforts to save lives with what was emerging biologic understanding was inspiring.

It was time for me to move from medical school to medical training, the apprenticeship time in becoming a doctor. Where you do that, your internship and residency, shapes everything about your future. It shapes how you think, how you relate to patients and colleagues and the breadth of your horizons. I knew I wanted to be in a place where medicine was twined with science: where the culture championed making decisions based on scientific evidence and where the goal was not just to deliver the best care based on today's understanding but to help make tomorrow's medicine better through research. I thought the Brigham and Women's Hospital in Boston represented the best of that, deeply entrenched in the standards of excellence by being adjacent to and a part of Harvard Medical School but openly emphasizing new approaches and challenging established ideas. On the day every medical student both dreads and dreams of, Match Day, I learned we had matched: I ranked the Brigham first, and they ranked me in their top tier. I was given a slot at the Brigham. It truly transformed my life.

Bruce Walker, my good friend in medical school, also interviewed at the Harvard hospitals and was most interested in Massachusetts General Hospital (MGH). We vowed that if we both got our first choices, we would find and share an apartment midway between them—and we did. Bruce and I had one of those odd bonds unique to medicine: we had been anatomy partners. That meant we learned anatomy together by working on the same cadaver. It is a rite of passage not very common in medical schools today, but then, it was an emotional and ghoulish experience, and also a deep privilege. The body is a sacred space. We were given the right to see and the responsibility to know it. We and the other two members of our team took it very seriously. Bruce and I did some extra work to really figure out the complicated structures in the head, so we shared some knowledge compulsions that made us compatible. That made living together easy, as we both tolerated heaps of medical journals and books with the bonus that we both thought a pint of ice cream was a darn good meal. With only spoons to wash!

Bruce was from an academic family and had studied chemistry, so he was much more able than I to get engaged in the science behind what we were learning. He knew that he wanted to do science as well as treat patients, and he knew he could do it. He shared my interest in the immune system. And like me, he was both frustrated by the limitations of treatments we could offer patients and intrigued by what organisms, including humans, could do on their own against disease. For every time an invading germ, an injury, or a genetic mutation made someone sick, there were countless times every day when the body resisted disease or repaired itself. And these were just the ordinary illustrations of what the body could do. Like many medical students, we had been impressed by phenomena like the abscopal effect—*ab* for "away from" and *scopal* for "target"— observed when radiation or other local therapy that hit metastatic cancer in one part of the body could destroy it elsewhere. It seemed that somehow the immune system learned something from the local death of cells and then applied it to the body as a whole. There was a resilience in the body that was sometimes evident. Commonly it involved the immune system and the blood, but it could also apply to other tissues like an injured liver. Cut out up to a third of the liver and it will grow back: remarkable regeneration, not unlike the odd salamanders I used as my specimens growing up. That seemed an area of medicine that begged to be exploited. Something that offered more than the drugs that simply try to reduce symptoms or slow but not reverse disease. The immune system seemed like the place where this was most evident and most important across medicine, so we were naturally both drawn to it.

Although neither of us was so impressed with himself that he would have said anything about making discoveries, Bruce and I felt somewhat prepared to care for patients and hoped to make some contributions, as scientists, in the area of immunity and disease. When he and I got to Boston, we found an apartment to share on Marlborough Street in a neighborhood called Back Bay, which really was a bay until it was filled in during the nineteenth century—430 acres of what was tidal marsh between the mainland and the hub of rocky prominence that was old Boston and its Beacon Hill. It was filled with redbrick town houses that persist to this day. Although the area is now gentrified, in 1980, Marlborough Street was still a place where there were boardinghouses, and many of the Victorian-era houses were poorly kept. But it was roughly halfway between the hospitals where we would be working and accessible by a combination of buses, the train known as the T, and, in good weather, bicycle.

The Brigham, where I worked, sits in the heart of an extraordinary concentration of medical facilities. It had been pastureland when the Brigham (then Peter Bent Brigham Hospital) received its charter to serve the poor and Harvard Medical School outgrew its downtown location. They served to anchor the subsequent growth of the Longwood Medical Area (named after Longwood Avenue), which grew to be a neighborhood of twelve irregular city blocks and home to three teaching hospitals, a massive cancer research center and clinic, a famous diabetes research center and clinic, the Harvard School of Public Health and the dental school, and literally thousands of labs. About fifty thousand people commuted to work in these places in 1980 (the number would more than double by 2015), and patients came from all over the world seeking care.

It was an awe-inspiring place to enter postdoctoral training. That was before seeing the portraits on walls of the legends of science and medicine. I didn't take lightly how high the bar was set by all that history or by patient rounds with people whose names I knew from my Cleveland textbooks. Anxiety nearly crushed me. I only hoped I could give compassionate and reasonably errorless care to my patients before the gods of medicine found me out and sent me packing. What saved me was the open-mindedness of senior doctors who genuinely wanted to hear what the newly graduated might have to say and by colleagues who bantered ideas for sport. It became clear that by getting my wish to be a part of place where the science of medicine was king, I had entered a world where the unknowns vastly exceeded our knowledge and the pursuit of greater understanding was, by turns, grueling, inspiring, uplifting and devastating to experience. And sometimes you experienced all of it in a single day.

I was lucky to have, in Bruce, a roommate who understood my day-to-day experience. He would also play a central role in the most momentous night of my life. The occasion was a party I organized to celebrate his engagement to be married. I invited a crowd of our friends, including a psychologist named Stephen Shirk. For months, Steve had been telling me about a friend in his apartment building. He said, "Her name is Kathy and she's perfect for you." On this night he brought her as his plus-one.

Kathy, who was an artist, a one-time college art faculty member and also worked at a gallery on Newbury Street which was then, and remains, Boston's fanciest shopping street. When she came to our apartment, I noticed. Despite the Jack Daniels and not because of it, I knew this was an exceptional spirit. We talked; she sparkled. I had to mingle and so did she; still she sparkled. It wasn't bewitching as she's too genuine for that, but there was a special presence and a laugh that really struck me. Everyone there was already part of the crowd. She was the only newcomer. But she wasn't a bit fazed and engaged people with sincerity and ease. I realized that Stephen actually did know something special about people and had the two of us pegged just right.

Although I knew Kathy was special (and when my mother met Kathy she made it clear that she thought she was getting the better half in the in-law deal than Kathy's mother was), an event a few months later made it clear. My closest friend since I was four years old phoned from his home in the Virgin Islands with a medical emergency. Tim Reynold's wife Karen had just given birth to a baby who needed complex and delicate surgery. As they caught the first plane that would get them to Boston I set about making the arrangements with the top specialists in town.

When they got to Boston, Tim and Karen camped in the front room of the apartment I shared with Bruce. Kathy quickly became central to the support system we created for the family as days turned to weeks and then months. Someone else in a new relationship might have experienced a few days of this crisis and made other plans. Kathy did everything she could think of to help Karen and Tim and never missed a beat, never did anything without love. It was a crash course in what it means to live with the possibility that a medical crisis could, at any time, overwhelm other plans. She took it with good cheer and with grit; nothing deterred her optimistic, caring way.

After Kathy and I got engaged we went to Western Massachusetts to see her parents. We went to dinner at one of their favorite spots and noticed a couple who were in their eighties, or perhaps nineties, sitting together and laughing repeatedly, even uproariously, at some shared story or joke. We looked at each other and knew that if we could make each other laugh, we could get through whatever came our way. We married in a rainstorm of biblical proportion on June 2, 1984. My father was my best man, but had a mismatched tuxedo that Bruce Walker's new wife had to urgently remedy. The bride's ride got lost. An ever helpful clergyman cousin decided at the alter to change our already memorized vows (awkward pause) and guests had to slosh through Harvard Yard from the church to the reception. But we had a blast and were the last danced-out couple to leave the party, by cab. We had our first child, Margaret, in August 1985 when I was a tutor in one of the Harvard dorms. Next would come Elizabeth in 1987, and Edward, nicknamed Ned, in 1991.

As much as I tried to involve myself, Kathy unequivocally was the parent of record. She worked full-time at Payette Associates, one of Boston's premier architecture firms, but made the balance work as best she could. I was mostly useless as I was doing clinical work at the hospital, conducting research, and moonlighting weekends as a physician to make enough to buy ourselves a home. Our first one was a two-family that we shared with another couple. When my mother-in-law first saw it, she cried. My choosing research meant I earned less than the baggage handlers at the airport and it was not the life she had hoped for for her daughter. As a child of the Great Depression herself and having had family struggles in a financial crisis during Kathy's youth, Geraldine Elliott knew of money problems. We were confident that better days were ahead, but there were moments, particularly when something unexpected arose, that reminded us that my choosing research was not without its strains.

One evening, when Margaret was only a few months old, Kathy brought her to the hospital to visit me in the on-call room where residents retired during break periods. I was stretched out on a bed, and Kathy put Margaret down next to me. She grabbed my necktie and, as babies do, put it in her mouth. In a flash I suddenly realized that earlier in the day I had been working in a lab with radioactive materials. In leaning forward, had I dragged the tie over 'hot' materials? Indeed, a Geiger counter revealed that I had. The radiation safety officer was called. His response was all irritation about the forms to be filed. Nothing was mentioned about the child until I wouldn't relent, but nothing could be done. The incident further raised the ante on what the research path might cost our family. I knew it was right for me, but was it right to ask so much of Kathy and the children? It had to mean something more than what doctoring would. I was pretty comfortable that I could help patients as a doctor, and I knew that would be easier for us. If research was the choice, it had to be for a pretty high calling.

THREE

CANCERLAND

When her doctor got the marriage license test report, he sent her to the hematology clinic at Brigham and Women's Hospital. She arrived with her fiancé, and I brought them into a private office to break the news. The tests showed she had chronic myeloid leukemia (CML), a type of cancer in which the bone marrow produces abnormal granulocytes, which are a type of white blood cell. The best option was chemotherapy and a bone marrow transplant. Without them, she would die of the disease.

I don't recall the precise words I used, but the situation was not hopeless, and I would have said as much. What I do recall is that my patient's eyes filled with tears and her attention began to wander the moment I used the word *leukemia*. Prior to meeting me, she had felt perfectly fine and was thrilled about getting married. Suddenly I was telling her that she was in the chronic phase of a certainly fatal form of cancer. CML is best treated at this moment, when people do not feel sick and fewer than 10 percent of the blood cells are involved. Untreated, the disease can advance and become less vulnerable to medicines. When this happens, people really do feel marked fatigue and fever increasing as they approach a crisis phase where the abnormal cells multiply in an out-of-control fashion, crowding out the normal blood cells needed to sustain the body.

The about-to-be-married young woman I met at the Brigham left without making an appointment, and in the weeks that followed, she wouldn't respond to any of the calls we made or the letters we sent. Did she know all that awaited her if she chose treatment? I doubt it. But most people knew that chemotherapy at that time was inadequate and bone marrow transplantation, which then was the only hope for curing CML, meant high risk and life trauma. In general, transplant procedures were improving, with immune-suppressing drugs that could reduce some of the transplanted cells' attack on the recipient's body (GvHD). There was also an increasing public awareness of transplantation. While it is a totally different matter when an organ like a kidney or liver is transplanted, growing success in those areas did shed some reflected positive light on bone marrow transplant. When the press reported on transplantation, the stories were generally positive, highlighting lives that were saved.

However, the press accounts generally obscured the details of the procedures, which could be harrowing for everyone involved, including the teams of professionals who performed them. The hematology group at the Brigham did bone marrow transplants, and trainees like me also cared for patients who made the pilgrimage to Boston for treatment at the neighboring Dana-Farber Cancer Institute. The Farber was one of a small number of comprehensive cancer centers scattered across the country. At these places, science and treatment lived side by side, with the balance not always favoring the experience of the patients. Indeed, in the 1980s, Dana-Farber was the kind of place where many patients were pushed to their physical limits by doctors who considered themselves part of a warrior tribe. The chief warrior was Emil "Tom" Frei, who had, with colleague Emil Freireich, made extraordinary, lifesaving advances in the treatment of childhood leukemia with just such an all-out approach at the National Cancer Institute in the 1960s.

With the official title of physician in chief, Frei was understandably very aggressive with therapies, and his attitude set the tone at Dana-Farber. While surgeons generally followed a "cut-it-to-cure-it" philosophy, oncologists in the Frei mold who gave chemotherapy were testing giving patients the biggest dose of chemotherapy they could survive, on the belief that this afforded them the best chance at cure. "More is better" had worked for childhood leukemia, and now with new drugs being developed, maybe finding the right mix of highest-tolerated doses could do the same for the much more common cancers of adults. Great effort was made to push doses while improving the care used to save patients from the life-threatening complications. The all-out ethos of the place could be seen throughout the building, which had both high-tech labs and patients' rooms. Sometimes, like all research-focused hospitals with the imposing equipment, constantly beeping monitors, and bustle of intensely focused people in medical uniforms, the place seemed one part hospital, one part science fiction battleship.

The culture and environment at Dana-Farber were particularly reassuring to patients who wanted the most modern treatment and who believed, given the stakes, that they had to struggle and suffer like prizefighters if they were to survive. This perspective of mortal combat had its downsides. First, it could enhance the guilt of those who feared, either consciously or subconsciously, that they were somehow to blame for their diagnosis. Rarely can a single factor, even smoking, be sufficient by itself to cause cancer, so this self-blame was often unscientific as well as unnecessary. However, it was also rooted in the all-too-human need to make sense, even self-punishing sense, out of events that are beyond our control. It also turns disease progression into a personal failure, a lack of sufficient fight. That is just wrong. While attitude can change the perception and particularly the family's perception of events, it will not change the rate of tumor cell growth. There is evidence that the immune system responds to input from the nervous system and so could be modulated by thoughts, but the response is not sufficiently robust to consider it central to the outcome of malignant disease. Spirited resistance is worthy in itself. Putting the burden of progressive cancer on one's spirit is just not fair. Unfortunately, biology always wins.

The tendency to self-blame runs deep, however. It is supported by some religious traditions that teach that one's physical, emotional, and even social well-being are proof of either virtue or sin. In the eighteenth century, theaters were filled by crowds eager to see the public dissection of executed criminals by so-called anatomists who sought to demonstrate that the criminals' inner organs showed signs of their moral corruption. Today, only a tiny fraction of society holds such extreme beliefs about the body and the soul, but they haunt many more who just have a feeling—as much a sensation as a thought—that they are responsible for their own suffering. This feeling, layered on top of the natural motivation to do all they could against the cancer, sometimes reduced willingness to speak up when suffering exceeded reasonable bounds. It could unfortunately work against people already dealing with the weight of their diagnoses and the rigors of their treatments.

But care at a research hospital really does translate into distinctive care. Almost never is a patient treated with just one person's opinion guiding decisions. Almost never is care delivered without consideration of what new developments might improve his or her chances. Almost never is the patient seen just as an individual; he or she is seen as an individual and as a representative of a disease. The implications of such a culture are of course both positive and negative. Care based on the personal needs of an individual accommodating his or her life priorities is an ongoing aspiration not always realized. The name of many cancer centers does not help. They are often titled "cancer institutes." That does not convey caring as central to their mission, though in most places it certainly is. It conveys a central paradox in much of modern medicine. Medical care remains largely primitive and will only advance by scientific study, but when we are sick, it is deeply personal, and we all want a comforting hand, a healing touch, not statistical analysis.

I lived this one unforgettable day during my internship. We were on call every other or every third night. That meant that we were essentially awake and available in the hospital for thirty-six hours followed by either one night sleeping at home before doing it again or getting in a twelve-hour day in the hospital and getting one more night in our home bed. During the every-third-day-on-call months, we had one Sunday free every three weeks. Otherwise, we were in the hospital, so doing laundry, buying groceries, getting to a bank, and socializing presented a challenge. The daily 10:00 p.m. meal was the social life for most of us. It was difficult to even stay connected to family, so it was notable when a phone call startled me from sleep on a night in my apartment. My parents were on the line telling me that Dr. Baldino, my paragon of a good doctor, had told my mother that she had colon cancer. She had been very reluctant to inform him that she'd noticed blood in the toilet bowl intermittently over a month or so. He examined her and sent her for a colonoscopy and biopsy that revealed the bad news. I couldn't think clearly, but I knew that I had to bring all the expertise I felt surrounded me in Boston to bear on her health.

It was a struggle to ask for help, but the colon cancer expert physician whom I trusted, Robert Meyer, and the surgeon whom I knew to be outstanding, Robert Osteen, were extraordinarily gracious and helpful. They immediately made themselves available, and my mother arrived in Boston to see them. When my parents and I were walking to Dana-Farber, a trip I had made dozens of times as an eager physician in training, the steps seemed to go into slow motion. Previously, I had regarded the place as somewhere where I could be useful and where I could learn to be more so by the fabulous physician and scientist teachers within its walls. Now that shiny panache turned gray. When my mother reached the sign by the door—Dana-Farber Cancer Institute—she could not go on. She wept. Her fear, her mortality, were in those letters on the wall. I had seen my mother as always cheerful, always ready to go forward, and now she was a patient walking in to confront a reality that could not be denied or made light of; this was life-and-death for her and for our family. We were all entering Cancerland.

As my mother steadied herself outside the doors of the Dana-Farber Cancer Institute, my heart broke and I understood, for the first time, what every patient who approached that door surely felt. For me, Dana-Farber had been a place of intense work and education, a crucible where I was becoming a better doctor and scientist. For people who came seeking treatment, every visit was accompanied by existential fear. Seeing that fear in my mother's face made me appreciate every patient's experience and motivated me to remember, in every encounter with a patient, that I was treating a human being who was scared and searching for a lifeline to hope.

What patients know, and I could see through my mother's eyes, was that a cancer diagnosis sends you into an alternate reality, *Cancerland*, where the usual things in life recede and it's easy to be overwhelmed by your condition, your treatment, and your prognosis. In Cancerland, you learn a whole new language related to blood tests and imaging technologies, and you scan the horizon for signs of hope or danger. People who spend months or even years in this environment can become so familiar with their own disease that they could pass for medical specialists.

Cancerland is not always a dismal place. Those of us who work there every day consider it a privilege to spend so much time in an environment free of the artifice that you find in more ordinary realms. Few things can make a person more engaged, authentic, and real than a serious diagnosis. Encounter people in this state of prolonged peril and you discover them without pretense and prejudice. They laugh and cry more freely and are less reluctant to say what they think. With some exceptions, love and empathy flow more readily. It's a bit ironic, but true, that gratitude and generosity come to the fore when we fear that time is running out.

Accompanying my mother through her treatment also gave me the chance to learn how people experienced the doctors, nurses, and everything that made up the system of care at Dana-Farber. My mother's doctors were people I knew as colleagues, teachers, and supervisors. I knew how these physicians thought and could imagine how they might discuss her care in a conference. But they did a good job of sharing the essential facts without overwhelming her when she was already feeling vulnerable. One of the best things they did for her was conclude each consultation with a review of the next steps to take. This information reassured her that though she faced a steep climb, there were toeholds and resting spots for her to anticipate. A clear plan makes any ascent easier.

As I watched my mother navigate cancer, I also came to understand the limits of transparency. In private, professionals who discuss a case together might consider many options that in the end are inappropriate in a given case. If you let a patient or his loved ones into these conversations, you run the risk of creating confusion— or worse, after-the-fact conflict. People are likely to recall the option not chosen and ask, "Why didn't you take that path?" Sometimes no amount of talking can reassure someone that it wasn't incompetence or neglect that determined the choice. The same trouble can arise when you share test results or imaging without interpretation and the filter that experience and judgment provide. Leaving it for patients to interpret them for themselves is both unkind and unwise, sending people adrift who most need a strong anchor.

My mother's course was set. She had a hoped-for curative resection that failed. Surgery left her with a humiliating colostomy that tested her dignity and sense of humor. These attributes she never lost in public, but I knew they were sorely tested even among close friends and made her feel outside the circle of the well even before she knew of any disease progression. She relapsed repeatedly over a number of years. These might have been prevented if the studies that came to completion five years after her death were available, but they were not, and I am only grateful that research has now spared other families what we experienced.

Each of my mother's relapses was viscerally felt, consuming dread by all in our family. My mother truly was the light we circled around. Each time, I reached out to senior colleagues whom I thought balanced expertise with humanism, and each time, they responded in ways I can only consider heroic. They represented ideals of medical and surgical care to me. But sometimes I wonder if my desire to do everything that could be done may have tipped even their best judgment on whether something should be done. When lung metastases were found, lung resections were done. One of my most awful memories of medicine came during that effort. The chest is richly wired with sensory nerves. Given how critical the contents of the chest are for us as an organism, it is no wonder that that is true. When surgery is done on the chest, particularly when horrifyingly medieval chest spreaders pry open the ribs, raging pain results. Those were and often still are necessary for resecting tumors in the lung. I sat by my mother's bed in the recovery room as she gradually came awake. Her first moment of glancing over came with a smile that quickly transformed into screams of pain. It was like a blowtorch had been applied to her skin, she later said. Such roaring misery was foreign even to my professional self; as a son, it was sickening. A well-placed nerve block finally put out the fire.

She healed, but then developed dizziness. Rarely does colon cancer go to the brain, but it did for her. Radiation was followed by more surgery to pluck out the metastases. On its face, that sounds entirely reasonable, and I am grateful to the surgeons who did it. But entering the skull alone can change a person. Entering the skull, cutting away some brain, and having radiation damage it as a whole leaves only a shadow of the former self. It did get my mother back to some function; enough to attend and dance at Kathy's and my wedding. That was a gift. But she then drifted, and finally it was Dr. Baldino who came to our house and said to me, "It is enough; she can only suffer from here."

As I look back, I see my optimism drove much of what happened. Not that my mother's doctors suspended their own judgment, but there are so few firm guidelines that naturally they shaded decisions in favor of being active in helping. This desire to help is perilous ground for physicians. It is often made the harder by the sense of some nefarious, legally based overseer peering over the shoulder. I don't regard it as something that affected those who cared for my mother, but I know in many circumstances it does and confess that at times it did when I was deciding what to do. The notion of defensive medicine is very real. For some, it becomes reflexive: do all that can be done so no one can accuse you of not taking action. That is mindless and drives costs, though for some reason health economists don't find it in the data, perhaps because no doctor would admit acting that way. It can also be more subtle and is the way I know I behave, and I suspect my mother's physicians did too. The impulse to be helpful is in all of us and is a deeply felt compulsion among most physicians. When approaches are available that have even a slim chance of helping, the default is to want to try. This "just do something" impulse (?) is what compels much of oncology care, even when the odds strongly favor that the action is prolonging death, not meaningfully prolonging life. It is made worse by FDA approvals of oncology drugs that induce remissions, but do not alter survival beyond a few months.

For the patient, the reflex is of course to do what is recommended. That was certainly the case for my mother: if an option was available, she of course said yes. She was an active, can-do person who felt it was her duty to family and friends that she pursue every meaningful option. Part of her role as a cancer patient was not just to fight the disease the way our language encourages people to do, but also to prevent others from suffering for her. She could not bear the notion that what her family experienced was loss. To try and mitigate that, she took every medical option she could. Almost comically, her baking schedule increased. She filled even more cookie tins and put more pies in the freezer, even a second freezer in the basement. Noble suffering meant doing whatever was recommended and then some.

After four years of struggle my mother died in 1985, at the age of sixty-five, which is the age I am now. She was savoring every moment as a parent and recent grandparent. It seemed unjust. Small-mindedly, I couldn't help but see injustice when I was "moonlighting" rare weekends taking care of nursing home residents. For many, they had no awareness of family or events around them because of advanced dementia. It seemed that a just universe would allow bartering a few of those seemingly hollow years to give those taken in their vitality. However, she had taught me gratitude as a way of living. I couldn't let those lessons turn bitter. Rather, I had to make what I saw and what my family experienced become fuel for more urgently working on ways to change what others would go through. I could not let that pain simply echo and fade. It made clear that nothing was more important than bringing new light, new light, new approaches to the dark shadow of cancer. What was available was crude: poisons, surgeries, and radiation. Like shielding from a hurricane with your hands, these were simple and hopelessly overmatched approaches to the complex biology of cancer. More science seemed the only way forward. I was lucky enough to be in a place where science stood tall and I was given a chance to engage it.

Moving science to create better clinical approaches is an almost painfully incremental affair, which meant that, as a clinician, I often found myself in the position of explaining the slow pace of research. Everyone hopes to learn of a new treatment or a drug in clinical trials that will provide a cure. Although all clinical trials are conducted with the hope that the impact will be great, the reality is that very few are, particularly in cancer. The work that can go on in the laboratory to determine whether a drug will work or not, be safe or not is improving, but still very limited. We were frequently implored to look for the breakthrough therapy, we almost never found one. Fortunately, most people accepted this reality, especially if we take took the time to explain things well. Most people still wish to participate, in part based on the hope for them, but at least as often, in the hopes that someone will ultimately benefit.

The hope for scientific progress is part of the pact willing doctors and patients implicitly make. It helps to justify the fact that most trials need people to be in the "control" group. That may be a group that gets only the standard therapy and not the treatment with a new agent. It is essential to do in order to define just what is added by the new drug. But it is an extremely difficult situation to discuss and for patients and doctors to accept. If you really believe that the new drug is worth testing, why will you not be giving it to me? Often, it is just because side effects, toxicities might be worse. That makes sense and is easier for all to accept. But people come to research centers seeking what is new and are generally willing to take a risk to receive it. Being part of the group with only what is already available hardly keeps with their expectations or desires.

The tension that creates for all involved is real and challenging. It is then that I have experienced the pulling of strings by people of influence. Efforts are made to game the "randomization," but fortunately modern clinical trials block that. It is impossible to be anything other than an identified "number" in the process that determines what particular drug or "arm" of a trial a patient will get. People push and try to use connections and even offer money for a chance at a new drug. Part of our oath is literally to take the same care of any and all regardless of station. Compassion and good care are not bartered for cash. In principle and in practice, we do what we can for all.

However, when you are working in matters of life and death, there's every incentive to push considerations of status and power out of the picture. When I became responsible for patients, many of the things I used to care about just didn't matter as much to me, and that included what was happening in popular culture. I also found I had to try a little harder to get into the social flow outside the hospital and the lab. It's a small example, but I once ran into a friend leaving work who offered me tickets to a game at Fenway Park. I like baseball, and as always, the Red Sox were a hot ticket, but I couldn't muster the enthusiasm to take the tickets. At around this same time, I had a second experience that I took to be a signal that I needed to make an effort to lead a more well-rounded existence. On my way home from the hospital, I had gone into a place where I expected to have a quick dinner alone, and I saw some people I knew at a table. I thought, This is great! Somebody I know. I was so out of practice socially that it didn't register in my mind that they were there alone, together, and intentionally. When I asked if I could join them, they said, "Well, we're kind of having dinner." In the pause that followed, it dawned on me that I had failed to detect all the social cues and intruded where I really wasn't welcome.

Miscues in the outside world were inevitable for anyone who worked in the land of cancer where every day we experienced drama or trauma in ways that both truly heightened our experience of life and numbed us to its nuances. People were saved, and people died, and amid the intensity of this experience, we had to create a kind of normality that allowed us to function well. This was accomplished, in part, using a kind of dialect that allowed for us to talk among ourselves, and with patients, in a way that evaded certain realities. We spoke of "harvesting" marrow from donors and "conditioning," "giving" it to recipients who had undergone chemo and radiation therapy so intense it was fatal without the new marrow cells coming in to "rescue" them. The marrow was taken from donors who were wheeled into operating rooms and placed under general anesthesia before we used big needles to repeatedly pierce the pelvic bone and attach syringes to draw out the marrow cells. This was strenuous labor involving up to one hundred insertions, which became a bit easier because the bone became sort of spongy under the assault of the needle.

With each puncture of the bone, a small amount of reddish-brown, gelatinous marrow was drawn into a syringe and deposited in a sterile bucket until a quart or more was collected. This was done with some risk to the donor, including, in some rare cases, nerve damage that could cause long-lasting pain and numbness. Back then, recovery involved as long as a week in the hospital. Although it sounds like we removed a substantial amount, in fact we took only about 5 percent of a donor's marrow. The portion left untouched continued to function, and the places that were harvested recovered quickly.

For recipients, the transplant odyssey involved two days of intense chemotherapy followed by total-body irradiation, which killed all their functioning marrow cells. We could give the chemotherapy at the Brigham of Dana Farber. As we did this, our patients would lose the ability to fight infection, which meant we had to confine them to special environments sealed by sterile plastic. They ate food that was irradiated to kill all germs, drank sterile water, and breathed air that was cleaned of all contaminants. No one could enter these spaces without donning sterile gowns, masks, and gloves, and in some cases contact was achieved only via sleeved gloves that were built into a plastic barrier that separated patient and caregivers.

After the chemo, we had to complete the patient's preparation for transplant with total-body radiation. The linear accelerator that delivered the radiation was in one spot, underground. We reached it via a network of tunnels that connected the basements of the hospitals. I can only imagine what someone lying on a gurney, whizzing through this space and staring up at the passing light fixtures, must have thought and felt. With careful technique and advanced medicines, the outcomes for bone marrow transplants improved steadily. In 1984, the number done across the United States exceeded five thousand per year, and the risk of death declined to 30 percent. (This sounds high, but for a radical and dangerous therapy in the early stage of its use, it was a decent record.) We did better than average, which meant that the great majority of our patients recovered and left the hospital with their cancer in remission and their new immune systems functioning well. One of my mentors at the Brigham, Joel Rappeport, achieved many milestones in their period, including the first effective transplants to cure a number of immune-related diseases, including one that was always fatal in children.

Our successes were thrilling. The trouble for everyone came when patients died of infections that occurred despite all our efforts, or could not be cured with even the most powerful drugs at our disposal. For people with CML, the outcome depended mainly on whether they were at the beginning stages of the disease or the more virulent, so-called blast phase. In the late 1970s and early 1980s, a little more than 60 percent of people with early-stage CML were alive three years after transplant. Only 16 percent of blast phase patients lived this long.

The losses were especially hard to take because during treatment we became attached to our patients and their friends and families. No amount of professional distance prevented us from becoming emotionally drained by our work. More than once, I left the hospital so exhausted that the bus driver would reach the last stop on the line, park, and walk back to awaken me because I had fallen asleep and missed my stop. At other times, I would become so discouraged that I came close to giving up my career. No one case dragged me down deeper than caring for the father of a friend. We just couldn't do anything more and watching this distinguished, well-loved man drift away was more than I could take. The night of his demise, I was on call. I was paging the senior physician, but in those days before cell phones, he had to find an exit off a highway before he could get to a pay phone to return my call. It was agony to have to speak to the family as a mere doctor-in-training. Finally, he made his way back providing the calming comfort the family needed. Fortunately, something positive would always happen to lift my dark mood. In the early days of my work on transplants, it was common for residents to leave the hospital in scrubs. One day, I stopped in a shop near the hospital to buy a bottle of wine before heading home, and a man in the store noticed what I had on.

"Excuse me," he said. "Are you a doctor?"

I said yes and made some sort of quip about how there were so many doctors in the area you had to walk carefully to avoid stumbling over them.

While I paid for what I was purchasing and the clerk made change, the fellow asked about my medical specialty. I mentioned hematology/oncology, and he said, "Do you work on bone marrow transplants?"

Given my experience, I wondered for a moment if he had known someone who had undergone the procedure and, perhaps, died. I gathered my courage and said, "As a matter of fact, yes." His next words almost shocked me.

"Good," he said. "I had one, and it saved my life."

After a brief chat about his recovery from CML, the man shook my hand and we parted. What were the odds of such an encounter?

I guess the fact that we met in the Longwood Medical Area meant they were higher than they might be anywhere else. But still, it was such an unexpected exchange that it took me a few moments to let it sink in. It was an incredible uplift. It made the drama of caring for the complicated process and its untoward consequences seem trivial. Nothing could reduce the extraordinary lightness of being in one young life pulled back from a certainty of death. It made cancer seem more vulnerable and it made transplant seem the ultimate extension of scientific reasoning turned into palpable tools of hope. That hope was changing dramatically. It was clear that what my classmates and I had tried to understand as we raised questions with George Bernier at Case Western was coming into focus. Much was still seen through a gauzy haze of only partial understanding, but it was making a difference. No area more limited in understanding but rich in potential than that of stem cells. But as so often happens in science, we were working with phenomena that we didn't fully understand and getting results we couldn't predict.

Bone marrow stem cells are the reason we are capable of making blood cells, lymphoid cells, and the whole range of infection fighters we call our immune system. These cells are remarkably varied. The neutrophils, for example, take more than a week to be made, but then generally last less than a day. Stem cells are the stark contrast. They have an ability to divide asymmetrically with one "daughter" cell going on to mature to a fully functioning cell while the other becomes a replica of the parent cell: a process called self-renewal. This perpetual regenerating ability is one of the distinguishing features of stem cells. But unlike cancer cells that also can self-renew, a normal stem cell has the ability and inherent function of moving offspring or itself into a differentiating process. Blood stem cells can keep on creating new functional blood cells (proliferation) and new copies of themselves (self-renewal) indefinitely. If transplanted, they will take up the same work and, again, do it until the recipient dies. Should the transplant be repeated, ad infinitum, they could be considered immortal.

Bone marrow stem cells also create most of the cells that monitor the body for malignancies and pathogens, including viruses, bacteria, and parasites, and mobilize against them. One of the most intriguing theories about how this system is able to act against specific invaders was devised in 1957 by an Australian doctor named Frank Burnet. Burnet suggested that particular blood cells, so-called B cells made by marrow, stood in reserve in the lymphatic system and then, when called upon, produced antibodies tailor-made to deal with specific invaders. Remarkably, this system also

seemed to form memories of defeated invaders and thus confer immunity to future attacks. He was largely right though it was years
before it became clear how some cells in the immune system could
be able to respond to only specific targets.

Lymphocytes—of which B cells are one type (the other major
type being T cells)—have an inherent ability to undergo a set of genetic mutations that modify a particular part of their genome. That
part of the genome represents genes that encode receptors expressed only in the particular lymphoid cell. That is, B cells express
the B cell receptor (also functioning as an antibody) and T cells
express the T cell receptor. The mutations occur at a particular
point in the maturation of those cells. When the mutations begin,
they undergo a beautifully choreographed set of maneuvers that
involve cutting the receptor gene and repairing it, but adding some
random variants into the repair process. As the pieces are recon-
nected, some are lost and some have new bits added to them. That
controlled chaos is what converts the receptor gene that starts out
the same in every cell, into a collection of distinctive receptor
genes. Each receptor gene then can have its own special "signature."
That signature is what allows the receptor to identify specific targets. It is remarkable on many levels. First, it allows for an immense
diversity in what targets can be recognized. By allowing some random variation to become part of the cell's DNA, individual lymphoid cells now have their own special identity and capability. That
builds in response to a range of targets that can be as diverse and
subject to chance as are the invaders the cells have to face. Our
genes could never have encoded for all the new invaders that nature throws at us. Instead, our genes accept a degree of random-
ness that allows for new abilities of B and T cells to be generated
and emerge as needed, allowing new defenders to be forged with
an ability to adapt to new enemies. It gives us both adaptability and
resilience, keys for success in any endeavor, but particularly necessary for protecting us in the ever-changing world of microbes.

The second lesson from this aspect of the immune system, is that not all mutations are bad. We tend to regard genetic mutations like a bad accident. And mutations in the wrong place are how cancers begin and progress. But most mutations are silent. They happen and are of no major consequence. This is most evident in skin cells. The constant bombardment of radiation from the cosmos induces mutations in most of our skin cells. Fortunately, few of those are of any consequence. And some mutations are good, as in the case of the B and T cells of our immune system. There, the powerful good of mutations is evident in providing new capability: diverse recognition of invading microbes. In evolution, mutations are of course how new adaptations emerge. When mutations result in better tolerance of a stressful challenge, those mutations are preserved. If they occur in our germ cell stem cells, the cells that form sperm and eggs, the mutations pass along to new generations.

The lymphoid cells bearing their newly mutated recognition receptors do not all survive. Some are selectively killed, culled from the herd of cells. They die for two reasons. Some have mutated receptors that just don't work. They are either not produced by the cell or recognize nothing of consequence. They serve no purpose and so die out. Others recognize something within the body and are so overstimulated by it, that they trigger a process called programmed cell death: a kind of cell suicide. Even among cells that survive, if they react to the body, they often reprogram to become inert or nonreactive, or become cells that actively suppress the immune system. These mechanisms result in what is called tolerance, an enforced calm against ourselves while allowing a fierce rage against outside invaders.

In the twenty-first century, it is common for scientists to imagine that the body is comprised of networks and systems—including living cells—that could operate with the seeming intelligence of the immune system. But in the early 1980s, when I began my career in science, little was known about how cells accomplished this work. One of the first to think very deeply about the question was a molecular biologist named Joshua Lederberg, who, after winning a Nobel Prize for his work in genetics, began to study artificial intelligence. Lederberg was interested in understanding how a computer might be trained to respond on its own to inputs and "learn" on its own. He also theorized about how collections of different types of cells might do the same.

Lederberg first proposed his concept of "tolerance of self" in the late 1950s, hypothesizing that lymphocytes do learn from what they experience in their development. If they are responding too vigorously, it is likely they are responding to the body itself and they are instructed to just sit down and shut up. And for the most part, they do. It wasn't for three decades that any mechanisms for how this happens were evident, but his concepts are now validated and well defined; defined enough to be turned into methods for manipulating immune tolerance and reactivity as clinical therapies.

The fields of stem cell transplantation and organ transplantation were those where tolerance and reactivity meant everything. A lack of tolerance in the immune system and the engrafted organ or bone marrow would be immediately targeted and rejected. In the 1980s immune typing was becoming increasingly sophisticated. It had started as just mixing blood cells from the donor with those of the recipient and seeing what happened. That was how blood typing got started. Literally, Lederberg mixed patients' blood and, depending on who clumped with whom, he broke them into groups, A, B, and so forth. For that he won the Nobel Prize in 1930 and revolutionized blood cell transfusion. Immune typing progressed beyond that by measuring whether mixed lymphocytes from donor and host resulted in proliferation, growth of lymphocytes, as evidence of activation. The basis for some people's lymphocytes reacting against another was being defined and was the basis for Human Leukocyte Antigen (HLA) typing that is a critical component of defining who can safely donate to whom. Developments in that field in the time I was in training made transplantation far safer and far more accepted as a reasonable approach to devastating disease.

Even with typing, however, the process of transplantation was still brutal for patients. The immune system of donor and host battling each other required use of intensive therapies to suppress immunity. That was so harsh that transplantation was seen as only the course of last resort. It was used in people who had no other options. Those people often had aggressive blood cancer so they also got intensive therapy to kill the tumor cells. With the early success of intensive therapy curing some people with blood cancers, it was hypothesized that maybe bone marrow could be used not just for transplanting from one person to another, but as a backup for oneself. The major toxicity of intensive cancer therapy was in killing bone marrow cells and intestinal cells. At least one of those could be collected before intensive therapy and stored in the freezer while the chemotherapy poisons did their work on the cancer. The bone marrow could then be thawed and infused, rescuing the ability of bone marrow to make new blood cells. That is known as autologous bone marrow or a stem cell transplant. It worked powerfully well, for some.

Success using people's own bone marrow or blood stem cells to rescue the effects of intensive therapy was curative for about 40 percent of those who had specific lymphomas and had failed every other therapy. People who had run out of options got their life back—nothing short of wondrous. So the question became, "Why not try this for patients with other cancers?"

At the hospitals where I worked in Boston, we began using high-dose chemotherapy and radiation followed by bone marrow transplants to treat malignant blood and immune systems. Among the first patients enrolled in trials of this treatment were women with breast cancer that had relapsed and metastasized after conventional treatment. Because they possessed healthy marrow, we first drew their own cells from their bones and then processed and preserved them in liquid nitrogen. (This is the first step in what's called autologous transplantation.) After patients endured life-threatening treatments with chemicals and radiation, we put the marrow back in with the hopes that their immune systems would recover fast enough to save them from death due to infection.

Autologous transplants to treat solid tumors were eventually done at research hospitals across the United States and Europe, but no one was more assertive about using this strategy than Emil "Tom" Frei. Like all oncologists, Tom was unhappy about the limited success of chemotherapy. In far too many cases, cancers seemed to be eliminated only to return in a genetically new form resistant to the treatment that had seemingly succeeded. Frei had reason to feel almost personally offended by the slow progress in our field. He had, with Emil Freireich, devised the combination treatment called VAMP—vincristine, amethopterin, methotrexate, and a derivative of the drug prednisone—to treat children with leukemia at the National Cancer Institute (NCI) in Bethesda, Maryland. VAMP was exceedingly and sometimes lethally toxic, but they ultimately made the regimen work with the help of interventions that rescued their young patients from side effects and infections.

In developing VAMP, Frei endured the trauma of giving the treatment as a last hope for dying children, only to see it fail. He heard protests from colleagues who deemed his methods unacceptably brutal and, presumably, wondered if he was doing the right thing. But like everyone else, doctors live with a confirmation bias that elevates successes and pushes failures into the far recesses of the mind. We need this psychological defense because, contrary to the widely held belief that caregivers always maintain professional distance, we get attached to the people we treat. We wouldn't be human if we didn't. Add the natural self-doubt that comes with the responsibility of directing the care of a person in crisis, and a focus on our successes makes it possible to carry on after experimental therapies fail and patients die. How else could we console a family in one hospital room and then walk down the hallway to greet someone who is very much alive and depending on our care?

In Frei's case, experience might have encouraged the development of an especially strong confirmation. As recalled in a book by his colleague Vincent DeVita, Frei was generally regarded as a "maniac" when he began treating children with VAMP. Words like butcher were hurled at him during meetings, and his patients suffered terribly. But his unorthodox methods sometimes worked, and every time a child endured the treatment, recovered, and seemed cured, he was motivated to continue. With enough of these successes, he was able to refine his protocols and increase the odds that VAMP would cure a previously incurable disease. With every child saved, the brutal treatment regime gained more acceptance among doctors who helped their patients, and their families, endure the process that brought them to a cure.

Decades after he left the NCI, Frei was director of Dana-Farber and could count hundreds of acolytes among the world's prominent oncologists. When he raised the possibility of using aggressive therapies followed by autologous transplants to treat solid tumors, he encountered no real resistance. An imposing figure, certain in his own mind and respected by other giants of the field, he was not someone who would tolerate much dissent or pleas for less aggressive science. At the time, the use of toxic chemicals against leukemia represented state-of-the-art practice, and many doctors hoped that chemotherapies would be developed for many other cancers if we had the courage to push beyond the usual boundaries.

In an echo of his early work, Frei devised STAMP (Solid Tumor Autologous Marrow Program), which involved high-dose chemotherapy and bone marrow transplant. He declared it to be "the cure for breast cancer." In a short time, Dana-Farber became a world leader in this kind of therapy for solid tumors. One of his partners in this endeavor was a colleague named George Canellos, whom he had known since the 1950s when they both worked at the NCI. Doctors like Canellos, Frei, and others enjoyed such high status that they found broad support for their ideas. Among their first STAMP patients, they saw solid tumors shrink markedly in a matter of weeks. Frei kept tweaking his technique, as he had in the development of VAMP, driving toward a combination of drugs and supportive care. The number of breast cancer patients who would get high-dose chemotherapy and bone marrow transplants (HDC/ABMT) would rise steadily from about one hundred per year in 1985 to four thousand in 1994. Although truly definitive data was lacking, patients and their advocates pressured insurance companies to pay for the treatment, and some who were denied filed lawsuits to win coverage.

The press was filled with reports of women and their families fighting to receive the treatment, which cost, on average, $200,000 per patient. Despite the limited evidence of effectiveness, the debilitating nature of the treatment, and all the risks, the high-dose chemotherapy and transplant protocol for breast cancer spread to centers around the world. In the United States, advocates argued that those who denied breast cancer patients access to this treatment were discriminating against women on the basis of gender. The demand became so great that investors backed dozens of new for-profit clinics that undercut the prices charged at more established cancer centers. (An early example of what came to be called "entrepreneurial oncology.") Some doctors also began offering the treatment to patients with ovarian cancer and prostate cancer even though, in the latter case, chemotherapy was generally considered ineffective.

Those breast cancer patients who survived bone marrow transplants sometimes suffered permanent damage to their heart, kidneys, or other organs, and as the years passed, we saw their cancers could return. More, it seemed, was not always better when it came to chemotherapy. As a fierce debate raged, advocates for this aggressive treatment thought their patients deserved the option of waging a last-ditch battle against death. Although randomized trials had not offered definitive proof that it worked, they considered it unethical to deny patients a treatment that showed promise. This is always the argument made by those who believe a useful intervention is being delayed unnecessarily as researchers dot their i's and cross their t's. At the Albert Einstein Cancer Center, the director of oncology wrote that he did not consider bone marrow transplants for breast cancer experimental. Why, he and others asked, should some people die for the sake of a research protocol that denied some patients the treatment just to prove a scientific point?

For those of us who treated patients and knew that one person's suffering and death rippled outward to affect great numbers of people, experimental treatments could be painfully tantalizing. I have had to tell people they were not eligible for studies, and these conversations were devastating. I also tried to push people on to trials when, by objective standards, they didn't belong in them. In these cases, I usually had a hunch that they might do well and felt pressure to find help for someone with a profound will to live. In most cases when these patients were admitted, the cure didn't come, and it was often hard to tell whether our effort brought any benefit other than a feeling that we—the person with cancer, his or her loved ones, and the caregivers—had done everything possible. I don't discount the reassurance people feel when they know that everything possible has been tried, but in making the maximum effort, we put a burden on the health care system and often diminished the quality of someone's last days. Prolonging death is not a kindness.

The treatment picture was further complicated by the fact that for every instance where it seemed someone died awaiting a drug's regulatory approval, there were cases where severe and unexpected side effects arose in medicines that had been approved for patients. Those who were skeptical about bone marrow transplants for breast cancer—I was one because the tumors rarely had a "complete response" to any chemotherapy—thought it was unfair to ask people who were already in crisis to risk their lives on a hell-on-earth experience, or tell loved ones they refused a choice that offered a glimmer of hope. This was, it seemed, no choice at all.

In the Boston medical community, the controversy reached a kind of breaking point in the mid-1990s when Tom Frei's longtime colleague and collaborator George Canellos backed away from STAMP. This was as the number of patients who died while recovering from treatment reached 10 percent nationwide. Even with this risk, so many women sought access to the treatment through their physicians that researchers conducting formal trials, in which some patients got the medicine and others did not, were having trouble attracting patients.

Everything came to a head in 1995. First the press in Boston reported that an HDC/ABMT patient at Dana-Farber (who was also the science reporter for the *Boston Globe*) had died of heart damage after receiving a massive accidental overdose of chemotherapy drugs. Thirty-nine-year-old *Boston Globe* writer Betsy Lehman's death devastated her family and friends and shook the medical community. It also focused attention on the treatment she had been prescribed. Months later, at a big national conference called to review the BMT for solid tumors, it was compared to Halsted's radical mastectomy as an example of a severe therapy that turned out to be no better, in many cases, than a less debilitating one. In the years immediately following this meeting, a flood of data called the protocol into question. In 1999, results from four big trials were set for release at the annual meeting of the American Society of Clinical Oncology, but before this happened, the press reported that the studies showed the treatment was not reliably beneficial. The final blow came when a team sent to check the data cited in the single-most encouraging study, published by a South African group, discovered it was fraudulent.

In the end, roughly thirty thousand American women underwent the STAMP procedures, but fewer than one thousand were ever part of a formal research program. Many of the thirty thousand had chosen the grueling treatment as a last and only lifesaving option. Those who died may well have endured an unnecessarily miserable end of life because of the treatment. Those who survived could never know if it was because of the radical treatment or despite it. In the meantime, too little progress has been made toward a structural solution to the clash of values—scientific rigor versus compassionate care—that set the conditions for the race to an unproven cure. A move toward evidence-based medicine and more rigorous reviews of clinical trials was galvanized and continues, but the same tensions still arise as innovation competes with caution in an arena of life and death. The main sign of progress toward creating a more rational system for regulating experimental treatment is an evolving system for permitting "compassionate use" of drugs being tested for safety and effectiveness in carefully chosen cases where no other options are available, patients are fully informed, caregivers are protected from liability, and drug trials are not affected by the outcome.

As science gradually showed the limitations of bone marrow transplant, physicians began to see a new and dreadful disease that made people vulnerable to the same kinds of infections that we saw in patients whose immune systems had been ravaged by chemotherapy. These patients developed, among other illnesses, pneumonia, tuberculosis, herpes, toxoplasmosis, and even cancers associated with immune disorders. The most notable of the cancers was Kaposi's sarcoma, which shows itself in the form of purplish, dark-colored raised lesions on the skin.

First called GRID (gay-related immune deficiency), the mysterious illness that was reported by the federal Centers for Disease
Control in 1981 appeared in Boston that same year when a single
patient was identified at a health center serving the gay, lesbian,
and transgender community. A year later, the disease was renamed
acquired immunodeficiency syndrome (AIDS), and the number of
cases nationwide grew to 771, with 618 deaths. In 1983, the death
rate rose to 100 per month. Massachusetts governor Michael Duka-
kis created a task force to plan a response to this health crisis, which
was sparking fear and prejudice. At Boston City Hospital, one doctor even ordered a patient to leave when he arrived for a lymph
node biopsy and said he had AIDS. This was not an isolated incident. In 1987, Nathan Link of New York University published a
study that found 25 percent of doctors he surveyed believed they
had the right to refuse treatment to people with AIDS.

By this time, it was clear the infection was spread by blood and
perhaps other bodily fluids. Veteran doctors and nurses, me included, had to adjust to taking precautions about exposure to
blood, which had previously been of such limited concern that
young interns considered a splash of red a sign that one was a real
doctor. When I worked in the intensive care units, we sometimes
worried about transferring the virus by mistake. In one case, a
technician who had finished using an ultrasound machine on a
man with AIDS asked me if it was okay to then use it on a pregnant
woman in the room next door. We were so early in our experience
with this disease that I didn't know the right answer. We opted
to forgo the ultrasound on the second patient, just to be on the safe
side.

The first big breakthrough in AIDS science came when Luc
Montagnier and Françoise Barré-Sinoussi of the Pasteur Institute
in Paris, identified a retrovirus—the human immunodeficiency
virus—as the cause. Robert Gallo, who worked at the National Cancer Institute, is credited with demonstrating that the virus was the

cause of AIDS. He had previously discovered the only other known human retroviruses, HTLV-1 and HTLV-2. Like all viruses, retroviruses have to invade a host in order to replicate, but retroviruses are a bit more devilish. They literally insert themselves into the genome of their host cells and turn them into factories, producing large quantities of new viruses that depart to spread the infection. Retroviruses were known to cause cancer in some animals, so Gallo's work on HTLV-1 and HTLV-2 was of keen interest to everyone in oncology. The discovery of HIV gave impetus to everyone who had turned to AIDS research or took care of people with the disease. In Boston, that included people still in training, like Bruce Walker and me.

In the early days, we had no treatments to use against HIV itself, only its many complications like infections and cancers. Much of what we did for patients seemed like fighting one complication only so they could develop another that was often worse. The physical wasting, severe pneumonias, and endless diarrhea was misery writ large. Often without meaningful therapy to offer, care reverted to just fighting infections and trying to help patients feel a bit more comfortable. In many cases, we employed the same medications used to treat the effects of chemotherapy, including anti-diarrheal, antinausea, and, in one of my cases, you may be surprised to read, cocaine to relieve severe nosebleeds. Not quite identical to the street version, this drug does constrict blood vessels and is used by some doctors who perform sinus surgery to limit bleeding. But if our dying patients also got some momentary relief from their psychological distress, this was a positive secondary benefit. In these cases, I was often guided by one of my more difficult experiences in the intensive care unit at the Brigham. We were treating a man who was teetering on the edge of death when we saw his blood pressure and other vital signs decline. Doctors can find it too easy to start thinking in terms of the numbers, and in this case, I went in and I gave a drug that reversed all the narcotics and that brought all the numbers back to normal. But it made this man feel miserable, and of course, he died the next day anyway.

When I saw my patient's daughter after he died, I said, "You know, we tried our best to keep him alive." And she said, "But why did you do that?" When her question sank in, I found it hard to breathe. I just realized I had acted for me and for my peers who I worried were judging my decisions. By intervening, I had improved the numbers for a few hours, but it was not the right thing to do for the patient and his family. Inevitable death is a diagnosis no doctor should miss because to act against it costs much in agony experienced and resources squandered.

As we cared for people who had AIDS in the days before treatments were devised, it was commonplace to deal with similar edge-of-death moments, but it was often in young people who otherwise were a rarity when dealing with such issues. The inevitability of death from AIDS created the sword of Damocles hanging above all who heard this news as their diagnosis. It was an unthinkable clash with vigor of the young age of most patients. In the gay community there was often enough information and community support that people were aware and prepared to consider the measures that should and should not be undertaken long before any emergency arose.

AIDS patients experienced every kind of suffering you can imagine, including deep psychological pain. In many instances, the search for equilibrium prompted families and friends to come together. We were privileged to see love and reconciliation help many people get through those terrible times.

Very few people maintain their emotional façade in the face of death. Instead, they recognize the value of the time they have left and strive to make the most of it. But sometimes even the state of emergency is not enough to heal a rift. Almost thirty years have passed since I cared for one young man who died of AIDS while refusing to reconcile with his mother. Although family conflict can still arise over issues of sexual identity, back in the 1980s, it was far more common, and the rifts that opened in relationships could be wide and deep. In this case, as in many, I came to know my patient's family and friends, and I heard about the pain his mother felt. But her son was firm in his decision, and it was not my place to argue. In the end, he died estranged from her, and she would suffer more as a parent who lost a son in more ways than one.

Experience with HIV/AIDS patients gave every doctor, nurse, therapist, and technician the chance to become a better caregiver. Because it was a viral disease that affected immunity, it also pointed us to avenues of inquiry that were closely related to the most exciting areas of cancer research. For a century, scientists had debated the possibility that infectious agents cause cancer, but with the rare exception like Burkitt's lymphoma, proof had been lacking. Stronger evidence supported the importance of the immune response in protecting people from cancer, and the Kaposi's sarcoma we saw in people with HIV added to this evidence.

One of my earliest projects in the area of infection and cancer was done when I got a chance to work in the lab of the Harvard faculty member and virologist Jim Cunningham. In time, Jim's work would range across a spectrum of important diseases, from HIV/AIDS to Ebola. He would also train a small army of scientists who would go on to do important work around the world. He was more willing than most laboratory chiefs to assign members of his team to various avenues of research on the same general topic, putting us in direct competition. (This is not something I would do today in my own lab.) Then, as now, Cunningham's goal was to understand how retroviruses caused leukemia in mice. (One had recently been worked out, the so-called "Friend" virus, which was identified by scientist Charlotte Friend, who died of lymphoma in 1967.) What drew me to it was the fact that viruses were relatively simple entities and might be a good tool to get some glimpse of how cancer develops. The retrovirus-mouse-leukemia process was a particularly

good model for anyone who wanted to explore the relationship between infection and cancer. The virus was readily available, the
mice were easy to manage, and the leukemia cells could be generated in abundance, which meant that studies about molecular mechanisms could be done and the molecular reagents could be isolated
in sufficient quantities

It was a time when the retroviruses seemed like they could
provide deep insight into cancer. Work done by Harold Varmus and
Michael Bishop, who were eventually awarded Nobel Prizes, revealed that some viruses are capable of picking up genes—the ones
that control cell growth—from the cells that were infected. What
was so shocking is that the cancer wasn't developing because of the
virus' genes. Rather, the cancer was driven by the genes that were
hitchhiking in the virus. The cancer came from the genes of the cell
itself. Extrapolated to humans, cancer wasn't coming from being
invaded by a virus, it was coming from within—the enemy is us. It
was by picking up growth controlling genes and expressing them
differently, expressing them under control of the virus, that the cancer emerged. That meant that our own genes were the culprit. When
corrupted, they could become "oncogenes" (*onco*: tumor causing):
genes that normally allow us to grow could lose control and drive
the unregulated growth of cancer.

Varmus and Bishop would influence generations of biologists,
and they would, as evangelists for scientists, use their own experiences to urge people who didn't fit the cliché most people imagine
when they think of scientists to enter the field. As a young man,
Bishop thought more about being a historian or a writer than he
did about becoming a researcher. Varmus would describe himself
as a good but not super student who enjoyed going to the beach more
than working on science fair projects, and he didn't pick a direction
in life until college, where he spent most of his time at the student
newspaper. As someone who was an English major in college who
sometimes doubted his place in the laboratory, I was reassured to

know that a background in the humanities didn't preclude, and might even enhance, the ability to creatively contribute to medical science. The complexity revealed by Varmus and Bishop—who would imagine a virus hijacking DNA?—reminded the scientific world that biology is a sea of remarkable nonlinear feats of nature. Any one of them could be distilled down to the fundamental chemistry of the molecules involved or the physics of particle interactions, but knowing the chemistry and physics could not result in predicting the biologic outcome. Despite the advanced understanding of chemistry and physics by 1976, the Varmus and Bishop discovery was as surprising and as it was awe-inspiring. And it totally changed the focus of cancer research. It was no longer a search for what might come from the outside to cause this horrible disease; the answer was deep within.

The Varmus and Bishop discovery was that our cell's own growth governing processes could go awry. It was clear that growth involved signals in body that were transmitted to the cells to turn on genes promoting cell division. Their work discovered genes that executed the growth program, but others then found viruses could also reveal the signals that triggered growth. One virus induced a red blood cell leukemia despite being able to infect a number of cell types. This so-called Friend virus apparently took advantage of some signaling process restricted to red blood cells. Studying it finally revealed that the virus worked by attaching to a receptor on the cell surface and that receptor regulated signals the body uses to make more red cells after a bleeding episode (or high altitude). Viruses might then teach us not just about the internal executors of cell growth but how signals from the outside can turn cell growth on or off. That was where I came in to the field: on the idea that knowing how viruses entered cells might lead to discoveries of new growth regulators at the cell surface.

A new Harvard faculty member was trying to discover the portals or receptors that other retroviruses used to enter cells. His name was Jim Cunningham and he had come from the lab of Robert Weinberg at the Whitehead Institute, a giant in the oncogene field and a personal hero of mine. Jim was thought sufficiently brilliant that he was given a Howard Hughes Medical Institute supported position, the most prestigious in basic life science work. I became his first postdoctoral fellow. I could barely speak the language of molecular biology when I started and had to learn it on the fly. I also still had clinical duties and the contrast between the worlds could not have been starker. Clinical decision making was based on limited data, was fast-paced and multidimensional: family meetings, reviewing x-rays, calling consultants, and deciding therapies filled every hour to overflow. Lab work meant thoughtfully designing and analyzing experiments where time lines were often long, never emergent, and all about precision. Jarringly different worlds with vastly different challenges and rewards, but all exhilarating. I loved it, but more than once nearly stopped the tough uphill climb of learning and doing science to embrace the clinical world I already knew and knew I could do with some competence. But the draw in the lab of affecting a disease, and not just the individuals suffering from it, was a Siren song I could not deny. Admittedly grandiose, it was the motivation that fueled me and I think most physicians who do laboratory-based research.

I was to find how the cancer-causing Moloney retrovirus got into cells. The approach was to transfer the DNA from a cell susceptible to Moloney infection into noninfectable cells. If cells acquired the ability to be infected, then they must have acquired the receptor that was the portal for the virus. That seemed like a straightforward, simple strategy. It was, in concept, and that is the beauty and the beast of science. Simple concepts are very compelling, but often inexplicably hard to execute. It's why it is so hard for people with an illness to understand why on earth it is taking so long to get something done. I will try to illustrate with my experiment.

The plan to take the DNA from one cell, break it up in fragments, and transfer all the pieces into a large group of other cells was technically challenging. Selecting the cells that became infectible was challenging. But technical challenges are just about rolling up sleeves and getting things done. Sometimes they bring things to a halt, but I have rarely seen that. Most of the time, scientists are creative enough to overcome or work around technical hurdles. Some win Nobel Prizes for doing so. The more difficult problem is interpreting the results.

When starting an experiment, you pose a question based on what you already know. In my experiment, we knew that we were moving DNA from one cell to another: one cell donating DNA to another. If that donor DNA allowed for virus infection, then the new genetic material in the now infectible cell had to be from the donor or the virus. So, we reasoned that all we had to do was find the donor DNA and exclude the virus genome, and we would have the gene that was the virus receptor. What we didn't know was that viruses are not very discriminating. They not only carry their own genome, which may include hitchhiker oncogenes. But, they transfer lots of other genetic material outside their genome. Who knew? I pursued lots of hitchhiker vagabonds until it dawned on me that my assumptions about viruses were very wrong. I learned something I think could still be relevant for viral diseases, but I went down too many rabbit holes because of my presumptions. Fortunately, my labmate, Lorraine Albritton, was pursuing an independent path and found the receptor gene. Wonderful person that she is, she included me in the success (and publication in the prestigious journal, *Cell*) while not discounting my stumbled-upon discovery (published in the *Journal of Virology*). I was delighted to have something from my lab efforts in print.

With the exception of my work under Adel Mahmoud, my only previous research project had been done as an undergraduate at

Bucknell in an honor's thesis on the poet William Butler Yeats. A complex and contradictory man, Yeats captured yearning, passion, ecstasy, and loss in lyrical, almost musical terms. And he often did it by invoking images of nature. That is probably what most drew me to his work, but there was resonance in so many matters of the heart that I stayed with him delving into his off-beat mysticism and seemingly stoic, art-obsessed personal life. Oddly, it was spending the time digging deeply into Yeats's work that convinced me I could take on scholarship and pursue bigger issues that were often complicated and difficult to conceptually unravel. It gave me the confidence to go to medical school and it gave me reference points for themes of personal life that I often heard in my patients. Yeats echoed often for me in hospital halls filled with people's struggles. His art seemed to offer transcendence as it made many of the specifics of the moment part of the nobler endeavor of life we all share.

Yeats was, as I suppose most poets are, also very nonlinear. He forced thinking about things obscurely referenced in his words, but captured in his rhythm or in the associations of objects in particular settings. For me, it stretched my thinking. The closest connection was not the discussions of literature I had in most classrooms, but more the digesting of religious readings I had to sit through as a child. Bless my grandparents for making me, despite any and every effort to avoid it, attend church no less than once a week. The teachings were mostly deadly dull, but at least I had to do some tangential pondering. That's what I turned to to figure out Yeats, and I do think it helps me still in overcoming false assumptions like I had made with my first real scientific project. Some mixing of logic and "what-if" conjecturing about alternative ways to put things together is both the joy and beauty of science for me. Nothing as profound as a "Sailing to Byzantium," sadly, but complexity gaining form.

An enormously complex situation was playing out around me, when I was studying viruses as a simple form of cancer model. That was the AIDS epidemic that transitioned from rare curious case to a full-on epidemic of furious consequence during the time of my clinical and laboratory training. While I was working on retroviruses a specialized type of that kind of virus was identified as the basis for AIDS. I started my work on the idea that retroviruses had much more to teach us about cancer, but the cross-currents of science are such that, ironically, it was a failed cancer drug that provided the first glimmer of light for AIDS

Azidothymidine, which came to be called AZT, was developed in the early 1960s by a Wayne State University researcher named Jerome Horwitz. When AZT failed against leukemia in mice, Horwitz concluded it was a medicine "waiting for the right disease" and turned to other projects. Two decades later, as scientists and doctors scrambled to find something that might work against HIV, the drug company Burroughs Wellcome asked the National Cancer Institute to test AZT. The NCI, which was acting as a screening center for drugs submitted for testing by scientists, companies, and institutions, had a system for determining in a matter of days which substances were active against HIV. In early 1985, azidothymidine was one of a small number that showed promise. In July, it was ready to try on human subjects.

The first HIV/AIDS patients who received AZT developed moderate fevers, and their blood showed an immediate rise in the "T-helper" cells critical to immunity. In addition to the evidence found in the blood, doctors saw patients who were sick improve markedly. Their fevers subsided, and they started to recover from the opportunistic infections that were part of the HIV syndrome. The trial was stopped because patients on the placebo were dying and it seemed unethical to deny them the medicine that was working for those who received it. Burroughs Wellcome filed for the patents that Horwitz and Wayne State had neglected to obtain.

With AIDS deaths rising to forty thousand per year and advocates building a political movement to demand action, the Food and Drug Administration accelerated the process it used to consider the safety and effectiveness of new treatments. Rumors about AZT spread throughout the community of people with HIV, and patients clamored to join the few trials under way. A few, including the Republican power broker Roy Cohn, used their connections to jump the line to get it. (His illness was too advanced for the drug to help him.) In March 1987, FDA approval was granted, and thousands of prescriptions were written. Within a year or two, it became clear that the drug wasn't equally effective in all cases, and HIV developed resistance to the medicine.

How did this resistance arise? For the most part, it was a matter of accelerated natural selection. Like cancer cells, which tend to grow faster with more DNA mistakes than normal cells, viruses that evade the immune system move quickly and mutate wildly. In the case of HIV, this frenzied activity inevitably produces some viruses that can survive in the presence of the drug. These survivors in turn produce copies of themselves and pick up where the original infection left off. But the fact that AZT had some positive effect pointed to promising areas for research. It also encouraged efforts on antivirals to treat a host of diseases. For generations, we knew that bacteria were vulnerable to attack by all sorts of medicines, from penicillin to ceftolozane. However, viruses had generally defeated the science applied to stop them. With the impetus of the AIDS crisis, crash efforts yielded other drugs that worked like AZT and could be used to treat herpes, flu, and other conditions.

AZT was followed by new categories of drugs, including protease inhibitors, which stop the production of new viral material. By 1996, combinations of drugs that were called HARRT—highly active antiretroviral therapy—produced a steep decline in AIDS deaths. It was a truly extraordinary time. Patients who had written their wills and said good-bye to family and friends were, within months, up and resuming a full life. Comparing some to Lazarus of the Bible was not a stretch—they literally arose from their death bed. It was also at this time that I was recruited to the Massachusetts General Hospital where I joined my dear friend Bruce Walker and the most extraordinary oncologist I have ever met, Bruce Chabner. Bruce Chabner was fabled for his leadership at the National Cancer Institute and was just arriving at the MGH to establish a patient-focused clinical Cancer Center: one that could leverage the new science emerging from Boston's burgeoning megaplex of biopharma. But what made Bruce special was his humanity. He sincerely cared about patients and the people who took care of them. The explicit ethos was always, patients first. It sounds so obvious, but it is often left unspoken in the flight plan of academic centers. That was not true at the MGH and one of the reasons I love being a part of it to this day. In one of my first meetings with Bruce after he recruited me, we were speaking about my plans and as I was about to leave, he said, "And how can I help?" I had never heard that said in over fifteen years of various meetings with Harvard hospital and medical school leaders. It sounded a bell for me that I was now in a place I could call my professional home. I try to echo his words and sentiment in meetings ever since.

The MGH at that time had whole floors of patients in various stages of dying from AIDS. It was horrifying to see such young people in such misery. But MGH was one of the places where AIDS research was a priority. Bruce Walker was asked to head the AIDS Research Center and he invited me to be its codirector. He focused on the immune response to HIV and a vaccine, I focused on the consequences of immune deficiency and how that led to cancers. We shared lab space and constructed a shared office suite. It was a rare moment when professional commitment, friendship, and the opportunity to do something of importance all came together: a true gift.

The cancers that occurred in AIDS were not those that happened in most other settings. They were due to poor immune control of viruses or the immune system itself. Kaposi's sarcoma and lymphoma were of extraordinary frequency and we tried to develop new therapies for each.

Nearly all of our patients were too sick to endure the typical chemotherapy used to treat these cancers. (This despite new drugs that could relieve the nausea, anemia, and low white cells that are among the worst side effects of chemo.) For Kaposi's sarcoma, my friend at University of Southern California had found that lower doses of a chemical called paclitaxel, which had helped some patients with various malignancies including breast and ovarian cancer. In many patients we saw the cancer retreat and even disappear.

Paclitaxel, which is known by the brand name Taxol, was derived from the bark of the Pacific yew tree. Long known for producing poisonous leaves, which were sometimes used in suicide, yews have a particular place in history. Yew pollen can cause allergic reactions, and in some cultures, even sleeping beneath a yew is considered to be dangerous. Richard the Lionheart and King William II were supposedly killed by arrows shot from yew bows, and the tree's boughs were incorporated in funeral rites in ancient Rome.

The yew bark that produced the first paclitaxel was one of two hundred samples collected in the Pacific Northwest by Arthur Barclay as part of an ongoing effort by the National Cancer Institute to discover potentially useful molecules in plants. Much of what we use as medicine is derived from plants and primitive animals like fungi, which have been producing chemical compounds to defend themselves for roughly four billion years. Aspirin, opium, quinine, and digitalis are among the better-known, plant-derived medicines. Fungi gave us penicillin. Some cardiac medicines are based on substances from lower vertebrates like snakes. The value of natural chemical sources has remained quite constant over the years, with between 12 and 50 percent of new medications credited with origins in the plant or animal kingdoms.

Years passed between the collection of the yew bark and the

discovery that it contained a substance that could kill ovarian and breast cancer cells. This research set off a scramble for the great volumes of yew bark needed to conduct more studies. Loggers in economically depressed communities hoped for a big new business. Environmentalists rallied to protect the forests and the animal species that depended on the yew, including the northern spotted owl. A fierce political debate, which was sometimes framed as a contest between human life and environmental protection, ended when chemists figured out how to synthesize the key molecule.

The federal government promotes and funds research but isn't in the business of actually marketing drugs, so when Taxol was eventually approved for use in patients, the National Cancer Institute sought a partner in the industry. The contract was won by Bristol-Myers Squibb (BMS). The drug became a blockbuster, with sales that exceeded $1 billion per year. The company's profits far exceeded the few millions in royalties paid annually to the federal government, and this sum grew as science showed that additional types of cancer were vulnerable to it.

When Parkash Gill and I contacted BMS to tell them of early success with low-dose Taxol therapy for Kaposi's sarcoma, and to ask them for help in conducting a more extensive clinical trial, they scoffed: the dose was almost half that used in other cancers; it couldn't possibly work. They refused to even allow us discounted access to their extremely expensive drug. We had to find the money ourselves to do the study, and fortunately we did. The results were quite dramatic and even people with severe lung disease recovered promptly. BMS took note. They also realized that their drug was soon to come off patent and our data combined with some from the NCI might get them continued exclusive marketing. Treating an "orphan disease" like Kaposi's sarcoma could result in seven years of exclusivity from the FDA, keeping any generic from coming out to compete with them. To do so, they needed our data. We were hopelessly naive about the pharmaceutical business. When they asked what we wanted for our data, we thought the right thing to do was to only ask for the reimbursement of our costs. In hindsight, we could have funded our research for seven years. They got their "orphan drug" status for Taxol and made billions.

As most Americans would eventually learn from political debates over our health care system, and occasionally from personal experience, drug patents produced great flows of revenue. Unless academic centers hold the patents or, like in our case, can pay for and own the information from a clinical study, there is nothing beyond covering the costs. The revenues all go to the drug makers. While they have handsome profit margins, in their defense, the costs associated with successfully moving from research to drug are unfathomably large—estimated to exceed $2.5 billion in a 2016 analysis by the Tufts Center for the Study of Drug Development. The reasons are multiple but include the terrible inaccuracy of research models in predicting what will happen in patients. Much of what is done in research is to reduce the complexity of disease to as simple a set of models as possible. It is the only way to get a handle on the details of what is happening. In drug research, the emphasis is often on molecules: specific enzymes or single receptor molecules that have been implicated in a disease. In cancer, the focus is often on what gene is mutated and whether that mutation causes the molecule the gene makes to be more active or less. Anything that is more active is a more desirable target to go after because it is easier to inhibit something than to make it more active. Finding a good target is often where discovery labs in academia make their contribution. Sometimes they add identification of a chemical compound that might affect the target. But it is the pharmaceutical companies that have the expertise to go from a compound to a drug.

Getting to a drug involves an enormous team of people who contribute pieces of the process. Chemists modify the original compound to identify variants that might be more specific in what they target (almost all drugs are "dirty" in affecting more than their intended molecular target). Medicinal chemists also define variants that are more easily soluble in water, or more stable in storage, or more able to get inside a cell without being destroyed. Cell biologists assess how the compound alters cancer cells, killing them, just stopping them from growing, or changing their differentiation state. Pharmacologists measure how the compound is handled by the body: whether it is absorbed in oral form, how long it lasts in the bloodstream, and whether it is cleared by the liver or the kidneys. Toxicity is then evaluated in both Petri dish–based assays and multiple different animal types, but none of them completely mimic what will happen in a person. Most drugs end up failing in the late stage of development because of this reason. We just still don't have decent ways to determine if a drug that passes all the tests will not harm people. Once a drug enters into clinical testing the costs exponentially increase and failure collapses down immense efforts by dozens if not hundreds of people.

Prices in the U.S., build in virtually all the costs of developing the new drug. They also include the costs of other drug candidates that might have failed. Other countries with national health systems negotiate drug prices. That is not the case in the U.S. where Medicare and Medicaid are forbidden from doing so. That results in pricing strategies by pharmaceutical firms where the U.S. prices are substantially higher than elsewhere (often twice the price of other developed nations) and projected to be the major source of revenue. It is an increasingly contentious debate. Clearly the companies need to cover their research and development costs and return a profit in order for new drugs to be made. It has to be lucrative enough so that new companies, whose risks are amplified by the limited number of new drugs they can work on, can be attractive to investors. The large pharmaceutical companies are highly averse to risk. It is the small start-ups that are required for innovation. Those start-ups depend on venture capital that has to tolerate the long interval between investing in a company and having a medicine that can be sold—a time estimated to exceed a decade. Investors have lots of options for their money, so to take on the high risk and long duration of new drug development, the possible returns have to be high.

The true cost of a drug is often obscured from a patient's view because it is paid by an insurer. This divide means that the insured and their doctors are shielded from the cost-benefit factor and can simply demand treatment, even if it is extremely expensive and of limited benefit. When the insurance system was first devised, few medicines were priced so high that the cost mattered much. If a treatment offered a potential benefit, no matter how limited, it was easy to go ahead with it. But as costs rose, the people who ran the system began casting a wary eye toward medicines that produced only incremental benefits.

In the case of Taxol, which cost about $35,000 per patient when it was approved, the benefits were impressive in certain advanced breast cancer patients, reducing the risk of progressive tumors. In some cases, it was even prescribed to prevent recurrent cancer in women determined to be largely cured by surgery. The drug works by interfering with the division of cells, including both healthy ones and cancerous ones, and ultimately killing them. Drug resistance was common in patients who received Taxol. Nevertheless, oncologists could prescribe Taxol where other drugs failed and to help some patients live longer. When resistance arose, they could switch agents, though inevitably cells start to become "cross resistant," resistant to many types of drugs.

Drug resistance hinges, in part, on a survival-of-the-fittest process that allows a small number of cancer cells that aren't susceptible to a drug to replicate until the body is repopulated and illness returns. This dynamic mimicked evolution run amok, with drug-resistant cells thriving as susceptible ones became extinct. It is why most drugs are given in combination with others. The idea is that if you first give medicines that work by different mechanisms, a cell may be resistant to one mechanism, but is unlikely to be resistant to the mechanisms of all the drugs. Combinations of drugs with distinct mechanisms of actions are often designed and some have worked spectacularly well. The cure rates for childhood leukemia, testicular cancer, and lymphomas are stunning successes. But most cancers that come from what are called epithelial cells, the cells that make up and are the basis for cancers of the breast, lung, colon, prostate, stomach, pancreas, bladder, and liver, can withstand the multipronged attack. This is also true of cancers from the brain and many from our musculo-skeletal system that are called sarcomas. As this process became better understood, oncologists adjusted the timing, the dosing, and the variety of drugs used to try to find some way around the cancer cells' defenses. The strategic use of medicines sometimes extended life, but this shuffling of the deck didn't represent real progress. And in the long run, many cancers came back in more virulent forms, and many patients rightly thought they were playing for time, hoping to live long enough for science to produce a definitive cure It made going to clinical oncology meetings almost unbearable. It seemed that innovation was reduced to just recombining already poor performing drugs and the results were at best tiny increments in patient survival.

Although hope was ever present, the 1990s brought far too many profound disappointments. One of the most crushing began with a front-page article in the Sunday May 3, 1998 edition of *The New York Times* that announced that two naturally-occurring proteins—angiostatin and endostatin—seemed to halt the development of blood vessels that tumors required to survive. The scientist leading this research, my Harvard colleague Judah Folkman, had devoted decades to the study of angiogenesis—angio for "blood vessel" and genesis for "creation"—and did impressive work on the way that tumors produce chemicals to stimulate nearby capillaries to develop new blood vessels to nourish the malignancy. Folkman's team did painstaking work that included processing, literally, gallons of mouse urine to find proteins that could shut off the blood vessel growth. When this success was announced Folkman was cautious, saying, "If you have a cancer and you are a mouse we can take good care of you" but others were not so measured. Nobel laureate James Watson predicted, "Judah is going to cure cancer in two years."

In the days after the article appeared a drug company that made the two medicines experienced such a surge in investments that its stock price rose 50 percent. Patients all over the country clamored to be treated with these proteins even though they had never been tried in humans. One oncologist in New York reported that a very wealthy patient called to ask if "a large infusion of cash" could get him treatment based on Folkman's science. A large contract to produce a book about Folkman's discoveries was part of the enthusiasm.

All the attention affirmed what was a lifetime of work for Folkman, who had sometimes been the only prominent scientist devoted to the angiogenesis puzzle. Remarkably empathetic and kindhearted, Folkman was so brilliant and precocious that he was admitted to Harvard Medical School at age nineteen and while there helped develop the first heart pacemaker. By thirty-four he was surgeon-in-chief at Children's Hospital Boston. His first application for a grant to study angiogenesis was rejected by National Cancer Institute reviewers who thought he had gotten the relationship between tumors and blood vessel backward. The rejection letter offered the blunt assertion that "tumor growth cannot be dependent upon blood vessel growth any more than infection is dependent on pus."

For decades Folkman's research into blood vessel growth as a target for cancer treatment yielded little progress. Folkman was a fabled figure by the time I arrived in Boston, beloved by people who appreciated his enthusiasm, intelligence, and dogged spirit.

He was also a living example of the tension between scientific passion and realism. Technical as it may be, science is a human and therefore social endeavor. This fact was illuminated brilliantly by Thomas Kuhn, a physicist, historian, and philosopher who pioneered the study of scientific progress. Kuhn was interested in the ways that communities of scientists respond to new ideas and noted that, at first, concepts that deviate from accepted wisdom are rejected, often at great pain for the men or women who devise them. A classic historical example involved the Hungarian physician Ignaz Semmelwies, who suggested that contamination caused high rates of death among women who gave birth at a hospital where he was chief surgeon. An experiment involving handwashing by doctors cut the fatality rate by 90 percent. However, the concept, which was proposed before germ theory was developed, was roundly rejected and its proponent was scorned by his colleagues. Semmelweis was emotionally devastated by the way he was treated by his peers and by the knowledge women would die because he couldn't make his case successfully. He died, in 1865, after being forcibly committed to an insane asylum. He was just forty-seven years old.

Like many rejected scientific revolutionaries Semmelweis would not be affirmed until decades after his death. Today he has been memorialized by statuary and coins, and a university has been given his name. The honors came as his concept attracted support and the accumulated work created a "paradigm shift" (Kuhn coined the term) that changed baseline assumptions about postsurgical disease. The scorned scientist became an acknowledged genius, textbooks were revised, and countless lives were saved.

Every scientist dreams of making an advance of the sort Semmelweis achieved but dreads the experience he endured. The trick here involves a balance of respect for yourself and respect for others. If you lose confidence and abandon an idea too soon, and it yields a great breakthrough for someone else, you will never forgive yourself. However, persevering in the face of reasonable criticism can also bring you to a place of regret. In the end, you discover nothing. The tension between confidence and realism is made even more intense by the ever-increasing competition for scarce research funds meted out by government, foundations, and industry. As much as we'd all like to think that data speaks for itself, you must be a good enough salesman—self-confident, energetic, and optimistic— to make funders enthusiastic enough to give you money. If there was a knock on Judah Folkman it was that he sometimes showed an almost messianic zeal for his ideas. However, his zeal had won him the support from funders who helped him create the entire field of angiogenesis research.

The excitement that came with the big press reports was soon overwhelmed by controversy. Scientists who tried to replicate Folkman's results, which would be required if his findings were to be accepted, struggled to do it. When this failure was reported, Judah explained that the process his lab used was complicated and, as he explained at the time, the two substances he isolated could fail for some weird reason, but the principles were sound. However, the news about these failed attempts at confirming Folkman's results was painful for him. At a conference where he was honored for his work he wondered aloud, "How long can one persist without the acceptance of one's colleagues?" Judah's experience was not his fault. His had been the first and the loudest voice that insisted it was too soon to talk about cures. Oncology may be the one field where good news travels too fast, and the consequences of this problem can be devastating to scientists. In the case of angiogenesis, the replication problem was solved as other scientists also saw mouse tumors shrink. More ups and downs would follow as hundreds of labs pursued variations on Judah's original research on the way to chemicals that would ultimately prove useful. However, Folkman's name would long be associated with a flash of false hope, much of it created by those like James Watson, who seized on a new idea as finally providing some scientific basis for hope in cancer therapy.

While angiogenesis research didn't cure cancer in two years, it did and does still offer new approaches. A nuanced view of cancer at the end of the twentieth century would have revealed that painstaking work on a number of fronts was yielding real, if not-quite glamorous results.

Most notable was the fact that the death rate for all forms of this disease had peaked in 1991 and have dropped slightly every year since. Much of the reduction was caused by antismoking campaigns and the decreased incidence of tobacco-related cancers in men. Screening for colon cancer, and the removal of precancerous growths during colonoscopy, also helped. The 1990s also saw the emergence of testing for genetic abnormalities known to raise the risk of cancer. Two genes in particular—BRCA1 and BRCA2—were so strongly associated with breast and ovarian cancers that many women who were found to carry them underwent preemptive surgeries. These operations reduced the odds of a woman developing breast cancer by half. The risk of ovarian and fallopian tube cancers was cut by more than 70 percent. But all of these can be seen as the fruits of cancer research—some from epidemiology, studying the basis for outsized risks in groups of people, and some from basic research.

For people diagnosed with cancer, improved surgical and radiotherapy techniques also brought better outcomes. However, the advances imagined in the 1960s, when scientists began to speculate about intervening at the genetic level to stop cancer, had not arrived. In 1990, the first patients to receive human gene therapy for any illness—a severe combined immunodeficiency—did well when a functioning gene was delivered to their white blood cells with the help of a virus modified to be harmless. The fix could be permanent and it was promising enough to drive intense research for more and better gene-based therapies. Then the worst of the fears

expressed decades earlier by those who doubted the safety of genetic therapies came true. In 1999, an eighteen-year-old named Jesse
Gelsinger died after receiving an experimental genetic therapy for
a metabolic disorder.

The genetic cause for Gelsinger's disorder had been discovered
as scientists mapped the genetic causes for a host of illnesses. His
treatment had been approved by federal authorities who had considered more than three hundred proposals for experimental therapies and approved forty-one that targeted conditions caused by
single gene mutations. Gelsinger, who developed the disorder in
childhood because his genetic deficiency was only partial, required
a severely restricted diet and took dozens of pills per day to survive.
He had told a friend that his death would be the worst possible
outcome of the experiment but then added, "If I die it's for the babies" who had the same disorder at birth. But if their deficiency was
complete, it was invariably fatal.

Jessie Gelsinger died of multiple organ failure likely caused by
an immune response to the virus that carried the genes he needed.
The virus used was not a retrovirus, but an adenovirus to which
most people have some degree of immunity. An investigation into
the tragedy pointed to the possibility that researchers overlooked
signs of trouble, rendering the patient more vulnerable to an immune injury to the liver, and may have been unduly influenced by a
financial interest in the therapy they were developing. As news of
these findings spread, scientists working on gene therapies saw support evaporate. The federal Department of Health and Human
Services imposed new regulations on gene research and sent teams
to review work going on around the country. Harvard was one of
ten places that would receive extra scrutiny. The local paper, the
Boston Globe, discovered that roughly one-third of the gene therapy trials involving patients would be closed. When I was asked to
comment for the article I stressed the positives that might emerge
from the crisis. "The field is chastened in a way that will ultimately

help it," I said. "The more we can do to avoid ethical or safety issues that undermine the science the better."

Shaken by the Gelsinger tragedy, the angiogenesis controversy, and other factors, public trust in science and medicine, as measured by the University of Chicago's General Social Survey, would drop sharply between 1999 and 2005. Nevertheless, doctors and scientists enjoyed a higher level of public confidence than the members of other professions, including civil servants, business leaders, lawyers, and politicians. People may have been impatient for us to make the kind of progress promised when I was a kid reading *Life* magazine, but they continued to have faith in us.

I would argue that generally this faith is well-placed. Scientists and, I should add, the families of scientists, sacrifice a great deal to the cause of advancing our understanding of the world and to keep in check the competitive drive that can motivate some people to take shortcuts. At my house, Kathy, Margaret, Elizabeth, and Ned put up with my absences and the fact that even when I was present I could be distracted, because they knew that what I was doing was extremely difficult and might just be important. Much as I tried, my schedule was unpredictable, and too often I would find myself delayed in either patient care or as our group labored over a paper or a grant proposal that lacked some important detail.

Sometimes the sticky problem that kept me working later than expected was something as mundane as a misplaced illustration. This is precisely what occurred one evening as we tried to address a critique we had received for a paper we had submitted to the journal *Science*. At that time, we worked with printed photographs of images of cells or other data. We had to paste those into composite figures, sometimes of many parts. Late that night as we were assembling the final versions to tuck in the mail, one small image had apparently fallen off and we could not locate it. We searched for seemingly hours and finally gave up. We resigned ourselves to taking up the search the next day and I drove home having missed one more dinner and one more round of bedtime rituals. At home I went to the kids' rooms to check on them as they slept. When I leaned over Ned's crib the photo fell out of my shirt pocket and landed faceup on his forehead. The dear boy saved the day without even a pause in his rhythmic slumber. If only I had come home earlier.

FOUR

CHEMICALS IN CONVERSATION

Chemistry is the language of cells. The conversation begins with deoxyribonucleic acid (DNA), which directs the assembly of life in all its forms. Chemistry is also the science that brings precision to biology. Decipher how chemicals communicate to direct the activity of a cell, and you are on your way to finding interventions to halt disease and enhance health.

In oncology, as in all areas of medicine, how chemicals communicate is through the vehicle of the most fundamental unit of life, the cell. Understanding how cells behave and how that behavior is corrupted in cancer is the holy grail. Yet, studying the cancer cell in isolation is not necessarily the way to gain understanding or dominion over cancer. A case in point can be found in James Allison's work on T cells.

Born and raised in a small town in Texas, Allison showed early signs of a strong and persistent intellect. In high school, he refused to take a required biology class because the teacher omitted all discussion of evolution. The board of education let him take a college correspondence course instead but did nothing to stop the taunting Allison endured from the school's athletic coaches who spied him studying in the gym. In college, he chose science over medicine for two reasons. First, as he readily confesses, he wasn't very good at learning vast amounts of factual information, and doctors need to know a lot of facts. Second, he feared making mistakes that might cause grievous harm. As he would say, "Doctors *need* to be right. Scientists are *supposed* to be wrong."

After earning a doctorate in biological sciences, Allison went into immunology and cancer research. He was, like me, fascinated by the powerful potential of the body's ability to defend and heal itself, yet unlike me, intrigued by the chemistry that enabled this process. The most tantalizing aspect of the process was the immune system's ability to identify and react to a huge variety of targets. In many instances, this process also produces long-lasting immunity that protects us in future encounters with the same virus, bacteria, or even cancer cell. This is the activity triggered by vaccines. But while we understood their general purpose, so little was known about how immune cells detected invaders and then became fighters against infection and cancer that an enormous scientific field was wide open for explorers like Allison.

In 1982, when he was at the University of Texas, Jim discovered a receptor molecule that helps T cells recognize antigens of unwanted objects like viruses and start the process of defending the body from infections or cancer cells. This he compared with the ignition switch on a car. A few years later, after moving to the University of California–Berkeley, Jim recognized that a protein called CD28 acted as a sort of gas pedal to further activate the T cells. Next came Allison's discovery, made with his colleague Jeffrey Bluestone, that a protein called CTLA-4, which protrudes like a little tail from the surface of T cells, acts like a brake to stop them from overdoing things. (When the immune system fails to stop at the right time, it creates its own problems—autoimmune disorders—that damage the body. Lupus, rheumatoid arthritis, psoriasis, and type 1 diabetes are examples of autoimmune disorders.

Prior to Allison's work, it was thought that the little-tail protein served the opposite purpose, signaling T cells to take action. This belief was so entrenched that for several years, controversy raged over Allison's finding. The idea that immune cells must be subject to more complex controls than simply "ignition" and "acceleration" made sense, but it was raised at a time when much of science was focused elsewhere. Allison would recall that during this period, he was sometimes teased by colleagues who thought his interest was so implausible that they would jokingly cough and cover their mouths as they said, "Jim is a"—cough—"*tumor* immunologist." Although he dreamed of developing chemicals that would work on CTLA-4 to treat people with cancer, Allison received so little support that his progress was slow. For years, he remained what he called "a mouse guy," testing his ideas in his lab and seeking both the breakthroughs and the backing to move from mice to human beings.

The T cells that Jim Allison sought to manipulate came from the bone marrow stem cells that provide almost all the power of the body's natural immune systems. Work done on other types of stem cells suggested the very strong possibility that they could be manipulated to produce remarkable results. In 1958, John Gurdon of Oxford University used ultraviolet light to kill the nucleus of a frog egg and then inserted a single cell from the lining of a frog intestine. Gurdon was testing what was unknown at the time: whether all cells share the same DNA. It was not known if DNA remained the same throughout the lifetime of a cell or if cells parceled out and lost some of the DNA as they took on the specialized characteristics of a mature cell. He ingeniously thought he could figure this out by taking the nucleus containing the DNA of a mature cell and putting it into a context where all the cells of the body needed to be made— the fertilized egg. He did it in frogs because of the large size and number of their eggs. They could be easily handled and a lot of them could be tested in short order. He turned out to be right, as the egg became a tadpole and then a frog capable of reproducing normally.

Gurdon's successful nuclear transfer marked a giant step forward in cell biology and suggested that actual cloning would be possible. It indicated not only that DNA stayed quite intact during the process of cell differentiation, but also what that DNA expressed. The genes expressed to make a cell of the intestine were very different from those expressed in a so-called "totipotent" (toti: all; potent: capable) cell like the fertilized egg. Yet, the intestinal cell DNA could be "reprogrammed" to express what it took to become totipotent and make a whole new organism. The implications were enormous and represented cloning. A new animal was made from a single cell of a fully formed one. Gurdon was so modest that he refused to speculate about its importance. TV newscaster Walter Cronkite visited him for an interview and asked him when cloning would be done with mammals and, ultimately, human beings. "No idea," replied Gurdon, "but somewhere between ten years and a hundred years."

Playful and self-effacing, Gurdon was the unlikeliest of scientific superstars and would long preserve an evaluation written by one of his teachers. It begins with the sentence, "It has been a disastrous half" and notes that Gurdon had "been in trouble, because he will not listen." The most revealing comments appear in the professor's conclusion:

> I believe he has ideas about becoming a Scientist; on his present showing this is quite ridiculous. If he can't learn certain Biological facts, he would have no chance of doing the work of a Specialist, and it would be [a] sheer waste of time both on his part, and of those who have to teach him.

Diverted by academic professionals, Gurdon went to graduate school at Oxford intending to study literature, but a mix-up at the admissions office allowed him to take courses in zoology. Here his creativity and spirit—the same spirit that annoyed his undergrad professor—flowered, and he became a shining light as an undergraduate and graduate student, eventually publishing his paper on nuclear transfer. The cloning question was exciting for people to consider but it obscured the more important issue of reprogramming that Gurdon's science illustrated. Theoretically this meant that science could turn back the clock on adult cells, making them behave like the most powerful stem cells of all: the fertilized egg. Those cells are capable of making every component of an organism and are therefore totipotent. In the human that roughly means two hundred and twenty different cell types. Taken to its logical end, Gurdon's work meant that cells and whole organisms could be rejuvenated.

Besides hinting at a pathway to cloning, Gurdon had also pointed to new ways to understand cancer. The first pluripotent human embryonic stem cells would be derived from testicular cancer cells. This was done in the 1980s by scientists who noted that the human cells behaved quite differently from those that came from mice.

Cardinal features of stem cells are that they can self-renew (make more of themselves) and differentiate. What Gurdon's work indicated is that differentiation is not necessarily a one-way street. Cells, or at least the DNA within them, can be made to reprogram and go backward to a more primitive state depending on the conditions. A question that is naturally extended from this work is whether some mutations could cause mature cells to reacquire the functions of stem cells? Perhaps not the differentiation property, but what if they could reprogram to become self-renewing when they should otherwise not have that feature? Such a cell, particularly one that was stuck at a particular stage of differentiation, would almost certainly be cancerous. The concept of cells in cancer reflecting features of stem cells was something tested by John Dick, a pioneer in stem cell biology and cancer. In 1994 in Toronto, Dick, who had been trained by fellow Canadians McCulloch and Till, published a paper describing leukemia stem cells. He did it by using the same transplantation techniques that his mentors had used to first demonstrate the experimental proof that stem cells existed. He did so by first generating a mouse so deficient in its immune function that it could tolerate human cells—it would not reject them. Stem cells from human blood engrafted in these animals and made human blood cells. Dick used the model to test whether some cells within the swarm of cells that were human leukemia could make the mouse leukemic. They were and did so even when transplanted a second time into another mouse. That provided evidence of cancer stem cells. He and others then went on to demonstrate that similar types of cells exist in some if not all human tumors. He has since used it to determine that the frequency of the cells was shown to correlate with poorer prognosis in some leukemias. He also looked to see if they could be targeted by chemotherapy. They would need to be if a cure was ever to be achieved for they are capable of regenerating a full cancer. If they were not wiped out, the cancer would recur. Targeting leukemia stem cells is an active area of research and it is not yet fully defined as the difference between remission versus durable cure.

That Dick's discovery would be made in the blood was to be expected. Blood is accessible and readily observed, and thus most useful for scientific inquiry. Fortunately, it often provides reliable hints for studies in other parts of the body. After Dick's findings, stem cells were identified in cancer of the breast, liver, brain, colon, and more. These cancer stem cells could be the result of random genetic errors or outside influences, such as radiation or chemicals. In every case, the cancer stem cells could both replicate themselves and create descendant abnormal cells that may not have the full features of a stem cell but can disrupt normal cell function and kill.

Cancer cells have long been understood as rapidly proliferating things. Some tumors, called teratomas, contain such varied types of cells—bone, muscle, skin, hair, teeth, and so forth—all jumbled together, that they suggest a kind of biological madness. In fact these grotesque collections are evidence of the power of stem cells run amok. Not only do they not know when to stop replicating, they don't know which cells they are supposed to create and how. In the 1970s, Martin Evans of the University of Cambridge was able to keep mouse teratoma cells alive and differentiating into various new cells indefinitely. Then, in the 1980s, Evans and others identified embryonic stem cells that could be cultured to create viable, fertile mice. If the culture was adjusted genetically the results would be mice with one or more genes "knocked out" (and sometimes replaced) to create the perfect specimens for research purposes.

The knockout mouse was a great boon to scientists because it gave them access to populations of identical animals—essentially clones—selected for a specific trait. If you wanted to find out what a gene does, the best way to do so was to engineer a mouse that was deficient in it. Eventually the technology also progressed so that it was possible to selectively deplete the gene in particular cells. What this has done is to allow the definition of what a gene does in particular organs or cells types—heart, blood, brain, for example. It is also now possible to do so whenever in the lifetime of a mouse was of greatest interest. Gene function early in the development of a fetus might, and has been shown to be for many genes, very different in an adolescent or even an aged mouse. This kind of precision has been enormously productive in teaching us about the particular functions of genes. It has also been helpful in defining how they relate to disease.

Engineered mice can be used to define how a gene might affect the response to particular challenges like infection or injury or even how drugs are metabolized. There continue to be new ways to use genetic modification to understand genes and their impact on disease, and they all depend on the original definition of mouse embryonic stem cells by Martin Evans. Those stem cells could be grown indefinitely and can be genetically modified. They are then injected into a newly formed ball of cells that will become the mouse embryo and eventually become mice capable of breeding and growing whole colonies of these highly valuable models for understanding and treating human disease.

What Evans enabled was undeniably good. What he also spawned was an effort to find whether embryonic stem cells could also be made from humans and that was laden with more controversy. For scientists, it would be a landmark achievement and open the possibility that embryonic stem cells might be able to produce human tissues in a petri dish—making their study possible. For others, it raised the issue that embryos were somehow being manipulated and destroyed for research—many mistakenly equated it with abortion. Embryonic stem cells were eventually made from humans using the discarded material from in vitro fertilization (IVF) clinics or, in some early experiments, material from an abortion. Generation of human embryonic stem cells after those first efforts was always from IVF; abortion was not involved. Certainly legitimate ethical debate was warranted around whether IVF material represented life, but it could not be regarded as the same as abortion: the IVF material was a collection of a few hundred cells that were not in the womb and could not survive without being so.

Although embryonic stem cells do not require material from abortions, other research does. For example, the immune-deficient mice that could allow human blood stem cells to make human blood cells do not make T cells. That requires human thymus tissue. By implanting thymus and blood stem cells from aborted material, mouse models of human immunity were made much more useful. That has allowed vaccine studies and work on HIV vaccines in particular to move forward. The area is controversial, to be sure, and qualms even among researchers are common. However, the reality is that the material would be incinerated. Using it in research at least offers some positive purpose. To me, that respects the dignity and sanctity of human life. Opponents of such research argue that fetal cell donation somehow encourages women to end pregnancies that would otherwise go to term. In fact, the decision to donate tissue is always made after someone has chosen abortion. Critics also raise a religious argument revolving around the belief that conception creates a supernatural soul that merits extraordinary protections. This idea is guided and validated by one's religious faith and so is not subject to debate. I personally do share reverence for the seemingly miraculous series of events that lead a single fertilized egg cell to become the complex, thinking organism that is us. Nothing is more awe-inspiring. Even when "lower" organisms are studied in the lab, the sense of reverence is there, for no matter how much we learn about the processes involved, exactly how cells know when to start or when to stop their actions, it is still profound.

For much of the world, the first hint that we might be able to unlock the secrets of life and perhaps even intervene arose when doctors began to treat infertility. As artificial insemination became a treatment for infertile couples in the twentieth century, social critics imagined a host of possible problems. Most alarming to social critics was the notion that one day egg and sperm could be united outside the body—in vitro fertilization—and then implanted in the womb. Aldous Huxley made "test tube" babies part of his dystopian view of the future in his novel *Brave New World,* and this writing contributed to moral objections to any effort that seemed like interference in procreation. By 1969 a Harris poll determined that a majority of Americans believed IVF was "against God's will."

As many religious and political leaders took stands against IVF, scientific progress was slowed but not halted. At the University of Cambridge, a gynecologist named Patrick Steptoe and a scientist named Robert Edwards were determined to discover, as Edwards would say, whether reproduction would be controlled by "God Himself" or "scientists in the laboratory."

They got their answer when the first IVF baby was born in England in 1978. A Harris poll done months later found a change of heart across America. Sixty percent of respondents said in vitro fertilization should be legal and half said they would opt for it if they needed it. Today more than 60,000 babies per year are born in

the U.S. with the help of IVF and, Huxley notwithstanding, no social crisis has arisen.

Because it was aimed at a specific, narrowly-defined medical
challenge, IVF research could be understood as a project with real-
life benefits. A healthy baby in the arms of a loving mother or father
settles things for most people. Far more difficult to resolve were
the questions arising from research on fetal cells collected after
abortion procedures and embryonic stem cells derived from fertilized eggs not used by couples involved in IVF. Because the science
was linked to abortion it was caught up in the highly-charged debate over the morality of terminating pregnancy. The disruptive
protests and occasional violent practices by abortion opponents,
who had bombed clinics and killed doctors, were enough to give
anyone pause when it came to taking a public stand on embryonic
and fetal stem cell research. (Those who actually did this work were
careful about security.) A great many doctors and scientists did trek
to Washington to testify in favor of continued federal spending on
this science and Harvard University took the unusual step of advo-
cating for it as an institution. A panel of medical, religious, scientific, and ethics experts convened by the Reagan administration
took the same position in an 18–3 vote. On the other side of the
issue stood those who argued on the basis of religious faith and
morality. I couldn't have disagreed more with those who acted on
their feelings of awe by trying to ban the use of discarded embryos
and fetal tissues in scientific research. In world where sick and injured people endure suffering and loss daily, we have a responsibility to learn all we can about the way we are created, develop, and
function so that we can ease at least some of the pain. This is where
protecting human dignity lies.

In the 1980s, even more than today, the federal government was
the most important funder of the kind of basic science—like Arthur
Barclay's collection of plant samples in the Pacific Northwest—
that can seem only vaguely related to something as concrete as a

specific drug to treat disease. President Reagan stopped short of seeking an outright ban on all fetal and embryonic stem cell investigations. But he and his successor George H. W. Bush, who were both committed to ending abortion rights, did withhold federal funds from this research. When Congress voted to override the executive ban, which was a sign of how contentious the issue was, Bush used his presidential veto to maintain it.

Scientists who continued their stem cell projects did so with other funds and were careful to use separate facilities and equipment. I still have equipment in my lab bearing the green stickers signifying private funding sources that did not restrict use of the equipment. These awkward arrangements and diminished resources slowed progress. Partisan politics being what it is, Bush's defeat by Bill Clinton brought a change in 1995. This opening was soon closed by a congressional ban authored by two members of Congress from the Bible Belt, Roger Wicker of Mississippi and Jay W. Dickey Jr. of Arkansas. They attached it as an amendment to an act of Congress that President Clinton felt he needed to sign and thus became law. Also known as the National Rifle Association's lead supporter in Congress, Dickey's other main accomplishment prior to entering his new career as a lobbyist was a ban on federal research on gun violence. (After the 2012 mass shooting in Aurora, Colorado, one of fourteen such tragedies that year, Dickey would confess he regretted his work to limit research on gun violence.)

Fortunately, my own work with stem cells was focused not on those derived from fetal or embryonic tissue but on the superstars of the immune system: bone marrow stem cells. As everyone working in this field knew, the valuable stem cells that could produce infection fighters were extremely difficult to identify and isolate from all the material aspirated from a bone marrow donor. At best, conventional techniques produced concentrations of 20 percent stem cells. In my lab, we developed a method that yielded a 75 percent concentration. We did this by taking advantage of the way the immune system worked.

In nature, the body holds its most potent bone marrow stem cells in reserve while others are activated to produce defender cells to fight pathogens and cancers. We used a chemical that would be toxic to those activated ones but not to the cells reserved in the marrow. This last-man-standing approach meant that we could harvest a bounty of the most valuable stem cells, and do so with such high enrichment that we could characterize the molecular features of the cells. We did this with human cells at a time before the mouse models allowing human cell engraftment were fully developed. Instead, we collaborated with a colleague in Nevada who had realized that if cells could be put into an animal before that animal developed immunity, then as the immune system developed, it would fail to recognize the donor's cells as foreign. The animal would be tolerant of the donor's cells just as it would its own cells. The trick was to get donor cells into an animal before the first vestiges of its immune system become active. My colleague, Esmail Zanjani, worked with sheep and showed he could use ultrasound-guided injection of the pregnant ewe to successfully implant human cells that would then give rise to human blood as the animal developed. He injected the human cells we had isolated and mature human blood cells of multiple types were present in the lambs after birth. The results demonstrated that we had bona fide human stem cells. The method never took off, perhaps because we published in *Science* before we had the sheep data, but perhaps also because it did not work in the prevailing model of the day, the mouse. Mice were enthusiastically embraced as the key model as the engineering methods I mentioned were really blossoming. We worked on human cells, which few people did then, and no easy model was available. The mouse has much more activity in its stem cells and so would lose stem cells to the toxin in our activation selection method. No mouse stem cells could survive. The mouse does not always mimic the human and when it doesn't skepticism emerges. I learned an important lesson and switched almost exclusively to mouse models. We validate in human cells when we can, but I learned that the difficulty of human cell research ran deep.

Working with mice often seems odd when your goal is helping people. Indeed, many things learned in the mouse have not panned out when finally tested in people. But some do and we were lucky enough to be involved in one such experience. We searched for a way to obtain bone marrow cells from blood, to spare patients, donors, and, yes, caregivers from the difficult job of withdrawing them by piercing bone. How did we do this? Well, previous research had established that the body produces "come-to-me" signals that tell cells where they should live. For bone marrow stem cells with a receptor called CXCR4, these signals provided the homing beacon that held them in place inside bones. When we gave mice a chemical that turned off the beacon, the stem cells migrated to the blood. If true in people, it meant that targeting a specific chemical mediator of stem cell location could result in harvesting stem cells from the blood without all the effort, expense, and trauma of going to the operating room.

Today the basic method of moving stem cells from the bone marrow to the blood is used by most bone marrow transplant centers, which takes almost all the pain out of the harvesting procedure. It involves an older medicine, the cytokine G-CSF, and a method to target the molecule we had worked on. But as luck would have it, the company that made the compound we used to prove our science didn't move forward to commercialize it. This is common in corporate medicine, where executives must make bets on future products without being certain of the odds. Another company wound up producing a different agent used for the procedure. It was an agent they had already tested in humans for another purpose (ironically, AIDS). They quickly showed it too moved stem cells into the blood. While the business windfall went elsewhere, we had the reward of knowing we had added something to the science that provided benefit to patients.

Big scientific endeavors can seem amorphous and are therefore vulnerable to misunderstanding. The $3 billion Human Genome Project (HGP), which was launched in 1989 by the National Institutes of Health, was typical. Some proponents stressed how it would yield progress against specific diseases, like Alzheimer's, cystic fibrosis, and cancer, which would make it relevant to every person on earth. However, this suggestion risked raising expectations too high. A more realistic view would note that genomic research would aid the overall science of molecular biology and perhaps associate specific genes with diseases. This would be painstaking work, and therapies based on it would lie many years—if not decades—in the future.

The genome sought by the HGP team would not be a complete and exact blueprint for a species. They were hoping to collect something more like a raw listing of the set of gene pairs stored in the nucleus of a cell. The pairs are made up of the nucleic acids adenine and thymine or cytosine and guanine. These AT or CG combinations instruct the development and activities of cells, organs, and—ultimately—human individuals. They are found inside the nuclei of cells in the twisted-ladder structure that James Watson and Francis Crick dubbed the *double helix*. Human nuclei contain 3.1 billion base pairs. Were they to be untangled and stretched out, the DNA from a single cell would produce a six-foot-long string.

The term *genome* was coined in 1920, and the first complete identification of a simple one, for a virus, was accomplished in 1976. The federal Human Genome Project became possible with the development of machines—DNA sequencers—that automated a labor-intensive process. However, the early sequencers were expensive—$200,000 in 2017 dollars—and would only report a string of six hundred base pairs with each run. These strings were similar to the list of words in a dictionary. And just as a page in a dictionary doesn't provide you with the sentences and paragraphs to make a story, a piece of a genome cannot tell you how, for example, something as specialized as a liver cell or a skin cell is created or performs its functions.

The government-backed genome project progressed slowly until it got a jolt from a competing team headed by scientist and entrepreneur Craig Venter. In 1998, Venter announced that his group, working at a new company called Celera, would use a new generation of sequencing machines and the data being generated by the HGP scientists to race ahead of them. His commercial goals included the patenting of genes and the production of a genome that could be sold to researchers at companies, universities, and institutes. Venter was extremely flamboyant, as scientists go. He sailed a big yacht that flew a ballooning spinnaker sail that featured a picture of himself in a wizard's hat. At one public event where he was set to speak, he walked onstage accompanied by sequined Broadway dancers.

Venter was so brash that he proposed to reach his goal while spending a fraction of what the taxpayers were investing in the Human Genome Project, and this made politicians in Washington impatient with the government's effort. His backing from corporate funders also raised concerns about how the results of his research might be used. Who would receive the benefits if the genome, or parts of it, could be patented with an eye toward profit? Would therapies derived from this science be so expensive that only the very rich could receive them? Shouldn't the general public expect to share in the gains if government research provided the foundational work for Venter's group? These concerns became more acute when Celera filed preliminary patents on 6,500 gene fragments that its scientists had identified. This move was particularly alarming to politicians in foreign countries where scientists had joined the genome project initiated by the U.S. government. This was a particular interest for British prime minister Tony Blair, who wanted the raw data of the genome to be freely available to all.

Although the iconoclastic Venter might say that a privately backed effort would be more creative, nimble, and driven to succeed, I would argue that only the federal government could have organized and initiated the great genome hunt. It was the biological version of Project Apollo, which the National Aeronautics and Space Administration (NASA) organized to put the first human beings on the surface of the moon. Accomplished in just eight years, Apollo did science, engineering, and manufacturing on a scale that no private group could match. If you are skeptical about this, consider that the first manned private spaceflight, which relied on technology developed under NASA, wouldn't be made until 2004, which was thirty-five years after the first lunar landing.

Of course, I'm not arguing that the competition Venter's group provided wasn't helpful. Scientists are no less ego-driven than anyone else. A few, like John Gurdon, may be so idealistic or self-effacing that they resist attention, but most of us are competitive sorts, and we enjoy getting credit for our work. Prestigious prizes, including the Nobel, are awarded in part to motivate scientists, and very few would decline to attend a reception at the White House or an invitation to provide the keynote speech at a major conference. But most of us understand that in the grand scheme of things, we are minor players and that progress depends on eventually sharing information and research results.

For a brief period, the competition between the genome teams overwhelmed the usual cordiality we expect in science. Venter, whose style departed from the norm, took much of the early blame for this state of affairs, but he had partners in the dance of dysfunction. The HGP's top leader, Francis Collins, believed he was doing work as important as the Apollo moonshot program and the splitting of the atom. This feeling and a sense of public ownership over the work, by many accounts, led him to resent Venter as an interloper—but he sought to accommodate him. In 2000, the two groups reached an agreement that resulted in a tie at the finish line. In 2001, on February 12—which was Charles Darwin's birthday—*two* reports were published with similar data. As often happens, *The New York Times* broke the news a day early, announcing to the world that the global consortium put together by the government and the Celera Genomic team led by Craig Venter had reached the goal. Their most startling finding was the fact that humans possessed far fewer genes than science suspected. Instead of one hundred thousand or more, the number would eventually be estimated at about nineteen thousand.

On the day the news was announced, the headline shocked a great many doctors and scientists. We knew that genes are required to direct countless functions, from the development of an egg and a sperm to the working of every organ system. This counts for all the roughly 3.2 trillion cells of varying types that make up the human body. The discovery that the human genome is much smaller than expected would frustrate some scientists who hoped to find a single gene responsible for a discrete illness, which might then become the source of a cure. It is true, of course, that lone mutations are responsible for certain illnesses. Mutation of the gene called TP53, which is responsible for controlling cell growth, is associated with some malignancies. However, simple one-to-one, genetic cause and effect seemed less likely with the news that the genome is so small.

Equally surprising was Venter's observation that only about three hundred of the genes his group identified were absent from the genome of the average laboratory mouse. The rest seemed to come from a common ancestor, some one hundred million years in the past. The government team, striving to make a similar point, said they found a baker's dozen of genes that human beings acquired from bacteria. They said they expected to find many more. This was, in Venter's eyes, part of the wonder to be appreciated in the genome. "Some have said to me that sequencing the human genome will diminish humanity by taking the mystery out of life," he said as the project was completed. "Nothing could be further from the truth."

On one level, the smaller genome and the idea that humans have so many genes in common with a tiny mouse suggested that we aren't such a special species. This seems doubly true when you consider that a certain translucent water flea, *Daphnia pulex*, has thirty-one thousand genes. It's a rather special flea, with the ability to sprout defensive armor and spines and to adapt to polluted water. However, it's still a flea. And the thought that such a lowly creature might surpass *Homo sapiens* in any measure seemed just wrong to many people.

In evolutionary terms, however, the human genome can be seen not as diminutive but as elegance itself because it does so much with so little. The only way this could happen would be if genes worked in concert to achieve the variety of expressions seen in the body. Instead of LEGO blocks clicked together or beads lined up in a row, our genes establish a huge variety of combinations similar to what you might see if you could gaze upon a city from a mile in the sky and recognize the myriad connections of the people who live there. If we could see how many people on a given block patronize the grocer on the corner, and then see how the grocer and his customers connect with others, we would be astonished by the diversity of their connections. It is in the coming together that individuals establish a functioning society, and it is in the coming together that genes create life.

Genes power the cells to interact, with chemical compromises creating orderly growth and functioning. This is the dynamic process described by Itai Yanai and Martin Lercher in a book called *The Society of Genes*. As they note, the sequencing of the genome revealed a "survival machine" that requires cooperation in addition to the competition that marked an older way of considering genetics, as reflected in Richard Dawkins's treatise *The Selfish Gene*.

Dawkins, who actually inspired both Yanai and Lercher to enter biology, depicted a Hobbesian kind of war among genes, with the fittest reproducing to live on and on. This does happen and can explain certain human traits. However, we now know, thanks largely to the genome projects, that our genetic selves are extremely complex. For example, most of our roughly 3.2 trillion individual cells must be signaled by others if they are to replicate and grow. Without these signals, they do not act. When a cell does divide, it provides each "daughter" cell with a copy of its DNA. This renewal is done at varying rates. White blood cells turn over in a matter of hours; red blood cells last 120 days; some neurons are made and live as long as we do.

Inevitably copying, which calls for each cell to reproduce over three billion nucleic acids in proper order, poses the possibility for mistakes in the form of mutations. Usually these errors are harmless. Cancer cells, as Yanai and Lercher point out, require several genetic mutations to cause disease, also known as multiple genetic "hits." Trouble arises in the body because the mutants may self-replicate more rapidly than normal cells, may have impaired repair of DNA damage, have impaired differentiation, have less sensitivity to death signals, or a host of other functions altered in cancer. Faster rates of proliferation or less efficient damage repair means that they are more likely to acquire a second, and then a third mutation. With each new mutation, cancer cells overcome more of the body's ways of defending against cancer until control can no longer be imposed and the cells take off as a full-blown cancer.

The cancer tipping point depends, in part, on how often cells are replicated and thus have a chance to collect mutations. Our skin cells, intestinal and airway lining cells, and blood cells are among the most active. The number of cell divisions ongoing at any moment in our bodies is measured in the hundreds of billions. Mistakes happen in the process of replicating all that DNA. When mistakes happen that change the cycling of the cells, their ability to repair DNA mistakes, or a host of other abnormalities, abnormal cells are made.

Many of them just disappear because of a natural self-destruct mechanism. The self-destruct mechanism—also called programmed cell death (PCD)—prunes away old and unneeded cells and makes way for newer ones. PCD eliminates the webbing in a developing fetus's hands to make way for fingers. It also helps govern the number of neurons developed in the brains of both children and adults.

Cancer cells may carry mutations that help them evade this natural process. With their systems stuck on "go," they consume far more energy than normal cells, crowd out healthy ones, and often travel to other sites to colonize the body. If they are cancer stem cells, they may also survive the onslaught of chemotherapy and cause both recurrences and metastases and ultimately death.

I was reminded of the relentless quality of metastatic cancer in the 1990s when my father was diagnosed with cancer. Like so many northerners he had moved to Florida to be outdoors more. I went to visit him in March 1995. He was fit and active and we played tennis but when we finished he felt some back pain. It didn't seem to get better even with rest and in May he had an x-ray. That was when his doctor called me, not my father, to reveal the news. By June 1995 he was being transported by ambulance, twice a day, for radiation treatments. I'm not sure there is ever a case when twice-daily radiotherapy is required for any patient. In his case it was certainly not the standard of care and it resulted in much suffering. The inevitable bumps in the road on transport were deep jolts of near unbearable pain in tumor-ridden bones. I could tell from my father's reports and from the information I gleaned from his doctors that he had only a few months to live.

When he finally talked with me about this, he accepted his prognosis philosophically, reassuring me that he felt he'd had a good seventy-four years.

I wasn't so philosophical. It seemed to me that my father was getting therapy that had no chance of curing him: the goals were strictly to palliate misery. Why then would twice-daily misery be considered appropriate since the long-term benefits of twice-daily therapy were unproven? It was hard not to draw the conclusion that for Medicare data support, Florida's senior citizens were considered by the unscrupulous as a kind of medical gold mine. Florida Medicare fraud stands apart from any other state in the country. For-profit hospitals certainly don't help. I visited my father when he finally had to be hospitalized to find that despite a less than one-week stay, he had been ignored sufficiently in the for-profit hospital chain to develop deep ulcers on his heels. Complications occur of course in every hospital, but experience with my father leads me to strongly support the policymakers emphasizing payment based on patient outcomes, not just procedures performed.

If the genome is considered a rough script for the development and functioning of living things, then stem cells are the star players in the production. They are the heroes that build the body, maintain it, and repair it. They even verge on superhero status because of their ability to create multiple types of offspring and their near-immortality. Similarly, cancer stem cells are like fallen angels, or the villainous Agent Smith in the Matrix movies. Smith replicates with terrifying ferocity and can reappear after what seems like a total defeat. So it is with cancer stem cells.

With stem cell features being shared by both cancer cells and the cells at the foundation of our body's well-being, it has to be an area rich with opportunities for scientific understanding of health and disease. The challenge is that stem cells for most of our tissues are only recently recognized so we have limited information about them. We also don't have good measures of how things change over time at the level of single cells. This means we mostly glimpse events indirectly and imprecisely in the body. This may partly be why biology is perceived as the least linear of all the sciences. It is very difficult to directly connect cause and effect. Although physics, chemistry, geology, and even astronomy have unresolved mysteries, they generally yield to mathematical logic: A interacts with B and you get result C. In biology, a cell labeled "A" may have dozens of vertices that can contact any number of adjoining cells conveying a range of messages with varying intensity. Some of the messages change the neighboring cell temporarily, others permanently, and messages convey very different meanings depending on the other messages that are happening at a given time. It is likely that as we gain quantitative measures of each message and each effect it elicits, biology will reduce to more discernable logic. However, it is now a science of complexity; progressively more awe-inspiring with each dimension we unveil. The processes that give us life, animate us, and burden us with disease are astoundingly complex.

That complexity is exemplified by the many unanticipated consequences that eventually show up with medical interventions. Breast implants have been used for purely cosmetic purposes, but are also often a part of the care for a woman with breast cancer. Breast removal is still performed (though not with the "radical" extremes that Halstead championed) for cancer therapy and is increasingly used to prevent cancer in women who have known genetic predispositions. Angelina Jolie is someone who preferred bilateral mastectomy to bearing the risk to her and her family of breast cancer. Undoubtedly, consideration of mastectomy is influenced by the ability to prevent disfigurement through breast implants. They may well be considered an ancillary to cancer prevention in such settings. Unfortunately, as with all technologies, they have a downside and, in this case, a cancer downside. While a rare event, women who have received breast implants with textured surfaces have increased risk of an otherwise very rare cancer of the immune system. They can get a so-called Anaplastic Large Cell Lymphoma of T cells. The T cells that are such an important part of immunity against infections and against cancers can be provoked in this setting to go sufficiently awry to result in a very aggressive cancer. Notably, this does not seem to occur with smooth-surfaced breast implants. The risk is not substantial enough to warrant implant removal, but the FDA does recommend increased awareness on the part of patients and their physicians. This one example points to the near incomprehensible complexity of the body and, in particular, the immune system.

Settings of chronic injury are known to increase the risk of cancer. Cigarette smoke and lung cancer is a classic example. Chronic liver injury from alcohol, hepatitis, or some parasites (including Mahmoud's Schistosoma japonicum) resulting in liver cancer is another. These are cancers of the cells within the injured organ and have some intuitive logic. The constant wounding and repair process might eventually end up with a repair process that is abnormal and eventually out of control: a cancer. Even a damaged immune system resulting in immune cancer makes some sense. People with some autoimmune diseases like Sjogren's syndrome or lupus have a slight increase in B cell lymphomas. But T cell tumors are rare, not associated with underlying immune disorders, and could not be expected to result from a specific type of implant. Why textured and not smooth implants? Why T cells and not breast cells? Why the particular type of T cell cancer? All are impossible to understand based on our current state of knowledge and could certainly never have been anticipated. Where to even begin to explore how an external stimulus like the textured implant could eventuate in a rare immune malignancy is unclear. I for one could never undertake investigating a problem for which there are so few clear threads of connection. It is important to be bold in taking on important problems, but scientists have to balance their desire to solve a problem with the hard-nosed judgment of whether they can. It is often a cause of great frustration by the public and, particularly, patients with the problem. Why can't doctors and scientists do better at solving my problem? It is not for lack of interest. It is for a lack of solid footing in a bog of biologic complexity.

Getting that footing often happens with the establishment of very discrete findings. Jim Allison provided those for cancer immunotherapy, Montagnier and Barré-Sinoussi for AIDS, and James Thomson and John Gearhart for stem cells.

FIVE

STEM CELLS AND A RENEWABLE YOU

James Thomson of the University of Wisconsin and John Gearhart of Johns Hopkins isolated and grew human pluripotent stem cells in their labs and reported their success within weeks of each other in 1998. The importance of this breakthrough was lost on no one, as it pointed the way to make any cell in the human body. These were the ultimate stem cells and no matter what disease or cell type you studied, these cells offered the possibility to gain more direct insight. Most prior work depended on getting rare samples from people and most such samples didn't last in culture. Or they depended on easier to culture cells from mice. Getting human embryonic stem (ES) cells meant human cells could be cultured long-term and then allowed to differentiate to become mature human cells of different types. Getting them to grow was pretty straightforward, particularly with Thomson's work as a guide. It required a special media in which to grow the cells, but once they were established they could grow indefinitely. Getting to become a cell type of interest was a challenge.

Sometimes, simply changing the media to a different type allowed the cells to spontaneously mature into a cell of interest. Looking into a microscope and seeing cells beat like a heart was pretty compelling theater. And pretty compelling evidence that heart cells could be obtained. Everyone in the field thought that was likely to be a shortcut to making cell patches for damaged hearts—a kind of therapeutic holy grail for people who suffered heart attacks and subsequent death because they had lost too much muscle. It has yet to be effectively done. It has taken years to learn how to make the cells not just any heart cell, but the ones of the adult heart that make up the parts of the pump damaged in heart attacks. Similarly, human ES cells spontaneously make neurons. That has certainly inspired much excitement about implanting cells for a host of brain and nervous system disorders.

There was no question that human ES cells would make a difference, though there was also no question that it would take the concerted effort of many. Assembling teams, aggregating data, and sharing ideas was essential. At Harvard, hundreds of people in various disciplines from hematology/oncology to neuroscience and embryology worked on stem cell–related projects, but we encountered each other mainly by accident. It didn't take a genius to recognize that this isolation deprived all of us from both raw information about important advances and the kind of water cooler talk that spurs new ways of thinking about difficult problems.

In the highly competitive world of science where people can be quite guarded about sharing what they know, lots of attempts have been made to create interdisciplinary teams to jump-start research. With the rare exceptions like the still fractious Human Genome Project, these collaborations tend to fall apart. However, stem cell research offered the possibility of regenerative medicine, an area of such profoundly humanitarian consequence that it seemed we simply had to corral our egos, and join our talents and resources to take a team approach. We had one member of our faculty who was recognized as an expert, and around whom we could rally. And by the way, it wasn't me.

Douglas Melton had done his doctoral work under John Gurdon, the pioneer who wasn't even supposed to be a scientist who had successfully cloned frogs in 1958. (Doug was five years old then.) In the 1970s, Gurdon headed Cambridge University's molecular biology lab, which had supported Watson and Crick and three other Nobel laureates. Gurdon would be awarded a Nobel in 2012, and many of the methods he devised in the 1950s and 1960s remain in use today. At Cambridge, Melton worked with Gurdon and managed to publish five papers on genetics and cloning before he was awarded a doctorate. This remarkable record helped him to become a professor at Harvard the next year. He was all of twenty-eight years old.

Although he was anything but one of those laboratory egomaniacs who bully their way to the top, Doug was confident in a way that I was not. He too had shifted focus from the humanities to science, having studied philosophy as an undergraduate at the University of Illinois. But his ability to flourish in the Gurdon lab seemed to give him grounding and his inherent brilliance typically had him a step or two ahead of his peers in ideas of consequence.

Doug's confidence was evident in the direct way he addressed people at meetings. He knew that audiences, even scientific audiences, really want to be told a story. Make the narrative simple and people will get it, remember it, and seek you out for more. As one of my colleagues points out, "No one walks out of a lecture and says, 'I wish that was more complicated.'" Doug is a master of the well-told scientific story.

With his narratives Doug can create enthusiasm, and find support, for projects that might languish in the imagination of someone with less drive and creativity. It's hard to overstate the importance of personal qualities when it comes to getting things done in science, despite what people often think about scientists as robotic in their dedication to work. It's just not true that scientists are the impersonal eccentrics often portrayed in popular media. Passion, creativity, and personality drive science as much as any field and are particularly crucial in new fields like stem cell biology. Doug was able to bring people and monetary support to stem cell research, not by the force of his personality—he is actually quite soft-spoken—but by making coherent scientific arguments and cultivating collaboration. Unlike some high-level scientists, Doug recognized the value of what others could bring to a project, and that included everyone from clinicians who worked with patients to venture capitalists who brought money to science. He looked around the Cambridge/Boston community and saw an unmatched human and technical resource.

For much of the prior two decades, Doug has conducted painstaking explorations of the ways that genetic code is written and transferred to create new life. He did devote much of his time to developing and testing methods for looking inside molecules to discover how so-called messenger RNA control the factory functions that link amino acids together inside a cell. A great deal of what he did involved eggs of the same *Xenopus laevis*, or African clawed frog, that John Gurdon had cloned. *Xenopus* are good test subjects because they are hardy, they produce a lot of large, resilient eggs, and they are a decent genetic model.

Science became a lot less abstract and much more personal for Doug when his six-month-old son, Sam, was diagnosed with type 1 diabetes. (His daughter has it too.) Type 1, which is the immune-based form of the disease, arises when the pancreas fails to produce insulin at a level needed for the body to process and use nutrients. Insulin insufficiency, which can be fatal, causes a host of terrible symptoms, including seizures. It can be difficult to diagnose in infants, and the Meltons went through much anguish as they watched Sam suffer and waited to learn the cause.

The experience, and the understanding that Sam faced a lifelong chronic condition with potentially dire consequences, motivated Doug to shift the focus of his science completely. This almost never happens in science because of the nature of funding—you can only convince funders of your future success by proposing to directly build on prior success. Doug was supported by the Howard Hughes

Medical Institute and so was not subject to the same constraints; he could shift focus with their support. And so he did, deciding to focus his science directly on diabetes and on stem cells that he rightly envisioned might produce a true cure. The stem cells that create the pancreas and populate it with new functioning cells during the lifespan fall into two categories. One kind creates enzymes that digest food. The second type of cell is founded in scattered pancreatic "islets" where they produce, store, and release insulin and other hormones that regulate our metabolism and other functions. People with type 1 diabetes have too few of the insulin-producing "beta" cells, as they are called, generally because of an autoimmune disorder that selectively destroys insulin-producing cells.

For Melton and others, the beta cell problem seemed ripe for a solution that might one day involve using stem cells to create an ongoing supply of productive islets. (Direct transplants from cadavers had been tried with success but were extremely complicated, required multiple donors for enough cells for one recipient, and often gradually declined in effectiveness over time.) However, a great deal of basic science had to be done before a treatment involving stem cells could be considered. Many questions had to be answered about how the cells that created the pancreas developed in the embryo and fetus and then came to sustain the organ throughout life. Working in animals, Doug studied, among other things, molecules called hedgehog ligands, which regulate how embryos develop different parts of the body. These ligands, and the pathways they travel to do their work, were also implicated in some cancers. This was no surprise as, over and over again, science was revealing that the mechanisms that governed development and growth were often implicated in the wildfire of malignancy.

In work done with frog embryos, Doug made key basic discoveries about how cells in the newly fertilized egg begin to create the neural tissue that will become the spinal cord, the brain, and the nervous system. This development process depends, as Melton and his group found, on communication from one group of cells that sparks changes in others. Although it would seem esoteric to many laypeople, this work answered some key questions about how complicated life-forms emerge from an amorphous ball of cells that are the pre-embryo.

Inevitably, however, Doug and other embryologists would run into the limits of animal studies. Big disappointments with drugs that worked in animals but not human beings showed that only so much could be learned from studying mice or frogs or other species. (One big problem is that they don't develop under the guidance of all the same chemicals.) Like others, Doug turned to the study of human embryonic stem cells. Since not all embryonic stem cells have the same functional properties, he developed many new lines using the fertilized eggs abandoned by couples seeking in vitro fertilization. These he made readily available to any scientist in the world who sought them to study. He was able to do so because of the Howard Hughes funding. Government bans on using federal money were already in place.

Unlike others who had been discouraged by the controversy around stem cells, Thomson and Gearhart had been able to create privately funded projects to advance their science. Thomson would eventually reveal that he had also been denied access to University of Wisconsin funds by those fearing negative publicity. The answer to his money problems came from an entrepreneur named Michael West, whose company, Geron, sought to develop, for lack of a better term, fountain-of-youth technologies. West had a doctorate in biology and had spent his entire career investigating aging and searching for ways to slow or even reverse the process. Because they venture close to concepts that can seem fantastical, scientists who work in this area must fight against being perceived as crackpots. West's interests were quite legitimate. He was intrigued by telomeres, which appeared to govern the vitality of chromosomes. And he was fascinated by stem cells.

Funded by Geron, which also backed Gearhart, Thomson set up

in a freestanding facility with equipment he acquired on his own, and he used the same techniques he had employed in primate research. Frozen blastocysts were thawed, placed in nutrients, and processed so the stem cells could be isolated. Once established, colonies of cells had to be monitored closely and separated with pipettes to keep them from overpopulating their environments and differentiating into various subtypes of stem cells (for muscle, bone, nerves, etc.). Properly nourished and safeguarded, the cell lines, as they were called, were essentially immortal. They could reproduce almost indefinitely and supply researchers around the world with cells for research.

The ES cell lines that Thomson produced were available for purchase, but at a price and with reporting requirements that were extraordinary for scientific reagents. This hampered many from working in the field. Doug's lines were available more inexpensively. However, they were still being developed in the early days of the field and so had less characterization. Both depended on private money to be generated, a highly inefficient method for developing reagents of such dramatic potential. A disconnect between funding and importance is not uncommon in life science research, but to have a primary driving force of science, the federal government, speak out and ban an area of uncontestably important work is extraordinary. Private foundation funding could help, corporate investment could help. Unfortunately, the latter source was rare because of the distance from ongoing work and clinical application, keeping even the company that might risk the public relations issues, at considerable distance. Private funding was possible, but the scale of need versus available capital seemed to create an enormous barrier. We needed to assemble scientists to improve the pace of discovery and to be better at making a case to potential donors. Harvard is spectacular at assembling great talent, including philanthropic talent, and needed only an activation signal to become a leading stem cell program.

Doug was, to my mind, one of the leading stem cell experts in the world and one of Harvard's best scientists. (He was also a member of the National Academy of Sciences, which is one of the most elite scientific groups in the world.) Doug was succeeding, but it seemed that the whole enterprise of stem cell research required a more concerted effort drawing more people into a team. I heard he thought the same thing. When I went to see him to suggest we create an interdisciplinary stem cell institute, I was a bit worried that this fellow who was truly a superstar in embryology might not be receptive to a lunch-pail hematologist.

People are often surprised to hear a doctor or scientist express the kind of insecurity I felt when I went to see Doug. Often they assume that someone who has survived medical school and works in the clinic or lab must surely be completely confident and at ease. But confidence about doctoring does not translate into confidence about science. I was, after all, trained to be an expert in interpreting people's words, symptoms, x-rays, and how their stomach felt or lungs sounded; that was no more about fundamental biology than selling a product is to making it. They are very different worlds and I was a newcomer to refined haunts of basic science in which Doug had come of age. One thing I did have, though, was confidence that I could connect with people. I had learned that at people's bedside. It didn't hurt that I have outside interests to which people can connect. Sometimes that is parenting escapades, a good book recently read, or love of the outdoors. My offbeat passion for fishing even helped. Few things center my being like being on or in water, throwing a fly line and occasionally connecting with vitality itself when a fish strikes. For many years I kept a boat in Boston Harbor and often rose before dawn so I could spend an hour or two on the water throwing flies I had tied before getting to work at eight o'clock. I generally released what I caught but when I netted a particularly big fish I delivered it to a restaurant near Mass General. I always gave them the fish, and they never let me pay for a lunch.

I don't recall if I went fishing on the day I went to see Doug, but he would likely say I didn't betray any of my insecurities. We immediately connected on both a personal level and in our desire to see stem cell biology deliver medicines that could make a difference in people's lives. He spoke to me about his desire to see his work translated into treatments and he would be happy to accept help anywhere he could find it. Embryology, his specialty, could yield therapies, and it seemed likely that by studying how pancreatic cells were created, he could devise a cure for type 1 diabetes. This would be no small accomplishment. More than 1.2 million American adults have this form of diabetes, and children are diagnosed with it every day. It exacts a huge toll in terms of human suffering and health care costs. A stem cell–based cure that could lead to normal pancreatic function would be a godsend. However, Doug's basic science related to all of cell biology and had the potential to seed breakthroughs in many other areas of research, including oncology, if only various labs and individual investigators were able to collaborate more freely.

As a large bureaucracy, Harvard was a balkanized place where brilliant and generally competitive people pursued their ideas with such intensity that they might not notice that someone nearby was doing closely related work. Funding methods generally supported single projects and not collaborations. In addition to this limitation, Harvard scientists, like all American-based researchers, faced the obstacle of constricted federal funding and controversy that made philanthropists and foundations wary of getting involved. The situation left the United States vulnerable to being overtaken by other countries in this area of science and medicine, but it also created an opportunity for institutions where leaders were willing and able to invest their own resources. Geron had done this by getting behind Gearhart and Thomson, but those efforts had been relatively small in scale compared with what Harvard and its affiliated hospitals could do.

Doug agreed that Harvard needed more than a passive approach to stem cells and by the time our meeting came to an end, we had sculpted out a vision for a trans-Harvard initiative. More importantly, I think we both felt we had found a partner to make it happen.

I had deep roots in the medical community and knew how the hospitals worked, Doug was an established leader in the Faculty of Arts and Sciences and was fully connected to University power centers. We also represented the spectrum of what was needed to make stem cells deliver. He was a superstar in the world of fundamental biology and I had some traction in the applied science of medicine. We knew Harvard had little precedent for organizing people across the broad universe of institutions that comprised it, but we also knew that scientists, though skeptical, would welcome the chance to engage in a larger effort. Finally, we were confident that Harvard alumni would look favorably on the university leading such a potentially transformative field and would get behind us financially.

Many factors would work against us in this endeavor. First of all, lots of people want to get Harvard's money for their work, and even with its big endowment, the university had only so much cash and fund-raising muscle to go around. Second, we were asking the university to take the risk of putting its imprimatur on work that some powerful people didn't want done. Also, we had to allow for the fact that this kind of research rarely proceeds in a straight line. To use the wildcatter term, we were bound to drill some dry holes. And there was no guarantee that our successes in basic science would produce treatments and royalty payments to sustain an ongoing effort. Although we would contribute to the public good and make Harvard a leader in the field, this could be science for the sake of science.

Neither of us would consider that success. We were in it to make new therapies and benefit those for whom stem cell science offered hope. We named our planned organization the Harvard Stem Cell Institute (HSCI), intentionally leaving out the word research. We did not want to simply foster great research.

Moving the HSCI from concept to reality was only possible if we could convince the leaders of the university, medical school, and hospitals that something positive would result. To that end, I had one advantage that I couldn't reveal to Doug at the time but which I can write about here. In 1983, I had been one of the doctors who treated a young Harvard professor named Lawrence Summers for Hodgkin's lymphoma. This type of white blood cell cancer can cause lots of unpleasant symptoms, including pain and fever and weight loss. It can be treated (generally with chemotherapy and radiation), but not everyone survives.

Larry had become quite sick and it was initially unclear what he had. He was finally admitted to the hospital where I was the fellow (a term for a subspecialty trainee) on the consulting Hematology team. We had to conduct numerous tests, including a bone marrow biopsy, that finally revealed his diagnosis. He spent considerable time in the hospital, where I was often involved in his care and got to know him reasonably well. To me, he was a smart, ever-curious patient stuck with a lousy fate. I knew he was an academic economist, but I only later learned that he was what might be called academic royalty. His mother and father were both professors at the University of Pennsylvania and by the time he finished undergraduate studies at the Massachusetts Institute of Technology, two of his uncles—Paul Samuelson and Kenneth Arrow—had been awarded the Nobel Prize in economics. Larry was following their footsteps with a reputation for brilliance in macroeconomics until his diagnosis, when his health became his first concern. But Hodgkin's' didn't affect his mind. Each time I saw him he asked so many good questions that I made him a proposition:

"I'll teach you medicine," I told him. "You teach me economics."

Summers took the deal and in the course of his treatment, which led to remission and cure, I learned a great deal (much of it now forgotten) about how national and global economies work. More importantly, I learned that he was fearless intellectually and personally. He would never shy away from anything, particularly an opportunity to do something important. Once recovered, he resumed his extremely active life of teaching and research and consulting. In 1991, he left Harvard to head the World Bank. He joined the Clinton administration in 1993 and ended his work for the president in the position of secretary of the treasury. When President Bush replaced Clinton, Larry returned to Harvard to take the job of university president. At age forty-six, he was one of the youngest men—to this point, all Harvard presidents were men—ever appointed to the job. And since Harvard presidents rival popes when it comes to their longevity in office, it was possible that he could serve for decades.

Summers's investiture took place on a sunny October day in a ceremony in Harvard Yard. He was accompanied by much of his family, including his twin daughters, who were eleven years old. In his inaugural address, he stressed only one major research goal, which he called a "Revolution in Science." This revolution would occur, he said, during the coming "century of biological and life science" and would be driven by the need to comprehend "the biological and chemical basis of life." Summers understood the context of this moment. He noted the "multi-billion-dollar projects [to] sequence the genome" and acknowledged that the university would have to "adapt its traditional structures to most effectively engage the adventure of science."

Harvard had missed a number of chances to lead in biology since I had been there and one was particularly poignant in my field. A young, wonderful physician/scientist named Brian Druker was affiliated with the university and Dana-Farber. He was particularly interested in proteins called kinases, which are able to activate molecules by transferring a high-energy phosphate onto them. Druker was especially interested in kinases that regulate the production of white blood cells. This process is a bit complicated, as stem cells first produce so-called "progenitor" cells that then supply the body with what become mature white blood cells. When stem or progenitor cells get genetic defects they can cause cancer, and one of the first cancers in which this was realized is a disease called chronic myeloid leukemia (CML). The genetic defect was known as the Philadelphia chromosome.

The most important work on the Philadelphia chromosome's role in CML had been done by physician-turned-scientist Janet Rowley at the University of Chicago. Rowley was a child prodigy who got her undergraduate degree at age nineteen but was shut out of medical school when she first applied because the university had filled its quota of women. (They admitted three for every sixty men.) The University of Chicago's Prtizger School of Medicine admitted her the following year, and she graduated at age twenty-three.

Rowley became interested in genetics while working as a physician at a clinic for children who had Down syndrome. (People with Down syndrome have an extra copy of chromosome 21.) Rowley moved from medicine into science when she accompanied her pathologist husband to England for his sabbatical and a prominent hematologist named Lazslo Lajtha gave her a job in his laboratory at Churchill Hospital in Oxford. Known as an "atomic hematologist," Lajtha's work included research into radiation-related illnesses. In Lajtha's lab, Rowley began to study chromosomal defects. When she returned to Chicago, she met with another well-known leukemia specialist named Leon Jacobson and persuaded him to provide her with a special microscope and a darkroom so she could take photos of the chromosomes she studied and enlarge them. It had already been noted by two scientists—Peter Nowell and David Hungerford—in, of course, Philadelphia, that people with CML had an abnormally small chromosome 22, but it was Rowley who understood why.

Since genes deal in chemical conversations, Rowley's discovery hinted at what must be going awry. It was subsequently shown that a kinase on chromosome 9 had been shifted over to chromosome 22, and in so doing was fused with another gene such that the kinase was always turned on. An always-active kinase was forcing the cells to continuously grow, a very destructive kind of communication. It was also a potential point of vulnerability since it was evident that chemicals could inhibit kinases. This is where Brian Druker entered the picture. He was intrigued by the idea that the genetic error identified by Rowley might be fixed with a chemical that would turn off the runaway production of cells.

The big challenge would be to identify exactly the right chemical that would do the trick without messing with others related to growth and energy production. A dogged investigator with a well-honed scientific mind, Druker had been, like me, a child chemist free to experiment despite the occasional fumes released into his parents' home. Serious and self-effacing, he had just the right temperament, including the ability to be self-critical, to do top-notch science. As a physician, he had treated CML patients and took their deaths quite personally, allowing the losses to motivate his research. He also believed, like I did, that by working with a readily studied cancer of the blood and bone, he could understand principles key to cancer more generally.

Unfortunately (more for Dana-Farber and Harvard than for him), Druker ran into a roadblock that made it impossible for him to get the kind of backing he wanted. The problem was that the key chemical compounds he wanted to work on, named STI571, were owned by Ciba-Geigy, a Swiss pharmaceutical company. Dana-Farber had entered into an agreement for related research on products made by the company's rival, Sandoz. Despite the fact that Druker had encouraged Ciba-Geigy scientist Nick Lydon to develop drugs like STI571 since they would be targeted therapies very different from the general poisons used by oncologists, the logjam could not be broken. Stymied at Dana-Farber, Druker decided to move across the country to the Oregon Health and Science University in Portland, where the administration was ramping up its committment to research.

Supplied with a small amount of Ciba-Geigy's chemical, Druker tested it in lab dishes that contained both normal white blood cells and CML cells. To his astonishment, it killed 90 percent of the CML cells but none of the normal ones. He reported this finding to his Swiss corporate partner in 1994. Next would come animal trials, which also went very well.

The role of major drug companies in basic research was both essential, as a matter of finance and expertise, and fraught. The money kept scientists around the world working on innovative concepts, and the larger companies operated facilities that could support them with the production of needed chemicals in substantial quantities. However, the relationship between industry and science was complicated by the need for profit, and by the varied activities undertaken by corporate conglomerates.

Drug companies are often engaged in such complex mergers and acquisitions that projects often just get lost in the high-stakes games of corporate strategy and corporate careers. A perfect example of this arose as Ciba-Geigy and Sandoz merged to create the second-largest drug company in the world, Novartis.

Novartis had little interest in developing drugs for rare diseases as they represented small markets and, per the wisdom of the day, would not generate large enough profits. Pushing STI571 forward for a disease that worldwide only represented 30,000 patients was challenging and were it not for the unrelenting efforts of Druker, the result would likely have been quite different. He got Novartis to at least support a first study. In that study, he had to rely on patients who had already reached the limits of other therapies. Nearly 150, including six children, were enrolled to take the compound in pill form, every day, in varying doses. As first one patient, then another, and then another began to improve, Druker began to feel excited. None of the trial subjects experienced serious side effects, and many got better. The improvement could be seen in their level of energy and function and in their blood tests, which showed that STI571 was normalizing their blood counts and reducing the presence of cells with the Philadelphia chromosome. If this finding held up, Novartis would have the first cancer drug that fixed a specific genetic defect that caused malignancy.

The phase I results were nothing short of remarkable, but there was no commitment from Novartis that more studies would proceed.

Indeed, Novartis had not made enough of the drug to do a bigger second study. But in an early example of social media making an impact, a patient-driven petition landed on the desks of Novartis executives and expanded trials got quickly under way. Hematologists who had never heard of STI571 learned of it from patients who wanted to be enrolled in trials.

In December 1999, I was in the convention hall in New Orleans as Brian Druker gave one of the closing talks at the American Society of Hematology's annual meeting. Although efforts had been made to keep the results of the drug trial confidential, the press had reported that some big news was coming, and it was a topic of great speculation at the conference. Every seat was filled as Druker began to speak, and the room was so silent you could hear the sounds made as people scratched notes as he described the parameters of the trial. As he described it, every one of the patients who got the drug were in a late stage of the disease and their doctors had exhausted all other options. Some were obviously dying. This factor alone made the odds for successful treatment quite daunting.

A slender guy with thinning hair and a quiet voice, Druker is not the type to show a lot of emotion. But on this afternoon in New Orleans, he looked like he was having trouble controlling his excitement. He described the research group's efforts to identify a proper dose and schedule for treatment and months of waiting for results. Finally, as the regimen was refined to three 100-milligram capsules per day, the benefits became apparent. All thirty-one patients experienced what seemed to be complete remission, with their white blood cells returning to normal and their health restored. In some cases, the chromosomal abnormality that caused the disease began to disappear. Indeed, when they studied blood samples, Druker's group couldn't find *any* evidence of the Philadelphia chromosome in some of their patients. The only side effects reported were fatigue, muscle cramps, and stomach upsets.

I think that most of us who listened to Druker's talk reflected on CML patients who had died and others who had suffered the grueling experience of bone marrow transplants, which only worked a quarter of the time. In comparison, STI571 seemed like a miracle, and scientists generally don't believe in miracles. Druker acknowledged this when he spoke with the press. "One of the problems I've had with this project," he said, "is that I oftentimes have difficulty convincing people that this isn't too good to be true. One of the major goals of cancer research has been to identify differences between cancer cells and normal cells so that these differences can be targeted with more effective and less toxic treatments. That's exactly what we've seen happen in these patients."

Eventually named Gleevec, the chemical that excited the conference in New Orleans would prove to be so effective in early trails that the Food and Drug Administration used a fast-track process to consider its approval for use. Approval came on May 10, 2001. Novartis, which had been gearing up for the moment, began shipping the drug the very next day. In less than six hours, every advance order for the drug—more than five thousand of them—had been filled and shipped. Soon doctors and patients all over the world were seeing dramatic remissions like the ones recorded in early trials. The number of cells bearing the Philadelphia defect declined. Healthy ones increased in number. People faced with imminent death recovered their strength, began eating, put on weight, and resumed their previous lives. I saw this happen and was astonished.

The basic action of Gleevec was so different from the cell poisoning done with traditional chemotherapies that most scientists and physicians hoped it would work for nearly all people with CML and provide a lasting cure. Strong evidence that the problem mutation was being eradicated with treatment reinforced this hope. Similar optimism attached to the idea that a new cancer therapy paradigm had

arrived. If Gleevec could essentially cancel out the effects of a mutation that caused one cancer, perhaps it could do the same with others.

Soon after it got FDA approval, physicians led by my colleague George Dimetri gave Gleevec to patients with a gastrointestinal tumor that can be caused by a mutation similar to the one
that causes most CML. It worked in about 60 percent of cases. Other
trials found it effective against additional bone marrow–related
diseases and against an extremely rare kind of skin tumor. However, the list of malignancies helped by Gleevec stopped at this
handful. And the much-hoped-for cascade of breakthrough drugs
that would work similar molecular magic did not develop at the
pace many hoped to see. Indeed, while Gleevac could control CML,
it didn't cure it—patients required chronic therapy and some inevitably developed resistance to the drug. Still, it opened the door for
developing drug therapies specifically for the genetic abnormalities
driving the disease. That was entirely new in the drug industy and
signaled a major shift in thinking.

Gleevec opened a vast biological territory. It showed that forms
of kryptonite could be developed against the superpowers evi-
denced by many cancer cells. Gene sequencing could be used to
identify specific abnormalities and drugs would be found to attack
them. That rational approach was as compelling as it was difficult,
but much progress has been made using this basic paradigm. Generally not curative, such therapies at least provide a temporary benefit for many patients and the agents can be used in a way tailored
for the specific abnormalities seen in a patient's tumor. Instead of all
patients with a given diagnosis made by the last century's techniques
of what it looks like under the microscope, most major cancer centers now genetically characterize tumors and select the medicines to
be used based on that information. Indeed, a cancer drug has recently been approved by the FDA for treating a specific genetic abnormality regardless of the kind of cancer in which the abnormality
appears.

·   ·   ·

The office of Harvard University's president occupies part of Massachusetts Hall, which is the oldest building on campus and the second-oldest college building in the United States. (The oldest, the Sir Christopher Wren Building, is at the College of William and Mary in Virginia.) Once a barracks for Revolutionary War soldiers, who likely absconded with much of its hardware, the building so reeks of history that you can almost feel the weight of the centuries as you enter. When Doug and I went to see President Summers to discuss stem cell research, we breathed in the atmosphere for a moment, noted the historic references, and then got to the point.

At the time when we went to see him, Summers was one of the most well-known academic leaders in America. On campus, he was so popular with students that many asked him to sign dollars bills that bore his signature from his time as secretary of the treasury. (He generally obliged them.) In this time, before controversies inevitably arose, he was considered a brilliant if occasionally difficult man. He is a tough nut, and if you went to him with a half-formed idea, he was likely to crack it open and demonstrate its deficiencies. Those who felt personally offended when he didn't act on their ideas thought Summers was insensitive. "Bull in a china shop" was the cliché most often cited. I never felt this way about him. In fact, in my experience, he was politically astute and always more interested in learning what he could from a given encounter than in forcing his ideas on others. He was very good at synthesizing a variety of ideas and opinions and pushing toward a consensus.

Larry understood the nature of bureaucracies, and as his inaugural address showed, he appreciated the importance of the research. These two points of agreement were not unexpected. However, Doug and I were pleasantly surprised to learn that he saw the difference between the genome project, which was essentially an engineering task accomplished by the massive application of technology, and the less predictable business of stem cell biology. Of course, there was a place for computing power in our work, but we would also argue that the systems we studied were so variable and interdependent that it was extremely difficult to construct a mathematical approach to the science. We believed that biology, interdisciplinary consultation, and even intuition, the tangential product of the human mind's computing power, can produce unexpected but valuable insights.

With rare exceptions, only universities provide the kind of support that tolerates the cross-pollination, and risk of failure, we thought a big stem cell program required. In academic settings, it is the power of your idea, and not your connections or money, that matters most. This isn't always true in industry, where executives fear risking capital on open-ended research or in big-government bureaucracies, where ideas are typically just one of the important currencies that matter.

Although economics is widely assumed to be a numbers game, it is also energized by psychology, which explains much of what occurs in markets. Summers appreciated this aspect of his own discipline. One of his most noted works concerned a prescient description of the social effects of economic booms, which spread a kind of euphoria that causes people to deny the obvious risks in their actions, which then produce calamity. This was, in economics terms, a "theory of mind" description of events, based almost entirely on psychological insights, that was more predictive than anyone in attendance could have imagined.

In our discussion, Summers was able to appreciate the points we made about the less-than-linear aspects of our science. He was excited by the suggestion that Harvard had the opportunity to build the right culture for leaps forward in biology. As a person who had overcome cancer, he was enthusiastic about the therapeutic possibilities in our work. And he had no qualms about the morality of the science. However, he was concerned about the possibility of resistance we might encounter from others.

"Do you think this is the kind of thing that could get grassroots support, both inside and outside support, that would let you get traction?" asked Summers.

The term *inside* referred to the university community. Here we could meet some resistance from those who had staked out areas for research and might feel we were encroaching on their territories. However, we already had an eye on the folks we wanted in our collaboration, and we expected that most, if not all, would see the value in what we proposed. The "outside" community included all the political, academic, scientific, philanthropic, and even religious leaders engaged in stem cell issues and the general public. Nothing had occurred to make stem cell science less controversial, and with George W. Bush's election, we expected things to become more troublesome, not less.

"This is why we need to lead," I said to Summers. "The usual base of support—government and philanthropy and industry—is just not there. If we don't step up, who will?"

The leadership needed was a matter of inspiring, rallying, and directing the development of a stem cell institute, as well as helping to fund it. As much as scientists may wish it isn't so, money is so important to our efforts that without a steady supply most research ideas won't reach maturity. In some cases, money can even give a team time to fail, perhaps multiple times, on the way to success. If Summers could get us financial backing from the university and pitch us to the major donors who regularly supported Harvard, we had a shot at getting sustained funding for a long-term effort.

At the end of our meeting at Massachusetts Hall, Summers said he would get behind everything we sought. He would even give us a lead position in his meetings with donors, asking them to support us with their checkbooks. Doug and I would sometimes be required to shine our shoes and put on neckties to help this effort, but we could rely on him and the clout of the university to make those connections and, more importantly, put the university's credibility behind what we proposed to do. This factor wouldn't be enough to change the minds of politicians who were opposed to federal funding for stem cell work, but it would assure the world that what we were doing would be mainstream science in a responsible way.

Some big scientific research institutes acquire (or build) large facilities and put up big signs to indicate their presence. In 2017, for example, Cambridge University in England embarked on the construction of a big, freestanding facility to study stem cells, molecular biology, and cancer. Other institutes are essentially virtual organizations in which colleagues are linked by managers and funding streams but do their work in scattered locations. Some of our scientists would be gathered together in roughly forty thousand square feet of new space being built by Massachusetts General Hospital, but we weren't going to get our names on the building, and far more of us would work in labs and offices around the greater Cambridge area.

The important thing wasn't for us to all be together every day. What mattered more was that an organizational structure be created—this is was what was meant by "institute"—and that it encourage and facilitate regular communication across disciplines. This was important to stimulate creativity but also to focus Harvard's energies in this area to set certain standards and expectations. We were serious about the lofty purpose of the university, so the institute's ultimate goal would be treatments for diabetes and a host of other diseases and conditions, including cancer. High standards would be required to protect all of us from the pressures that scientists feel when great sums are invested in work that is so full of possibilities. In a field like stem cells, it doesn't take much to attract the attention of the press—or, for that matter, investors—who want to be the first to learn of a breakthrough. These are just the circumstances when the temptation to cut corners, exaggerate results, or even deceive can be extreme.

We convened the first meeting of the stem cell institute in a conference room at the American Academy of Arts and Sciences in Cambridge. Founded by a group that included John Adams and John Hancock, two of the academy's first members were George Washington and Benjamin Franklin. Its history and membership make it one of those places where you feel a bit awestruck as a first-time visitor. But the whole purpose of the academy is encouragement, not intimidation. Like Harvard University, it is a place that gives you permission to think in an expansive way, take creative risks, and persevere. One the most sweeping studies of top scientists ever done showed that creative perseverance, which I believe is encouraged in the best institutions, is the key to success. This process was shown to be a critical aspect in productivity for scientists in any age group. According to the study's authors, big successes come when the right person takes up the right idea at the right time. Some hit this sweet spot when they are young and so energetic they can pursue lots of concepts at once. Others just never cease and, given the right support, reach their destination in due time. As one of the paper's authors noted, Jean-Baptiste Lamarck didn't publish his landmark book on evolution, which preceded Darwin's *On the Origin of Species* by fifty years, until he was sixty-six. *Philosophie Zoologique* was the product of nearly thirty years of work and was followed by a seven-volume *Histoire Naturelle*.

Our group at the academy ranged in age, experience, and scientific perspective and possessed, I believe, the hard-to-define quality that the authors of the paper on successful scientists called Q. Their Q referred to the ability to find a research subject suited to their abilities and to the needs of the day. Our group—which included, among others, Leonard Zon, George Daley, Stuart Orkin, Jeffrey Macklis, Richard Mulligan, and Gordon Weir—had Q in the extreme, with expertise in cancer genetics, hematology, pediatric cancer, neuroscience, diabetes, stem cells, and more. Being nerds, we had flip charts and a big board where we could create a matrix.

On the left side, we made a vertical column of interest areas—diabetes, cardiac, neuro, blood, cancer, muscle, kidney, and so on—and across the top, we listed research approaches. The more we talked, the more we realized that rather than compete with each other, we would wind up adding to existing projects and developing whole new approaches based on the fact that we discovered different people interested in the same problems—kidney disease, for example—who were making progress by approaching from completely different directions. Our institute could bring these people and concepts together. As word of what we were planning circulated, we began hearing from those who wanted to be a part of it. From this pool, we would settle on twenty-five principal investigators, who were already overseeing their own research groups, and an additional seventy-five scientists. We engaged seven of the university's degree-granting colleges and an equal number of hospitals.

The enthusiasm for the Harvard Stem Cell Institute suggested to us that we might have underestimated the number of our colleagues who were keen for collaboration. (I also underestimated Larry Summers's prowess as an advocate, as he turned out to be very good at raising money on our behalf.) In short order, we had set in motion the development of an independent lab space at Massachusetts General Hospital and were planning an outreach program to alumni, a group that included many prominent people who devoted substantial sums to philanthropy. We also began recruiting top scientists within the Harvard community and outside it.

We already knew many of the people we wanted to court. George Daley, for example, was a stem cell pioneer who had earned a doctorate in biology at MIT and a medical degree from Harvard, where he was one of only twelve people ever to graduate summa cum laude. As a young scientist, he had worked in the lab of Nobel winner David Baltimore, where he had beautifully demonstrated what Janet Rowley proposed for CML. He used a retrovirus to put the fusion gene from the Philadelphia chromosome into a normal mouse blood stem cell and converted it to a leukemic cell. That was proof that the fusion gene really did cause the leukemia rather than just being associated with it. He now wanted to see if he could make blood stem cells from embryonic stem cells. It sounded easy in theory because embryonic cells should be able to make any cell type, but it was very difficult to do. George would spend over a decade trying to do it with only now appearing to be close to the finish line. He was also a physician who wanted to see science deliver for patients. When he agreed to join us, adding the weight of his reputation to ours, the stem cell institute had more of the gravity needed to attract young stars.

As in most fields, the most promising newcomers in science can be a little picky about where they establish themselves. Most look for places where they might access the best technology, find financial resources, and build their own teams. The Boston area was home to at least four centers that would be on any well-informed scientist's top ten for biological or medical research in the world. This status put us at a distinct advantage when we approached budding young stars like Amy Wagers, who was working at Stanford with a legendary cell biologist named Irving Weissman.

(Weissman and I had a bit of a history. He had once written to me to complain, quite bluntly, that I hadn't credited him in a paper. I tend toward being extra generous in this kind of thing, so I was apologetic about the oversight. I immediately dashed off a note that said, in essence, "That banging noise you hear is me pounding my head against the wall." We eventually became friendly enough to go fishing together.)

As a child, Wagers had been part of a Duke University program for the gifted, where one of her first courses was in writing, which helped her develop superior communication skills, especially for a scientist. In high school, she studied animal behavior and primatology at the University of Arizona, beginning an intense review of the sciences that led her to Northwestern University and a doctorate in immunology. (Her first paper, published before she finished at Northwestern, opened a significant new avenue for research into immune cells.) At Stanford, Wagers was known for taking on so much work that Irv Weissman concluded that it was impossible to find the limit of her capacity. In our discussions, she may have been won over by the idea that her curiosity and energy would meet few obstacles and might be amplified by contact with the different perspectives we would recruit to the institute.

Putting together our group was a bit like assembling a college football team—the best players wanted to know they were headed for a place where they would find competitors at their level. Soon after Wagers agreed to join the institute, we also got commitments from Kevin Eggan, who was working with Doug Melton and Konrad Hochedlinger, who had been a protégé of cloning expert Rudolf Jaenisch at the Massachusetts Institute of Technology. Konrad was also being courted by Boston Children's Hospital and the Memorial Sloan Kettering Institute in New York. However, we managed to team him with a Harvard alumnus who would fund his work based at the MGH, and this dedicated stream of donations gave him confidence in his future with us.

As we put our team together, we learned that others were choosing the same path, hoping to keep stem cell research going in the United States without any federal involvement. Stanford University had created a $12 million fund for stem cell science, and New Jersey's governor made his state the first to create a local initiative, with a $6.5 million grant to Rutgers. Work was continuing at Johns Hopkins and the University of Wisconsin. In California, activists were writing a ballot initiative that would ask the state's voters to create a $3 billion stem cell research fund. This referendum, which would pass in 2004 with a significant margin, recognized both the scientific and economic value of this kind of work. Just as computer hardware and software development made Silicon Valley and the Boston suburbs into business powerhouses, stem cell research would bring development and wealth to the locale where the most successful work was accomplished.

The stem cell promise went beyond cancer, and even Doug's work in diabetes, to include other diseases that could potentially be improved under a new rubric called regenerative medicine. This science considered the challenge of creating human cells, tissues, and even organs. Although it verges on science fiction, the end goal was to restore and perhaps even rejuvenate the tissue of the human body. I had seen it happen with bone marrow transplantation, where normal blood cell production could be regenerated from terribly diseased bone marrow. It was an already practiced form of regenerative medicine, but the term wasn't regularly used until the early 1990s. Enthusiasm for the field was heightened by Thomson and Gearhart's work on human embryonic stem cells, and ongoing research considered cellular fixes for nervous system disorders, brain damage, endocrine illnesses, and even heart disease. While embryonic stem cells were the main focus of attention, there was already evidence that therapies could be developed without the use of blastocysts or fetal tissue. Stem cells could be found in adult tissue, as well as in the blood left in the umbilical cord at the time of a baby's birth. Although the potential of cord blood had been clouded by significant amounts of hype (some of it coming from commercial collection and storage companies), these cells were already being used in the treatment of leukemia. It was quite possible that they would be useful, with a bit of coaxing, in other diseases.

The ultimate end point for regenerative medicine, a point rarely discussed, could be the extension of the human life span. This was not something one discussed without great care because everyone is interested in living longer and any suggestion that such a thing is possible can lead to a realm of make-believe. The first recording of the human dream of an intervention to extend the life span is a reference in the works of Herodotus, which were written about 2,500 years ago. Herodotus's concept of a fountain of youth may have been formalized first in ancient Greece, but it's certain the earliest human beings fantasized about life extension from the moment they recognized the reality of death. In the early twentieth century, the Life Extension Institute of New York was formed with the philanthropic goal of extending human life, but in 1936 it entered into a consent agreement that prohibited it from practicing medicine in New York. In 1972, an Arizona-based nonprofit called the Alcor Life Extension Foundation was founded to begin freezing human bodies (sometimes minus parts) moments after death on the chance that one day the technology will exist to revive them. Clients remain at −320 degrees to this day, though, prospects for their revival aren't any better now than they were in '72.

Alcor's approach to longevity is a great example of the way that a little bit of scientific truth can be misapplied to reach an extreme conclusion. In reality, some substances like bone marrow can be frozen and thawed and retain their life-giving qualities. However, this can only be done with materials that don't allow water crystals to form. Once water starts to crystalize, the expansion that comes with it bursts cells just as it does frozen pipes. The chemicals used to store cells prevent water crystal formation, but they just cannot get into whole organs sufficiently to allow the organs to be preserved. Thus, a frozen organ, like the brain, cannot be frozen and thawed, no matter how carefully, and have any normal function. Perhaps fortunately, such limitations keep the events of Mary Shelley's *Frankenstein* fictional.

There is another reason why cells just cannot be made to grow forever and it is called the Hayflick Limit. Named after Leonard Hayflick, it is based on his careful work sixty years ago showing that cells can only grow and divide in culture forty to eighty times before they stop. The number of cell divisions varies depending on the cell type, and stem cells may be able to overcome the Hayflick Limit. But more mature cells cannot. The basis for the limit is thought to be the gradual loss of the ends of chromosomes called telomeres.

These serve almost as bumpers—caps at the ends of chromosomes to prevent them from being chewed away by enzymes or getting into mischief with other parts of chromosomes. The problem is that they do not get fully replicated with the rest of the chromosome during cell division. The telomere then gradually shortens until it is sufficiently depleted, at which point cells get into trouble with any further cell division and stop. Stem cells and cancer cells can rebuild those telomeres and so are less subject to the Hayflick Limit—they can keep dividing. But even our stem cells start to decline in function over time. It is thought that part of the limited ability to regenerate as we age is the loss of functional stem cells. Regenerating them is critical for regenerative medicine.

Pluripotent embryonic stem (ES) cells offered the possibility of making all kinds of stem cells for organs that needed regenerating. That was part of the hope in our nascent center: We thought the ES cells could make the mature cells of a particular organ and the stem cells of that organ to sustain it. We knew stem cells were also cells that could be genetically manipulated. If that could be done to replace missing or defective genes then the new stem cells might correct the basis for some diseases. Stuart Orkin was internationally recognized for understanding the genetic basis for horrible diseases like thalassemia and was a stem cell expert; his joining us made it possible to envision new blood-based stem cell therapies. Jeff Macklis was showing that neurons in animal adult brains could be provoked to reform the circuits necessary for function, giving us hope that we could develop stem cell approaches to brain disease. Doug Melton was showing the adult pancreas didn't have stem cells capable of making new insulin-producing cells, but he was systematically finding out how ES cells could. The possibility of regenerating or repairing injured organs using stem cell biology was the light that drew us together. The shadow was the possibility that these cells could teach us about or even cause cancer. That was a lingering issue only time could unveil.

SIX

SNUPPY THE HOUND AND ιPSCs

As we announced the creation of the Harvard Stem Cell Institute, the science around cancer and the other diseases we would study continued to race forward. Research on the immune system, which got a big boost with the work done on T cells—a subtype of white blood cells—during the AIDS crisis had progressed steadily under the leadership of scientists like Steven Rosenberg at the National Cancer Institute.

For years, Rosenberg had doggedly plotted the relationship between cancer and the cells the body can deploy to defeat it. The wellspring of these immune cells is the bone marrow, which deploys them via the bloodstream and lymphatic system. (Hence, the vital importance of blood and bone.) In 2004, Rosenberg started a small human trial—seventeen patients in all—using genetically altered T cells against the most serious form of skin cancer, melanoma. Perhaps the most intriguing thing about his approach was that it drew from the two most promising areas of cancer science: genetics and stem cells.

Understanding Rosenberg's work requires recalling that for every mutation that evolves into a disease called cancer, we experience countless ones that are identified and halted by our natural defenses. This defense depends on the fact that malignant cells emit chemicals called antigens, which signal the waiting fighters of the immune system to take action. These defenders, which are mostly T cells and

B cells, must also possess an antigen *receptor* that responds to the antigen and continues the immune response.

When cancer progresses, it's often because we don't have enough immune cells equipped with the right receptors. However, a few properly outfitted immune cells generally do appear, and they will get through to do a bit of damage to the growing malignancy. Rosenberg theorized that if he could find these effective immune cells and somehow create more of them, he might be able to intervene and tip the scales.

Rosenberg had become intrigued by the potential of the immune system when, as a surgeon, he performed a gallbladder surgery on a man who had had a stomach cancer removed in a previous operation. Reports from the original surgery noted that the cancer had metastasized to his liver, but when Rosenberg searched for those tumors, he couldn't find them. Further investigation confirmed the patient no longer had cancer at all. Intrigued, Rosenberg wondered if the man's immune system was somehow superpowered. Knowing that the blood was one place where he might access this power, he experimented with a transfusion of the cancer-free patient's blood to one with a similar malignancy. The transfusion didn't work as a cure, but it did set Rosenberg on a lifelong quest to discover how the seeming miracle of the missing metastases occurred. The key, he knew, was in the man's immune system, which had failed against the mass in his stomach but managed to succeed in his liver. "Something began to burn in me," explained Rosenberg later in life, "something that has never gone out."

Over decades, Rosenberg and others gradually deciphered the chemical process that guided the interactions between cancer cells and immune cells. In the late 1980s, an Israeli immunologist named Zelig Eshhar was the first to create T cells with artificial antigen receptors, called CAR T cells, or chimeric antigen receptor T cells. In 1990, Eshhar spent a sabbatical year with Rosenberg, and they worked on strategies for coaxing T cells to do their work against cancer. Eventually they focused on CAR T cells that targeted melanoma.

They used specific chemicals to give the T cells the ability to target melanoma cells and to heighten the power of their response.

Biology being what it is, the job of switching on T cells to produce a response that would stop the development of cancer would not be as simple as adding a couple of bits. However, the results of these first experiments were positive, and by the year 2000, work would be under way on a host of ideas for switching on immune cells. Thousands of proteins were being screened to determine which ones might be helpful in goosing the production of these cells or changing their activity. This was somewhat similar to what we were doing with stem cells, trying to affect their fate by testing the effects of hundreds, if not hundreds of thousands, of compounds to make the cells behave in a particular way.

Our many stem cell projects were aimed at the most basic science, including the problem of obtaining stem cells without the use of embryonic tissue. Two of our youngest team members, Chad Cowan and Kevin Eggan, plunged deep into this problem. Eggan had once considered becoming a medical doctor, but the cloning of the sheep Dolly, in 1996, had diverted him to basic science. Dolly had been created by Ian Wilmut of the Roslin Institute of Scotland, where he emptied a sheep egg of its nucleus, inserted DNA taken from an adult animal's cell, and implanted it in a ewe. The lamb that was produced was identical to the sheep that produced the donor DNA. Noting the material came from a mammary cell, workers on the farm named the lamb after the famously endowed entertainer Dolly Parton.

As the first cloned mammal ever produced, Dolly's mere existence shocked the scientific community. Princeton biology professor Lee Silver told Gina Kolata of *The New York Times* that Wilmut's achievement "basically means that there are no limits. It means all of science fiction is true. They said it could never be done and now here it is, done before the year 2000." Many young people like Eggan and Cowan found this prospect thrilling and contemplated using

Wilmut's techniques. Cowan had always aimed at molecular biology and had done postdoctoral work with Doug Melton. They needed an alternative to what Wilmut had done in sheep since it didn't work in humans. In 2005, Cowan, Eggan, Melton, and others reported that they had fused adult skin cells called fibroblasts and embryonic stem cells (instead of egg cells) and actually reprogrammed the adult cells, returning them to a state where they recovered the power to differentiate into any type of cell.

The team's success was dramatic, but not particularly useful as it depended on thousands of hours of solitary work, much of it performed while peering into a microscope and using foot pedals and a joystick to guide a needle into a single cell. Eggan, who would later describe this process as "the hardest video game you ever played," developed back problems while learning how to do nuclear transfer at the Massachusetts Institute of Technology. His biggest challenge was maintaining his motivation as he failed thousands of times in experiments with animal cells.

The exact nature of the fountain-of-youth process that Cowan, Eggan, and Melton tapped into wasn't fully understood, but the hope was that it could be used to return other cells to a youthful state where they could develop into vibrant, functional new ones. The ultimate goal here was therapies that replaced cells that were responsible for heart failure or diseases like Parkinson's. Such fresh cells, perfectly matched because they would be cultivated from the recipient's own tissues, would be the holy grail of the burgeoning field of regenerative medicine. It wasn't hard to imagine this science yielding improvements in existing treatments, like bone marrow transplants, rather quickly. Over the long term, it could even lead to the production of replacement organs. But as with every big scientific advance, regenerative medicine was bound to prompt worry and even fear in public officials and citizens. And once again, they would be given reason to be concerned about the integrity of those trusted to move research toward treatments.

.   .   .

The controversy around stem cell science, especially work that involved cloning and the use of embryonic cells, required us to be sensitive to the public relations aspect of our research. Even before the Harvard Stem Cell Institute formed, our goal of advancing stem cell research toward therapies was helped when Massachusetts General Hospital opened its new Simches Research Center and provided us with a big facility that was then named the Center for Regenerative Medicine and Technology. (In time the word *technology* would be removed from the name.) Stem cell research would occupy the core of the center's work, but the emphasis on the regenerative treatments we hoped to produce stressed the benefits that could arise from the work. (With the acronym CRMT, I thought we should try to enlist Kermit the Frog as a mascot, but fortunately that idea never went anywhere.)

The Simches building had been envisioned as a place for the most advanced types of medical research, and they admitted only five groups, including ones dedicated to genetics and computational science. The competition for these spots was quite intense and required that I present a proposal several times over. One stage of the process landed me before a review committee composed of top people outside Mass General. This was such an exclusive group that most had been awarded the Nobel Prize. Among them were Joseph Goldstein (cholesterol), Robert Horvitz (programmed cell death), and Phil Sharp (RNA). Although they did nothing to make me feel uncomfortable, I don't think I had ever been in a room with such an intimidating amount of brainpower. I was terrified.

Fortunately, in addition to making everyone without a Nobel Prize a bit intimidated, the level of excellence one encounters at Mass General tends to produce scrupulously fair processes that favor the best ideas. The review board, for example, was developed to assure that internal politics wouldn't drive the decision making. No one in this group had a favorite among the competitors or a stake in the outcome. The priority was to take advantage of the incredible resources available, especially the human resources, to accelerate the development of treatments. The possibilities for collaboration and, to use a tired term, *synergy*, were so great that once you tuned in to the possibilities, it was hard to contain your excitement. This is what happened with the board of consultants. Their faces showed they understood the possibilities at hand, and my heart stopped pounding. Soon we were talking about what would emerge *as* the regenerative medicine center was established, not *if*.

Frequently ranked the best hospital in America, Mass General excels at both clinical care and research. Many of our key allies would work in the MGH cancer center, where they were leaders in sophisticated molecular biology. The center's chief, Daniel Haber, ran labs with dozens of scientists and physicians who, like me, blended investigations with caring for patients. One of Daniel's big interests was cancer genetics, and he had recently assessed the genome of various lung cancer cells to discover why some could be stopped with a drug called gefitinib (the brand name is Iressa), but others could not. This was one of the early advances in personalized treatment for cancer patients. Daniel would go on to make great progress identifying how cancer cells circulated in the body, causing metastases even after patients were seemingly cured.

Patients who developed new cancers after they underwent successful treatments could be emotionally devastated by the appearance of a new malignancy, and doctors generally felt the same way. It was known that cancer cells circulate in the blood, but scientists had trouble tracking them. Larger cancer cells could be caught in a filtering system, but this method was rudimentary and missed many. Haber and his colleagues would address the problem from the other direction, capturing far more of the bad-guy cells by removing everything else. The process of doing this is part of a new field called microfluidics, which, as Haber describes it, allows for cells to be lined up and passed through a channel where they can be separated. Eventually this work would mean that a simple blood sample could be used to track the ways a cancer evolves in an individual and plan for treatments even before a person feels sick.

As he worked in the context of a one-thousand-bed hospital that accepted the toughest cases, Haber was driven by the needs of real patients facing life-threatening diagnoses. My own contacts with patients, most of whom had abnormalities, leukemia, or lymphoma, made me acutely aware of the fact that we weren't dealing with mere laboratory abstractions. We were seeking ways to help people who had received terrifying diagnoses and faced the prospect of difficult treatments, including surgery, radiation, chemotherapy, and bone marrow transplant. On the positive side of the clinical equation, we had treatments that worked and had refined them to reduce the suffering people experienced. However, everyone who came to us for care knew they faced a traumatic process. Treatment also meant helping people deal with the psychological realities of cancer, and this element of oncology always reminded me that our work in our sparkling labs equipped with DNA sequencers, centrifuges, and other pieces of expensive equipment should be devoted to the cause of the people we met in our clinics every day.

In rare cases, it seemed like the dreadful prospect of conventional cancer treatment, as people understood it, actually turned out to be fatal. I'm thinking of a man I tried to treat during the early years of the stem cell institute. He was in his midthirties and had Hodgkin's lymphoma. This disease is routinely treated with a drug protocol called ABVD, for adriamycin, bleomycin, vinblastine, and dacarbazine. The first component was found in the soil in Italy. The second was discovered by Japanese scientists working with bacteria. Vinblastine was derived in Canada from a plant found in Madagascar, and the dacarbazine was synthesized at a lab in Alabama. For people in my patient's age group, only 10 percent who got ABVD would have a return of cancer. It was less toxic than the regimen it replaced, but this improvement was relative. ABVD still caused much of the suffering associated with chemotherapy (nausea, vomiting, hair loss, intense fatigue, etc.), and it was hard for some people to accept that this was the pathway to a cure. However, I had never heard anyone decline it.

In this case, my patient was relatively young and strong and absolutely certain I couldn't help him. I worked with a team of doctors and nurses, and when we met to discuss his case, I said, "For some reason, I'm not getting through, but maybe there's some other direction that we can go in. Let's each try."

When one of the residents went to speak with this fellow, she asked, "Do you have a problem with Dr. Scadden? If you do, that's okay. Tell me. We'll find somebody else. We're here for you." Several people tried this approach, and no one could get him to budge. He understood he had cancer, but he wasn't ready to be treated. As he made his decision, he didn't have any particular organ involvement that would have caused him discomfort, like shortness of breath. Some people never experience acute symptoms. Instead, they just get progressively more fatigued. They stop eating, curtail their activity, and very slowly die. This is what he chose. It was heartbreaking for his caregivers. These are rare instances, but when they happen, they're just so striking you don't forget them.

Few things will bother a doctor more than a patient who chooses death over life, without offering any explanation. Years of experience don't make these cases easier, and despite my best intentions, I sometimes struggled to leave the feelings provoked by them at the hospital.

My family, like many doctors' families, did their best to accept that I was distracted, or impatient, for reasons that had nothing to do with them. Kathy had an adult perspective that helped her know what to ignore, but Margaret, Elizabeth, and Ned sometimes struggled to understand that my impatience really had nothing to do with them. They were also challenged to accept my clumsy efforts to make up for lost time with them. A good example would be the time I rushed home with the idea that we should all go pick raspberries because they happened to be ripe. In my mind, this seemed like a perfectly reasonable notion, but I hadn't slowed down enough to notice that no one else was interested in this activity. As much as I wanted to make up for my absences, for the times when emergencies took precedence, it couldn't be done on my schedule.

The burden of being a doctor's kid is always added on to the more typical challenges all children face. Our family had some idiosyncrasies that already made us "weird" as far as they were concerned. For one thing, we expected them to come to dinner every night ready to share something, even something very minor, that they had learned during the day. It could be a new word, a fact discovered at school, or an item they read in the newspaper. Kathy and I also required that our kids do all their school projects themselves, without our help. Our community was full of professors and scientists and engineers, so you can imagine what their peers brought in for the science fair.

Our hands-off approach to school projects was intended to encourage self-sufficiency. I'm not sure it worked. But if our kids were a bit frustrated, the experience hinted at the challenge adults face when they take on difficult tasks, from raising children to navigating a career, understanding that success is never guaranteed and that, generally speaking, no one is standing by to rescue you from a jam.

Stem cell science remained one of the most promising avenues for research that might lead to treatments. This work required the best technology and people, and our institute was well outfitted and staffed. Our gleaming, well-equipped space provided laboratory facilities and office support for dozens of scientists, many of whom would lead their own small groups. The work was a matter of developing and refining concepts, conducting experiments, and then reviewing the results to determine the next steps. Experiments with stem cell transplants take sixteen weeks, at minimum, to complete. The results often show that your original concept was not accurate and send you back to the starting blocks.

Frustrating as it may seem, experiments often end with a result that disproves your theory. Every finding has value, so I'd be reluctant to call these outcomes failures. But because eureka moments are so rare, I intentionally sought independent, almost-stubborn people to work with us. Colleagues around the world recommended candidates who possessed these strengths. We then searched among the candidates for a mix of backgrounds and strengths. We wanted some who had worked on genetic models in animals, others who had focused on bone, and some who had just worked on human cell lines and had done molecular biology techniques. We needed a spectrum of technical expertise as well as ways of thinking. It wasn't as specific as filling out the roster of a baseball team and thinking, *I need another infielder*, but we were mindful of getting the balance right and maintaining it as the science changed.

When people arrived, I encouraged them to speak frankly. Most, though not all, agreed to call me David and not Dr. Scadden. We did not assign research to people. Instead, we expected them to develop their own targets for investigation. They could ask big questions, and we would give them the tools to seek the answers. But I also required every newcomer to find a new collaborator for the lab. I never hired robots. I wanted people to connect with the fundamental humanness of what we were supposed to be doing, and I think unless people really feel that, it's hard for them to deliver on what I believe is our mission and our responsibility.

Most young scientists imagine they will one day have their own labs, perhaps at a university or in a biotech company, and we wanted them to develop the experience and talents to do this. But in addition to ability, top scientists must have the right temperament. They have to be willing to ask, "Am I crazy to be doing this? Is the data telling me to stop?" There's only so much time and so much money. If you can't interrogate yourself and decide when to stop, you can dig yourself into a hole. You'll be eight miles deep and thirty miles off course with no chance to getting where you set out to go.

Of course, no one is left alone to wander in the wilderness indefinitely. We regularly convene what's called the Lab Meeting, where people are required to review their progress and then the group offers both critiques and advice. We ask for all the available data and spend lots of time pushing to see if it's being used and interpreted in the right way. What is fact? What is opinion? Can you hold yourself to the standard of truth and ignore your desire for a certain outcome to your experiment? The point here is that everyone wants to find cures. But cures emerge from the kind of basic, incremental science that yields positive, negative, or ambiguous results. The key to thriving in this setting is to accept that a clear answer is the goal regardless of what the answer might be. Without this acceptance, you can become vulnerable to the forces that move people to fudge their results and commit fraud. The danger here is very real. Science itself is damaged by fraud, and those who commit it can experience such shame that they feel the only option is suicide. In 2014, Haruko Obokata, a Japanese stem cell scientist, published a fraudulent paper claiming a major breakthrough. After the fraud was discovered and investigated, her mentor, whose name was on the paper, killed himself.

Given the stakes, the Lab Meeting is a serious matter. The critiques can be done cruelly or collegially, and we always stress the latter. This isn't just to be nice. People cannot speak freely about their work if they fear being humiliated in front of their peers. Instead, they will hide their disappointing results, choosing to deceive rather than risk feeling ashamed. However, if everyone reports fully on results that are often puzzling or disappointing, we all get the idea that this work is extremely difficult and never proceeds in a straight line from problem to solution.

I try to set that tone, regardless of my frustrations or sense of urgency to move forward. Scientists come to our lab from many different cultures, and this can influence whether someone speaks up or hangs back. Temperament and personality come into play and gender is certainly something to which I try to be very attuned. It is a terrible loss for all when young women feel unsupported in science. Helping without patronizing, supporting while encouraging improvement, and being fair to all is my goal. Inevitably it is tested and nothing provokes me more than a sense of entitlement that disrespects others. One of the most hyperaggressive scientists I ever managed was a woman who seemed to think that a lab coat gave her the right to say and do whatever she pleased. No matter how much I value supporting women scientists, it cannot be at the repeated expense of others and our lab culture. That provoked the fortunately very rare moment of dismissing someone from the lab.

Being in an academic lab is inevitably a short-term experience. The point is to train people; educate them, and give them the skills needed for a successful career ahead. It is entirely different from a business where you hang on to talent. But we are not just educators, our product has to be new knowledge in addition to training effective seekers of new knowledge. We must be pushing innovation and testing new ideas of sufficient impact that we can fulfill our broader goal and frankly, gain funding. That creates an inherent tension of constantly taking in new talent, getting them up to speed and guiding them to move on successfully while also pushing to discover and deliver on the trust society gives us to make better medical care

Scientists in training are in a challenging spot. They have already spent years getting their degrees, five to six years for a Ph.D., four years plus three to eight years clinical training for an M.D., seven years plus clinical training for an M.D., Ph.D. The post-doc training is the apprenticeship they need to then get a job in a university or medical center; some may go to industry without this. The postdoctoral trainee spends three to seven years building a sufficiently impressive body of work to convince employers to hire them and a platform on which they can build their future independent research. Once hired, they usually have three years of "start-up" funding before they are expected to have produced work to gain the grants that will allow them to be fully independent. Once they are, they are essentially independent contractors, needing to find funding to do their work. Most universities provide only minimal if any research support. Some universities provide salary support, but hospital-based faculty do not receive this at Harvard and those based at the university (I am at both) get a portion of their salary covered for teaching (25 percent). The rest is theirs to go out and get. It adds an entrepreneurial edge that keeps people from getting stale, but it also pushes people to areas they think will fund them, not the ones that will allow them to be the most innovative.

Yet, innovators are what we need and we look for in hiring. My own trainee selection gives special attention to what I think might be a creative spark. They have to be willing to test a new idea. But failing at that could kill their career, so my job is to guide and shape them, and give the ideas the greatest chance of success. It is also to give them a safety net if they fall short. To do that, I have to encourage some who do not seem on track to choose another path, and do so quickly. Those are the toughest discussions. When people come to my lab they become family. Tough love is never painlessly administered, but finding a path that better connects with talents is part of the process. Life sciences now offer so many opportunities for fulfilling careers that the discussions about alternative career paths are getting much easier. The challenge now is to encourage the multitalented to see academics as a way forward. They are the ones who will sow the seeds of our futures through their teaching, mentoring, and research. The lack of stability and lower financial rewards are harder to accept when the industry offers so much good science and remuneration. Labs like mine have to help build the field in both private and academic settings, so we focus on building skills that serve them well wherever they go. Defending ideas, seeking and judging input from others, and clear communication are the keys.

Our Lab Meetings, Journal Clubs (reviewing published work by others), and Blue Sky, Bubbles, and Beer sessions (quarterly, end of day, big-idea debates) all try to push the skill sets and push the imagination. These are the give-and-take sessions where people expose their ideas, and that is not easy. It can feel personal when criticism comes your way, but it is essential to gain comfort with that and to interact with respect. Science is a small world and the person at the bench next to you today could be judging your grant application next year.

These sessions also reveal who has the habits of mind to be a first-rate scientist. What I'm talking about here is not a matter of intelligence, but of intellectual character. Basic honesty, integrity, and humility motivate good scientists to evaluate their own work and interpret their findings not just with creativity, but with caution. Seeing the bigger implications of any experiment is an essential trait for making contributions of substance. However, it can also lead to fiction. Clear-eyed analysis makes the difference. It is those who see with sharp focus the boundaries of their data, but allow themselves to squint and soft sketch a horizon in the distance, who make an impact.

Science takes grit. In fact, contrary to the nerd cliché most people conjure when they think about scientists, you'll find a remarkable number of athletes or fierce competitors in other domains in a typical lab. The first postdocs in my lab were sometimes hard to find because they were off heliskiing. One of my students performed cello for the Queen of England more than once and rock climbing is the workout of choice for my current lab group (subgroup meetings in the ER have been known to occur). Open chess games were what we did when I was a postdoc and losing was agony, made worse when a friend gave me a checkers set to commemorate a humiliating checkmate. Not quite the intensity of board games when I was a kid, when we would spend rainy afternoons plotting world domination in the game called Risk. (Scratch a scientist my age and you're more than likely to discover someone who played Risk.) Our games could get so heated that body slams would ensue and one of us ended up stuck, bottom first, dangling out of the drywall. Fortunately, this didn't happen at the Scadden house.

Transfer the intensity of those kids playing Risk to an arena where the same types of people are devoting years of their lives to work that may or may not achieve a breakthrough and you get some idea of the context in which high-level science is done. With vast amounts of money on the line and people literally dying for want of cures, the pressure to succeed is intense. It is amplified by the fact that it is a competitive enterprise, with people all over the world seeking to win the same game. In many countries governments invested heavily in biological research in a highly targeted and highly structured way because they recognized that progress might open big, valuable markets for medicines that the world would eagerly pay to receive.

In the United States stem cell science was clouded by ethical and regulatory debates. Here and in many other countries religion set policy in a certain direction. Those that were predominantly Catholic tended toward bans that reflected the traditionalist belief that at the moment an egg is fertilized it has the full status of a person. Israel, guided by the Jewish belief that human life doesn't begin until forty days after fertilization, and full status must await birth, almost every avenue of stem cell and regenerative research could be followed. The same was true in much of Asia, where government and religion occupied strictly separate realms. (The ethicist Art Caplan has said China is "an almost scientistic" nation where religion plays almost no role in policy development.)

With few social constraints, several Asian countries seized the opportunity to develop big research efforts with an eye toward the vast industry and profits that might arise out of the science. Most notable was South Korea, where government, universities, and industry came together to fund an ambitious agenda with $80 million and was centrally planned for maximum efficiency. Bureaucrats determined which research areas would be pursued by each lab, and overlap was discouraged. After visiting one of the labs engaged in this project, in late 2003, President Roh Moo-hyun said he would "not spare anything" in the pursuit of cloning research. The lab that inspired this comment, and the president's confession that he felt "electrified" by recent breakthroughs, was run by a Seoul National University animal cloning expert named Hwang Woo-suk. His main claim to fame was that he had used cloning to create animals that were resistant to so-called mad cow disease, which destroys nerve and brain cells and can be transmitted to humans.

The mad cow phenomenon led to news reports that showed wobbly and crippled cows and references to the tiny but terrifying possibility of human infection. As so often happens, the same people who might raise the loudest alarms because they feared some types of science were among those who wanted rapid and sweeping scientific responses in moments of crisis. News about Professor Hwang's cloned cow was followed by a surprise announcement that he had produced a clone of human cells by using one of the cells that surround a woman's egg at the time of ovulation—a cumulus cell—and the egg itself. He reported that he had transferred the DNA containing the nucleus of one cell and put it into a human egg cell. Egg cells have only one copy of DNA until fertilized by sperm and cannot divide or develop into embryos. Hwang claimed he had done for humans what John Gurdon had done for frog cells, moving the nucleus of a mature cell with two copies of DNA into an egg so it could now start dividing and making a new embryo.

The word *bombshell* doesn't go far enough to describe the impact of the results reported from South Korea. First, rumors of a cloned human embryo spread on the internet. Then press in Asia and the United States broke an embargo set by the journal *Science*, which was set to publish Hwang's paper on his success. HUMAN EMBRYO SUCCESSFULLY CLONED IN SEOUL, trumpeted *The Wall Street Journal*. The *New York Times* headline also used the terms *cloning* and *human embryos*, and its imprimatur made the world take notice. Americans who had made similar efforts, in many cases for years, were both amazed and astonished.

The first hints of trouble with the Hwang claim arose when he and the director of a South Korean stem cell research center joined with an editor for *Science* to meet with reporters. The problem wasn't that they seemed cold and aloof; in fact, they had so much fun dealing with the press, joking about chopsticks and chocolate, that they completely charmed the reporters. The seeds of doubt lingered in the caveats they offered about the difficulties of their work. First, they said that the cloning had been attempted with more than 240 cells, but they had succeeded with only one, ever. They also predicted that anyone who tried to replicate their success would have a very difficult time doing it.

Everyone who worked in nuclear transfer understood it was a technically challenging endeavor. And human eggs were particularly difficult to work with. For these reasons, the cautions raised by the South Koreans were sensible. However, they also had ample reasons to help others replicate what they had done. Without a second clone, produced by someone else, their achievement would be subject to doubt. Scientists from around the world, including three teams from the United States, sought to establish partnerships with the South Koreans. When Hwang elaborated on his technique, explaining he had slit the egg to make it more receptive to the insertion of cells, his success seemed more plausible to those who had worked with human eggs and found it difficult to pierce them with needles without causing too much disturbance.

In the months that followed the reported cloning, scientists, clerics, and politicians speculated about the potential cures that could arise and the moral hazards. Activists who opposed embryonic stem cell research raised alarms and pushed the United Nations to back a global ban on this work. Hwang fueled much of the speculation himself as he talked to visitors about experimenting with cell transplants in rats with spinal cord injuries and then, within two or three years, trying this therapy with human subjects in South

Korea and the United States. He told heartwarming stories about his rough childhood and the seven-days-a-week, round-the-clock work done by his team. He spoke of having staff members speak to the eggs they worked with so they wouldn't become lonely. South Koreans celebrated their nation's triumph over many wealthier scientific competitors, especially Japan and the United States. A stamp was issued to commemorate the clone. (It featured a person leaping out of a wheelchair.) Hwang's lab received big funding increases from the South Korean government, and in a move that could only be described as cheeky, he announced he would visit the British lab that produced Dolly to see if it was technically advanced enough to permit a collaboration.

Amid all the swaggering celebration, one of Hwang's young associates began to feel grave misgivings. Ryu Young-joon had authored the first draft on one of Hwang's most important papers but then left the lab for a new job. His departure prompted many more, and he knew that the work later claimed by Hwang could not have been accomplished by the team that remained. When he heard that his former boss had promised to perform an experimental treatment on a ten-year-old with a spinal cord injury, he became alarmed.

"I was furious," he would later recall. "I wanted to stop that."

Ryu took his concerns to a Korean TV news network, which began an intense investigation and soon discovered that Hwang's egg donors had included two women who worked on his staff, which was a violation of scientific ethics. Then came news that the majority of his lab's donors had received either money or low-cost fertility treatments as payment. Evidence of sloppy work, including mixed-up photos submitted to journals, was followed by a critique signed by thirty members of the faculty at Seoul National University. These experts expressed serious doubts about whether Hwang's results were genuine. Tests of the genetic markers in the supposed clones did not verify his claims. The credibility of South Korean science had been undermined by Hwang's work, they wrote, and only a serious investigation would resolve the looming crisis.

With its reputation at stake, the university created an investigating group that dug into Hwang's published papers, his records, and the methods used at his lab. Many on the panel were younger medical scientists with international experience and a commitment to the ethics that ensure both the value of scientific studies and the support of the public at large, without which science is impossible. In less than a year's time, they reached the conclusion that Hwang had fabricated his original claim of a human embryo clone and all his subsequent ones related to human embryos. (A rambunctious little Afghan hound named Snuppy—*Time* magazine's Invention of the Year—turned out to be an authentic animal clone.) Having turned Hwang and his colleagues into national heroes, the South Korean government and public were forced to accept that he was, in fact, a con artist.

The South Korean nation and scientific establishment moved quickly to accept the outcome of the investigation. Hwang's colleagues spoke of the way their probe asserted higher standards and signaled the world that they wanted to work in the mainstream. The government commenced a criminal probe. In his first response to the findings of the investigators, Hwang admitted his wrongdoing, saying, "I feel so miserable that it's difficult even to say sorry." However, he also tried to shift blame to his associates, and he continued to promote the idea that his work would lead to treatments in a very short time, insisting, "I think we can create patient-specific stem cells in six months if eggs are sufficiently provided." Eventually Hwang would be convicted of ethics law violations and embezzlement, but he would be spared prison time when a judge gave him a suspended sentence. When last seen in the press, Hwang was selling his services to dog owners, who, for $100,000, could have him clone their pets.

Hwang had generated such attention in part because of the

"yuck" factor: could a person really be the next Dolly? Horrible politicians now in droves? Great material for late-night comedians,
frightening in its potential for really awful misuse. What excited most
scientists I know was not about making new genetically identical
twins. That just wasn't going to happen unless women would agree
to carry such a creature in their womb, medical centers would agree to
let such procedures be done in their facilities, governments wouldn't
ban such efforts (which they did), and nature didn't prevent the process from being extremely rare and as often resulting in deformed
creatures as viable ones. What was exciting was the prospect that
reprogramming of nuclei could be done such that pluripotent cells
could be cultured. That would mean cells that were genetically
identical to cells from an adult but which had the potential to make
any cell in the body of a real person. Even if the eggs and sperm
came from related donors, the ES cells could not be any more closely
related to someone than a sibling or a cousin would be. By cloning
using nuclear transfer, the DNA would be identical to the donor of
the nucleus and therefore the cells would be too. That degree of
genetic sameness had powerful implications for generating cells that
ultimately might be used to replace a person's cells lost to disease.
It also had implications for being able to study the basis for someone's illness. What it didn't relieve, though, was the ethical freight
of stem cell research.

The process of cloning by nuclear transfer had one critical re-
quirement for success: lots and lots of human eggs. It is very uncomfortable and quite risky for women to donate their eggs. Hwang
had first gotten into trouble, not because he was a fraud, but because
he was coercing women in his laboratory to donate eggs. States like
Massachusetts banned compensating women for donating eggs for
research (despite allowing it for "reproductive purposes," like would-
be parents soliciting Ivy League women to donate for large sums of
money so they could improve the odds of a star child in the family).
Exposing the Hwang fraud helped reduce the concern about egg

donor coercion, but the ethical stains on stem cell research were mounting up. It didn't take much work for those opposed to stem cells to find a range of issues of concern from destroying embryos, to making clones, to exploiting women. Virtually all of the concerns were not real in substance, but perceptions can be all the matters, particularly among politicians—and they, of course, control the purse strings for research.

The year 2007 brought a remarkable scientific achievement and, with it, a freeing of stem cell work from many of the ethical concerns that surrounded it. A team led by a brilliant physician scientist named Shinya Yamanaka reported they had made adult cells into truly pluripotent stem calls without using a donor egg and nuclear transfer. Instead, he used four genes that coded for transcription factors—biochemicals that direct a cell's differentiation state—to wind back the clock on human cells. What the group produced were truly pluripotent stem cells, which could be used in research without any concern for the controversies around human embryonic tissue or cloning. These would be called induced pluripotent stem cells or iPSC.

Because he practiced science the way it should be practiced, and therefore shared his previous work in an open way, Yamanaka had provided a roadmap for anyone who wanted to join the pursuit of iPSC. James Thomson at the University of Wisconsin had first generated human ES cells and accomplished the same as Yamanaka at roughly the same time; George Daley followed shortly thereafter. When Yamanaka began publishing his work, our Harvard Stem Cell Institute colleague, Konrad Hochedlinger, discussed it with his former mentor at MIT, Rudolf Jaenisch, who initially expressed doubts about whether the news from Japan would hold up to close scrutiny. Konrad then assigned a doctoral student in his group to replicate Yamanaka's work. When she succeeded, he decided to move ahead on the idea of creating iPSCs that could be tweaked to become any of the more than two hundred types of cells found in the human body. Jaenisch quietly joined the race and all three—Yamanaka, Hochedlinger, and Jaenisch—published on the same day in June 2007.

A Hollywood-handsome young man with wavy brown hair, Hochedlinger had been a student at the Research Institute of Molecular Pathology in Vienna when he attended a lecture on nuclear transfer given by Rudy Jaenisch. It was 1999, and the world was still absorbing the news of Dolly the cloned sheep. Hochedlinger then found his way to MIT and threw himself into cloning research. Frustrated with the slow processes that were being used, he helped devise new ones and was soon coauthor on a growing number of papers. A laid-back guy whose demeanor masked intense ambition, he cloned a mouse. Hochedlinger then completed a nifty experiment that showed the therapeutic potential of this science by using stem cells derived from their own skin to cure mice with an immune deficiency. The immune system is implicated in so many diseases, including cancer, that this work would inform a great amount of follow-up experiments.

Skin cell / iPSC science would eventually lead to the astounding reality of mice created from skin cells in a process called in vitro gametogenesis (IVG). Speculation would rage over the ethical and theological implications of IVG being used to create a baby from any variety of cell donors, or even a single individual. However, in the near term, the development of iPSCs with mature cells foreshadowed the end of the controversy over the use of stem cell lines derived from embryos. It also advanced the cause of cell-based therapies for various cancers and diseases as varied as heart disease, diabetes, and Alzheimer's. A year after Hochedlinger published on his iPSCs, Amy Wagers reported that she had transplanted muscle stem cells to treat muscular dystrophy in mice. Soon after this discovery, she, Hochedlinger, and Kevin Eggan were among the first recipients of a new "early career" award from the Howard Hughes Medical Institute. The institute created the awards in order to ease the pressure young scientists feel to produce at a breakneck pace in order to keep their positions. The fifty winners were chosen from two thousand applicants, who were judged not on the basis of their proposed project but on their abilities and commitment to science. Each one received six years of salary and benefits plus $1.5 million to defray the cost of his or her research. We had hoped that one of our three applicants would get the prize. When all three were recognized, we were elated.

Our three young stars were focused mainly on the regenerative power of stem cells. Konrad Hochedlinger even put together a short film on salamanders, which can regenerate limbs lost to amputation. The film explained how stem cells mobilize at the site of an amputation and then differentiate to produce skin, muscle, bone, blood vessels, and more. In the end, he asked, "Why can't *we* do that?"

Although regeneration was an exciting topic, and the manipulation of iPSCs could potentially provide therapies to treat hundreds of illnesses, the work we were doing on stem cells also informed vast amounts of ongoing cancer research. In addition to exciting stem cell science, great strides were being made in the related field of immunology and in all of molecular biology. Intense studies of very specific chemicals were revealing their roles in cancer, and these revelations were being converted into therapies. A good example was work done on epidermal growth factor receptor (EGFR), which is involved in the development of skin (epidermis) and other tissues in the body.

Like all stories of discovery, the identification of EGFR is a great human tale. The leading investigators, who were on the faculty of Washington University in Saint Louis, were a former dairy bacteriologist named Stanley Cohen and a physician and scientist named Rita Levi-Montalcini. Dr. Levi-Montalcini had lost her job in prewar Italy when the Fascist dictator Mussolini declared that Jews couldn't work in universities, but she continued her research on nerve fibers in chicken embryos in a lab she set up at home. After the war, she divided her time between research centers in Rome and in Saint Louis, where Cohen also worked. Separately and together, they confirmed that when overexpressed, because of genetic mutation, this EGFR allowed for cancers to develop. (Cancer cells have one hundred times more copies of the receptor than normal cells.) In 1986, Levi-Montalcini and Cohen would be awarded the Nobel Prize for this work.

Twenty years after the Nobel award, drugs that inhibited the kinds of growth factors identified by Cohen and Levi-Montalcini were moving from trials to clinical use. They first targeted a part of a breast cancer cell called the HER2 receptor, limiting its activity, and also signaled immune cells to come in for the attack. It was given the brand name Herceptin and was found to be effective in some patients who had breast cancer and tested positive for an aberration in one growth factor gene. Women who received it for late-stage cancer got, on average, a 25 percent longer period of survival after diagnosis.

The first of what would come to be called precision medicines, because it was prescribed for patients with a specific genetic defect, Herceptin is far less toxic than the cancer drugs offered at the time it was introduced. Typical side effects were comparable to the flu, but nothing like the brutal nausea, vomiting, and fatigue associated with old-fashioned chemotherapy. Eventually the drug would be recognized as helpful to patients with early-stage cancer too. Some would live for ten years or more. Since Herceptin targets a particular abnormality, it is suitable for only one in five patients with breast cancer. And as with other drugs, cancers treated with Herceptin can return in forms that are resistant. However, doctors and scientists would continue to look for other types of cancer with similar genetic defects and try Herceptin as a treatment. The drug would work for some people with other types of cancer, most notably cancers of the digestive tract, but it was hard to predict the outcome for an individual patient, and Herceptin remained a drug that was added to other treatments. It did not replace them.

A second early form of precision medicine, which came into

common use under the trade name Avastin, depended in part on Judah Folkman's science of angiogenesis. As you recall, Folkman had observed that many solid tumors depended on a rich supply of blood, and he theorized that inhibiting the development of blood vessels would slow or even stop many forms of cancers. The substances he developed—endostatin and angiostatin—worked in mice but not humans. Avastin, which depended on a different mechanism, wasn't a cure, but it added months to people's lives. Results were less encouraging in trials of breast cancer, but then came good news from doctors using it against colorectal cancer, which is second only to lung/bronchial cancer when it comes to the number of people who die from the disease each year.

Avastin was such a significant advance that once again people felt as if the promised land of oncology was in sight. In 2004, Andrew von Eschenbach, director of the National Cancer Institute, talked of cancer as "a chronic disease we will manage much the same way we manage high blood pressure or diabetes." Eschenbach spoke as oncologists from around the world gathered at a big conference in New York. One of the presentations at the conference was titled "Therapy for Metastatic Colorectal Cancer: What Do We Do with So Many Options?" It was the kind of talk that made laypeople excited but annoyed scientists.

I happened to serve on an NCI advisory board at the time when Eschenbach delivered his speech, and he had opened each one of our meetings by declaring we would "eliminate [the] suffering and death" caused by cancer before 2015. Whenever he did, the people in the room who understood cancer to be incredibly varied and complex couldn't help but roll their eyes. This idea was a platitude one might offer to Congress, but saying it to experts resulted in whispers around the table, *Perhaps some nuance from the leader of the National Cancer Institute?*

The trouble with public statements that promised so much progress was that they created unrealistic expectations among patients and their families. Physicians were left with the work of explaining to patients that progress was slow and that cancer took so many forms that we were likely to need hundreds of new therapeutic tools to get where the NCI chief said we were heading. Genetic studies of specific cancers could turn up ten thousand or more abnormalities. And sometimes we couldn't even be sure why a treatment was successful or why it failed. In the case of Avastin, for example, the Food and Drug Administration backed off its early support for the drug's use against breast cancer, because the results were so mixed. However, the FDA would *add* approval for Avastin's use in some lung, kidney, and brain cancers.

For those of us engaged in the science every day, especially in immunology, hematology, and stem cell research, the tantalizing but limited successes that began the twenty-first century seemed to circle the target but not hit it. The challenge of cancer, as demonstrated by drug resistance, meant that dealing with it would likely require something vastly more complex than interventions that worked against a single genetic problem or acted on one chemical process.

Cancer arises, generally speaking, when the agreements that govern how cells cooperate in the body break down. In healthy animals, different kinds of differentiated cells regard each other respectfully, working together and behaving themselves. Through chemical agreement, growth is limited, energy is shared, and various duties are parceled out to be accomplished on the organism's behalf. Malignancies occur when, for lack of a better term, cells "de-differentiate" and revert to a more self-interested state. These cells become cheaters, taking more than their share of available resources, multiplying out of control, and neglecting their responsibilities, including the duty to die and make way for replacements. The one entity that can reliably rein in these rogues, and do it routinely, is the human immune system. It was obvious that we needed to work *with* the body to provoke the defenses that generally save us from cancer while avoiding unintended consequences.

SEVEN

PROVOKING A RESPONSE

If you stepped back from the bedside, or the lab bench, you could see the progress. In the late 1970s, more than half the people diagnosed with cancer would be dead within five years. The annual rate of new cases was climbing and would continue to rise. In the mid-1990s, it peaked at an annual rate of more than five new diagnoses for every one thousand people. Consult the data and you see that something wonderful began to happen. New diagnoses began to decline, and death rates began dropping by 2 percent per year. Now, two-thirds of all people with cancer will live beyond the five-year mark. The number of people considered cancer "survivors," which meant their disease was cured or well managed, was approaching fifteen million. This was five times the number who could be counted in 1971.

The biggest treatment improvements had been made in blood cancers, particularly non-Hodgkin's and Hodgkin's lymphoma, chronic myeloid leukemia, and eventually multiple myeloma. In the case of non-Hodgkin's lymphoma, a drug that is an antibody, called Rituxan, had a very substantial impact and every year since it was approved, increased the number of people cured. It is now estimated that 70 percent of those given the diagnosis will live at least five years, most of them cured. It was one of the first immunotherapy drugs, using a product of the immune system, an antibody, to target the tumor. Gleevec and its relatives have proven to be game changers in chronic myeloid leukemia (CML). Before Gleevec, a CML diagnosis was a death sentence. By 2006, 95 percent of people were living at least five years.

A host of antibody therapies like Avastin and Herceptin were being introduced and providing at least some benefit for so-called solid (not blood) tumors, though not the curative effects seen with blood cancers. Similarly, drugs targeting specific mutations, based on the model of Gleevec, became available for other solid tumors. The number of therapies increased and options beyond the first treatment choice greatly expanded. Improvement in outcomes could also be credited to technologies that allowed doctors to monitor and screen patients more closely. Colonoscopy, mammography, ultrasound, and other methods allowed for early discovery of new cancers and recurrences, and permitted minimally invasive procedures. In addition to improving survival rates, these technologies reduced complications from treatments. The use of real-time imaging by neurosurgeons, for example, allowed them to operate on brain tumors with more precision. Operations that once carried a significant risk of causing impairments to motor and intellectual functions became safer and more effective.

The most common form of brain cancer, glioma, originates in the glial cells, which literally glue together the nervous system. High-tech surgery, radiation, and chemotherapy can knock back glioma and even restore brain functions impaired by tumors. With careful monitoring and follow-up therapy, some patients live for five years or more. However, it is a very diffuse, invasive cancer so getting it all with surgery or even radiation is nearly impossible, which means it is likely to recur. And ironically, the return of the disease can involve malignancies with new genetic mutations that were caused by treatment itself. This dynamic was first noticed decades ago by physicians who used radiation against cancers. Later, the same effect was confirmed in people with Hodgkin's lymphoma who were given chemotherapy, which caused genetic defects that led to leukemia.

The problem of new brain cancers related to chemotherapy was reported by physicians and scientists at the University of California–San Francisco's Brain Tumor Research Center. One of the authors of this study, neurosurgeon Susan Chang, described it as a "natural history" of gliomas that evolve or "over enough time, progress to a higher grade."

In literature, works of natural history trace the life span and evolution of living things under observation. Natural histories always consider context, so the study of an animal would include reflections on its environment, predators, prey, and so on. Considered as a natural history, you could say the glioma paper published by the group at UCSF tracked the behavior of a kind of creature—the cancer cell—in the environment of the brain, over the life spans of people who developed this type of cancer. The authors documented the way some malignancies undergo a process of "hypermutation" that makes as many as two thousand genetic changes. These changes can make the cancer resistant or even invisible to both the immune system and medicines.

Ever since the discovery of the Philadelphia chromosome deformity, which is a defect found in leukemia cells, science had understood that cancer cells have genetic signatures. In some cases, like chronic myeloid leukemia, malignancies are genetically similar from person to person. (This commonality allows for successful treatment of almost all patients with one medicine, Gleevec.) However, some types of cancers are essentially unique in each patient, or they are so rare that little effort is made to find proper treatment.

The incredible variety of cancers can shock people who get a diagnosis but then discover that most of what they think about their illness is wrong. I once treated a middle-aged woman who had a form of leukemia so rare that hers was the only case I ever saw. The word *leukemia* is so closely associated with successful chemotherapy that many people hear they have it and expect to recover after grueling treatment. This did not happen in this case. Instead, my patient got sicker and sicker. She died, and to this day I'm not certain that she or her family truly understood what we were up against.

This terrible variety of malignancies explains more than the rare cancers that cannot be treated. It also explains why cancer therapy outcomes vary from person to person. It also suggests a pathway to better care. Knowing the exact genetic profile of a malignancy could permit far more precise treatment. This idea—that we could design therapies to exploit the exact genetic makeup of a malignancy—is what doctors reference when they use terms like *precision* or *personalized* cancer care.

The technology to readily evaluate the genomes of individual cancers didn't arrive until the start of the twenty-first century and the completion of the Human Genome Project. Then, in the summer of 2006, a group at Johns Hopkins University announced they had sequenced cells from twenty-two breast and colon cancer patients, compared them with normal cells, and identified an average of one hundred mutations in each tumor. Of those, about one-fifth seemed to cause malignancy. These findings, which with poetic justice had been funded in part by proceeds from lawsuits brought against tobacco companies, would contribute to The Cancer Genome Atlas Project.

TGCA had been started by the National Cancer Institute to create a public catalog of cancer cell mutations organized around types of malignancies. Theoretically, these mutational landscapes, as they were called, could be useful in developing treatments for specific disease and, eventually, for the specific cancers found in patients. As the first pages in the atlas were being written, the big excitement in oncology was related to immune response. In June 2006, the Food and Drug Administration approved a vaccine against the human papillomavirus (HPV), which causes about 70 percent of all cervical cancers.

It makes sense to mention, here, the double benefits of many vaccines. In addition to protecting individuals, vaccines also create what's called "herd immunity" by depriving pathogens of the reservoir of hosts they need to thrive. With the measles vaccine, for example, herd immunity occurs when 95 percent of children are immunized and infection becomes so rare that even the five percent who are not inoculated are protected. Unfortunately, this effect decreases dramatically when the immunization rate drops below the 95 percent threshold. A case in point arose in France in 2008 when measles vaccination rates dropped to 89 percent. By 2011, France had 15,000 cases, which caused the deaths of six children. This occurred in part because parents who believed unscientific claims about vaccines opted to forgo or delay them for their children. As this scenario illustrates, when it comes to infectious disease we are all in the fight together, and the best outcomes arise when we recognize our responsibilities to our communities.

The link between HPV and cervical cancer is one of the most well-established relationships in oncology. A vaccine against it took enormous effort but was finally available and represented an easy, cost-effective way to reduce the incidence of this cancer. While a relatively uncommon cause of death in this country because of PAP smears, it is a common cancer and the most common cause of cancer death in the developing world. A preventive vaccine could spare untold numbers of women a great deal of suffering, and save the health care system significant sums of money. Most effective if given before a person might be exposed to the virus via sexual activity, the vaccine would be recommended for preadolescent girls and would halve infection rates in teenager by 2012.

Human nature being what it is, the HPV vaccine's connection to sex, or more precisely the thought that young unmarried women might have sex, bothered people. In Texas, the state legislature prioritized sexual anxiety over health and voided Governor Rock Perry's order making the vaccine one of many required by the state. Later, during the 2012 GOP presidential primary, candidates Rick Santorum and Michelle Bachmann added their voices to the HPV

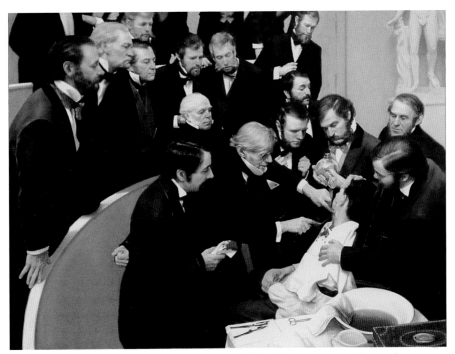

The Ether Dome, immortalizing the groundbreaking surgery when ether was used as an anesthetic for the first time. (*Massachusetts General Hospital*)

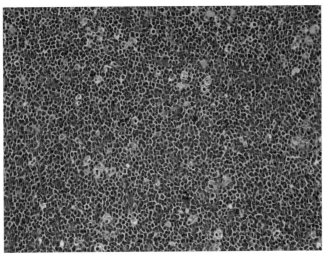

Burkitt lymphoma cells, a lymphatic cancer discovered by Denis Parsons Burkitt in 1958. (*Ed Uthman, M.D.*)

A leading expert on vaccine development and infectious diseases, Dr. Adel Mahmoud was David Scadden's mentor for many years. (*Merck & Co.*)

Donnall Thomas, the physician and professor who, along with his wife and research partner Dottie Thomas, developed the first bone marrow–transplant procedure. (*The Gairdner Foundation*)

Bruce Walker, M.D., director of the Ragon Institute and leading infectious-disease scientist. (*Massachusetts General Hospital*)

Ray Scofield (left), stem-cell pioneer, with David Scadden in Wales. (*David Scadden*)

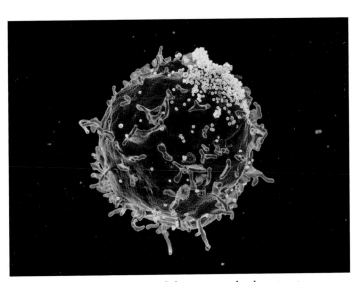

The Friend virus, a strain of the murine leukemia virus identified by Charlotte Friend in 1957. It served as a model for how a retrovirus can be used to gain insight into blood cancers. (*Elizabeth Fischer and Austin Athman, NIH Rocky Mountain Laboratories*)

The head of the Dana-Farber Cancer Institute, Emil Frei is best known for his work on the treatment of lymphomas and leukemias. (*Dana-Farber Cancer Institute*)

Taxol, or its scientific name paclitaxel (PTX), is a chemotherapy medication used to treat a number of types of cancer. (*George McGregor, National Cancer Institute*)

Douglas Melton, cofounder of the Harvard Stem Cell Institute, has twice been named one of the world's 100 Most Influential People by *Time* magazine. (*Massachusetts General Hospital and Harvard Magazine*)

Chromosome translocation is a chromosome abnormality caused by rearrangement of parts between nonhomologous chromosomes. (*Janet Rowley*)

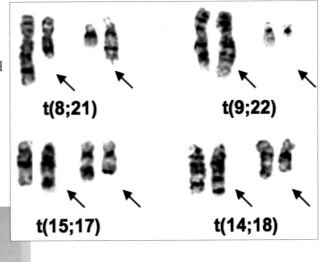

Physician/scientist Janet Rowley proved that cancer can have specific genetic causes and received the National Medal of Science. (*Dan Dry for the University of Chicago*)

Lawrence Summers, U.S. economist and former Harvard University president, who backed the stem-cell institute after a bout with cancer. (*Chatham House*)

A partially recellularized human whole-heart cardiac scaffold, reseeded with human cardiomyocytes derived from induced pluripotent stem cells, being cultured in a bioreactor that delivers a nutrient solution and replicates some of the environmental conditions around a living heart. (*Bernhard Jank, M.D., Ott Lab, Center for Regenerative Medicine, Massachusetts General Hospital*)

Researchers at the Zon Labortaory have created a model of cancer in zebrafish that allows them to capture live images of tumors forming and growing, in some cases from a single cell. (*Vera Binder, M.D., and Jonathan Henninger, Ph.D candidate*)

Leonard Zon (left) and George Daley (right) are physician-scientists focusing on the connections between stem cells and cancer at Harvard. (*Boston Children's Hospital*)

Dr. Scadden was inducted into the National Academy of Medicine and the American Academy of Arts and Sciences for his work on cancer and stem cells. (*B. D. Colen, Sr. Communications Officer for University Science, Office of the Vice President for Government Community and Public Affairs, Harvard University*)

Cover of the September 2016 journal *Cell* featuring "Lifting the Differentiation Embargo" and Dr. Scadden's research on effective differentiation therapy for acute myeloid leukemia. (*David F. Tan, Toronto, Canada*)

vaccine opposition. In Great Britain an antiabortion group opposed the vaccine with the argument that it "gives young people another green light to be promiscuous." The specious quality of this claim was refuted by a scientific study, done by researchers at Emory University, who found no correlation between the vaccine and sexual activity. Nevertheless, as of 2017 the vaccine was required for children only in Virginia, Rhode Island, and Washington, D.C.

A second oncological advance made on the basis of immunology was a prostate cancer therapy marketed under the brand name Provenge. This used patient's cells to make an antitumor vaccine for prostate cancer. This is not a vaccine in the traditional sense of something used to prevent a disease, but rather a therapeutic vaccine. It could be categorized as an immunostimulant as it uses dendritic cells: cells that come from blood stem cells and whose job it is to activate T cells. They process proteins and serve them up in a digested format that turns on specific T cells, selectively those T cells with a predetermined appetite. The Provenge approach is to isolate dendritic cells from the patient's blood, grow them and feed them a prostate cancer protein before sending them back into the blood to get the T cells going against the tumor. It is very patient specific and that makes it very expensive and complicated, but it is an FDA approved therapy.

Modern immunotherapies like Provenge descended from William Coley's toxins, which he developed after noticing that some of his cancer patients got better after they fought off an unrelated infection. The great hope for immunotherapies rested in the idea that they could work with the body, enhancing the natural response to malignancies. Patients, physicians, and the public were thrilled by reports on the early successes achieved in the development of immunotherapies, and research in this area attracted billions of dollars from the government, foundations, and investors attracted by the profits available in blockbuster drugs priced as high as $250,000 per patient, per year.

More than a little irony attended the fact that much of the scientific community and enormous caches of national research funding focused on the human genome and, particularly, the cancer genome while major leaps forward in benefit were coming from immunology, an area that was often outside the limelight in cancer research. There is no question that genome science was a powerful force for good in rationally designing therapies, but durable tumor responses were a rarity apart from Gleevec. Immune-based treatments seemed to offer hope for more effective cancer control. One of the leaders in this science, Carl June of the University of Pennsylvania, imagined a range of therapies that would depend on immune cells that had been genetically modified to do a better job of dispatching malignancies. June wrote of a time when transfusions of these lab-improved cells would be as routine as whole blood transfusions became in the early twentieth century. The goal, he said, would be a therapy that would be "clinically effective, scalable, reproducibly manufactured, appropriately priced, and marketed." When he outlined this ambition in 2007, it seemed like something beyond reach. Barring an unexpected new technology, the investment required to create the infrastructure for this type of medicine would compare with one of NASA's historic missions. And even if we had the money, we would have to solve an untold number of extremely difficult biological problems to determine *if* the idea was plausible.

Fortunately, science is generally done in the sort of step-by-step process that yields answers to questions and also points to the next challenge. This journey is inspired by the big goal, whether it's curing cancer or reaching the moon. But success requires organization, teamwork, and, for individual scientists, a devotion to solving the discrete puzzle that sits before you. You must enjoy this pursuit, even when you know that you might reach a dead end. Indeed, much of what can happen when you tackle one small piece of the work required to advance a huge scientific project might be considered bad.

First, you could fail to design your study in a way that addresses the question at hand. If you get the design right, you may run into problems with execution. Get over this hurdle and the accurate result from all your hard work may indicate that your theory about a gene or a chemical or a process in the body is all wrong. But say you succeed in moving from an idea to a promising result that fits into your team's larger, long-term endeavor. There's always a chance that the next step in the process will bring everything to a halt or some other group could beat you to the finish line. This is science. You think hard to come up with a big idea, work hard, and if you fail but have time left in your life, you start all over again.

Carl June's big idea called for exploiting elements of the immune system, including the fact that some cancer-fighting cells retain memories of the invaders they once dispatched and are primed to destroy them. This happens thanks to genetic mutations that occur as part of the normal process of developing the lymphocyte arm of the immune system: T and B cells in particular. Think of this as an example of gene mutations "gone good." Cells with a particular mutation that allows them to connect with and be activated by a particular target expand and durably remain. In this way, they serve to provide a kind of memory for the immune system. Upon encountering an old enemy anew, the memory-equipped immune cells possess extra power to deal with it and the ability to multiply to get the job done. When cancer prevails, however, the response wasn't vigorous enough.

As June imagined it, the solution to an insufficient immune response would involve interventions that improved the cancer-killing cells' ability to see, seek, and destroy while also multiplying and then creating something like a permanent rapid response team, ready to deploy when needed. The fix he would add to the immune cells was called chimerica antigen receptor. ("Chimeric" because, like the mythical chimera, it would be made from more than one animal source.)

"Antigen receptors" are chemicals that are the product of the controlled mutations in T and B cells. They can recognize particular targets, another name for which is antigens. Those that recognize targets on cancer cells can sometimes be identified and cloned. Once in the hands of molecular engineers, the antigen receptor can be manipulated to create a more potent activator of T cells by fusing it with other parts of the T cell activation molecular machinery. That chimera is then placed into other T cells to arm them for targeting a particular tumor antigen. Those cells can be grown to large numbers outside the body so you create a large army of cells with one target in mind. These CAR T cells are especially good at killing cancer cells that bear the target antigen. They are good at killing any cell that bears the antigen. Therein lies a problem. If cancer cells are from us, from genetic events that involve our own genes, how can normal cells be shielded or not attacked? That problem forced the field to focus only on targets that were malignancies of cells that were somewhat dispensable. B cell cancers have targets that are on both normal and malignant B cells, but only on B cells. B cells make antibodies that can be replaced by injections (so-called gamma globulin, an injection of which you might have had as a traveler to protect you from hepatitis A). So the pioneers of CAR T therapy, led by Carl June, focused on B cell cancers.

A lanky fellow with thinning hair and a pleasing, crooked smile, June is a determined scientist who was inclined to push forward on his ideas even though most major funders refused to support him financially and many colleagues doubted his ideas. This doesn't mean he was overly egotistical. In fact, when he was once encouraged to explain how he was trying to "cure cancer," he blanched at the thought and, in a stammering way, said, "Those words are hard to say." He added, somewhat shyly, "I think sometimes it's actually hard to think that you might actually succeed."

As a veteran of navy medicine, June was trained at Seattle's Fred Hutchinson Cancer Research Center (often called simply the Hutch), which is the world leader in blood stem cell transplantation.

He is also heir to a long history of U.S. military research into immuno-therapies that, at first, were imagined as a response to injuries caused by radiation accidents or nuclear weapons. One of the very earliest of these, and an example of cell therapy, was the bone marrow transplant procedure developed at the Hutch by E. Donnall Thomas. Recipients of this therapy produced fresh new armies of T cells that would confront their leukemia. June encountered the procedure early in his career and decided, by 1983, that he would devote himself to the science of immunotherapy.

In the late 1980s, I worked with June on an HIV study in an effort to help stem the AIDS epidemic. HIV is extremely good at getting into a particular kind of T cells that have a molecule on their surface called CD4. The virus uses the CD4 molecule as its doorway to the inside of the cell where it exerts its mischief. A colleague at MGH, Brian Seed, thought that it might be possible to use the viruses' dependency on CD4 against it. What he did was create a chimeric molecule that had CD4 on it as a way to create a Velcro-like connection with HIV. He fused the CD4 to the activating machinery of T cells. By placing that into T cells that were professional cell killers (so called "cytotoxic" T cells) he could generate an army of T cells capable of killing HIV-infected cells. A visionary physician-entrepreneur, Steven Sherwin, acted on that to create a company with the ability to move it from a laboratory to patients. Carl June was one of those who championed moving it to patients. I was a part of the group of physicians who joined with him to do so.

We treated patients with HIV who were also on medicines and we monitored if the new engineered T cells could persist in the body and attack HIV infected cells. I remember the first patient in whom we infused these cells at the MGH. Much trepidation on our part—my wonderful study nurse, Jocelyn Bresnahan, and I—at the bedside thawing the cells in a water bath and then infusing them like a blood transfusion. Our fears, kept private to not alarm the patient, were calmed by how smoothly all proceeded, how lively the patient was conversing throughout, and how nothing amiss was happening medically. The patient went home happy and well.

The cells are preserved in a solution called DMSO that prevents water crystals from forming. It has a particular and strong odor. When we saw the patient the next day in follow-up, we encountered an unanticipated complication: the patient's dog liked the scent of the DMSO. According to the patient, "he thought I was a pork chop." Fortunately, all lick and no bite. It apparently made for an entertaining evening rather than any trouble and the scent was gone by morning.

The cells targeting HIV were safe and stayed in the body for years. They appeared to have the activity we hoped for in killing HIV-infected cells, but we couldn't tell for sure. When new medicines are used, whether they are drugs or antibodies or cells, the first step is to be sure they are safe. That is called a Phase I study. It involves doses that gradually increase in a step-wise manner as safety information is gathered. A Phase II study is when activity is tested, usually at a single-dose level. The Phase III is when safety and activity have been established and the medicine can be tested against a control group of patients receiving the standard of care for the condition. These are generally very large and expensive studies that are often required by the FDA prior to approval of the medicine for sale. Phase IV studies are conducted after a drug is approved, with the intent of collecting information that might reveal otherwise hidden side effects. Not all medicines are required to undergo Phase IV testing.

The trial of modified T cells to attack HIV was somewhat different because of the complexity of making enough cells. It was small like a standard Phase II, but did include a comparison group who just received T cells, just not engineered T cells. The results were ambiguous so the funding for further testing dried up and the company died, despite its visionary leadership in engineering T cells. The idea and much of the technology resurfaced with CAR T cells targeting cancer.

Ironically, engineering cells often depends on HIV, or at least its basic composition. Putting new genes into cells like a chimeric antigen receptor takes advantage of what viruses do for a living— getting their genes into cells by infecting them. HIV is particularly good at doing that and having its genes remain durably present in the cell and all its descendents. Just as Mayor Vellucci and the Cambridge City Council struggled to understand and accept early genetic engineering work at Harvard and MIT, the idea that the most-feared virus of our age—HIV—could be used to devise some sort of therapy would unsettle many people. By the middle of the last decade, microbiologists and virologists had figured out ways to create a version of HIV that lacked the genes that cause AIDS but would be an effective delivery vehicle for genes.

"The disarmed AIDS virus acts like a Trojan horse," noted S. Y. Chen, of the University of California–Los Angeles. It is also helpful to think about the modified virus as a burglar who could defeat the lock on a door but forgot his purpose once he got inside the house. It penetrated into immune cells but couldn't deliver its virulent punch. It could, however, "infect" T cells with genes to produce chimeric antigen receptor and make them into superstars of the immune system.

In 2010, Carl June's team was working without much support. The National Cancer Institute, having seen failures in similar experiments, wouldn't back June. He found just enough funding from a small foundation created by Penn alumni to keep going. His group took roughly one billion T cells from the bodies of three men with CLL and augmented them with the chimeric antigen receptor genes. They added microscopic beads bearing proteins to the cell culture, which pushed the cells to divide and increase in number at a faster rate. (Earlier experiments had determined that the signaling molecules that were on the beads could accelerate cell division without causing any changes that diminished the cells' abilities to act against cancer or infection. These techniques had been used for years with consistent success).

The patients in Carl June's trial were at a stage of CLL sometimes referred to as "ultrahigh risk." This phase is reached when tests show increased numbers of cells bearing a defect in the famous p53 gene, which is a tumor-suppressing gene and in whose absence cancer can occur. In this condition, people with CLL progress more rapidly, and most will not improve with chemotherapy. Life expectancy is shorter than that of people who have CLL without a p53 defect.

The reality of late-stage CLL is much easier to discuss when you refer to genes and time spans and abstract complications. Turn to address actual human beings, who love life and are cherished by friends and family, and the conversations become exceedingly difficult. A recent study of patients at cancer care centers around the country found that of those with a terminal illness, nearly 40 percent had never discussed end-of-life options with their doctors. Only 5 percent could answer four elementary questions about the basics of their condition. Separate studies have found that people cling to the long-shot chance when they are told, for example, that they have a one-in-ten possibility of recovery.

It is the "optimism bias" that keeps patients and families seeking and believing in the chance to have the "Lake Wobegon effect" where "all of the children are above average." It comes with a tendency for people to believe they are special and will prevail where others do not. If they do not prove to be exceptional, those who care for them must work at persuading them that when it comes to cancer no one is at fault when they fail to beat the odds. Sometimes the belief turns to anger and suspicion when the crisis of failing therapies becomes real. Being caught in a raging wave of overwhelming cancer is brutal for all and people's worst fears emerge. Sometimes these feelings are amplified by events that occurred long before we meet a patient, and sometimes we wind up grappling with unstated factors in a family's history.

I once encountered deep skepticism while treating a cancer patient for whom no therapy was working. When I suggested a new, long-shot medicine, I could see her parents were gravely worried. When they asked if I was "experimenting," I realized from their accents and age that they were probably acutely aware of and may have lived through the horrors of the Holocaust. They were not sure if they could trust me or the entire medical establishment. I tried hard to reassure them, but even as I did this, I feared that I was talking too much, as if I were trying to talk them into something and that in doing so, I was likely making things worse. We went ahead with the treatment, but it failed and their daughter died. I would never learn whether they felt I was sincere.

Some people feel better after expressing these feelings, part of the job to remain calm and caring as they do. However, the words that are said can also be devastating. It is difficult to remain stoic and yet be authentic in such settings. Taking sometimes unfair words without giving in to the urge to protest is necessary. What sometimes comes out is a rote answer or false understanding, which is the last thing anyone needs from a doctor.

In time, oncologists learn to be guided by the person at the heart of the crisis: the patient. There are many ways to communicate the same information, and when you share a medical foxhole with someone, you get a good idea of what will work for them. In some cases, patients understand they face death but will not acknowledge the facts using the precise words. On the other end are those who need to say, "I know I may die soon," out loud, many times over. No matter where a person falls along the spectrum of reactions, love, friendship, psychotherapy, and pastoral care can be of enormous help. Everyone dies. Not everyone must cope with knowing that the event is imminent. These people deserve every bit of help we can offer.

The three patients who agreed to take Carl June's experimental treatment knew what they were getting into. They were told that augmented immune cells could run wild, as they had in one previous trial with a colon cancer patient who had suffered lung damage as a side effect and died. They also knew that as they underwent chemotherapy to destroy most of their existing immune system, which could otherwise inhibit the proliferation of the new ones, they would be vulnerable to potentially deadly infection. But patients who reach the end of conventional treatment options and are offered spots in a trial often seize the opportunity for multiple reasons. The chance for a cure, or even a somewhat longer life, is one big motivation. Another is a yearning, felt by many patients, to contribute something positive to others whenever the chance arises. Taking a chance on an experimental treatment can be seen as a great opportunity to serve in this way, and this service adds meaning to life.

Nothing notable occurred when June's patients had their T cells harvested and then underwent chemotherapy. (After many decades, transplant groups had reliable routines for managing the effects of the procedures so that the worst complications were avoided.) The lab-treated cells were infused back into the patients' bodies and began to replicate, but days would pass before signs of change arrived in the form of fevers and chills. Speaking later to *The New York Times*, one of the men said he became so ill that he was moved into intensive care and his loved ones were warned that he might die. Another of the patients recalled, "I was sure the war was on. I was sure the CLL cells were dying."

He was right. As June would observe, each of the trial participants became "a bioreactor," and the new T cells multiplied and went to work. Indeed, each one of the powerful T cells must have been capable of attacking and killing as many as one thousand cancer cells before it exhausted its abilities. Since the T cells were dividing, offspring cells would remain, which meant that CAR T therapy amounted to what June called "a living drug" that would last a lifetime.

Unfortunately, hugely successful cancer-killing cells can create problems of their own. Chemicals created as by-products of the destruction of malignant cells—a process called lysis—caused the fevers and other symptoms in June's patients. One developed cancer lysis syndrome. Early signs of this complication include exhaustion, emotional swings, and tremors. He hallucinated a vision of rain in the hospital corridor with his wife walking through it.

Cancer lysis syndrome is the most common treatment emergency for patients being treated for blood and lymphatic cancers. The word *lyse* means "break apart," and the syndrome begins, ironically, when a medicine that breaks apart cancer cells does its job too well. Each dying cancer cell contains lots of debris that's not good for you. When a treatment destroys the equivalent of two or three pounds of cancer cells, the body can be overwhelmed. Unable to handle all the circulating poisons, the kidneys start to fail, and the chemicals affect other key organs, including the heart and brain.

As the lysis syndrome accelerates, the basic chemistry in the body changes. If the kidney cannot filter properly, urine output plummets. The abnormal chemistry becomes toxic. Patients may vomit. They stop eating, develop cramps, and become disoriented. It's all quite scary for the person who develops it and for the caregivers who try to help, because we know it can lead to death by kidney failure, seizures and cardiac arrest. Various medicines can be given to restore normalcy to the body's chemistry, and some patients are put on dialysis. Most, but not all, patients survive.

When June's patient developed problems in his kidneys, the medical team went into action. The intervention worked. Over the long term, these patients would require regular injections of gamma globulin to help them fight off infection. This was necessary because in addition to destroying leukemia cells, the new T cells killed both the normal and malignant B cells.

In the end, two of the men in the trial went into complete remission and the third improved significantly. (By one published estimate, the T cells destroyed a full two pounds' worth of cancer cells in just one man's body.) Reports of this success were published with exciting headlines. On its website, *The New York Times* even posted a video clip that showed an engineered T cell attacking a tumor cell in a lab dish. In the video, the immune cell appears to crawl all over the cancer cell until the contents of its target start to flow out, like the guts spilling out of a fish sliced open by a filleting knife. Soon, the words *dead tumor* appear on the video. It's the kind of process anyone with cancer might hope to imagine taking place inside the body as a treatment takes hold and health is restored. In fact, many patients create movies of the mind that show their cancer cells dying, in just this fashion, and frequently meditate on the images. People did this long before anyone understood the mechanism of lysis. I don't know if this common fantasy was informed by some mysterious mind-body connection, but the fact that people were actually right about the cellular struggle taking place inside them is more than a little intriguing.

After his first small trial, Carl June broadened his effort gradually, refining his technique for delivering improved immune cells with impotent HIV. Unfortunately, his work provoked lots of over-the-top reporting in the popular press, where some found it impossible to resist shading the facts to suggest that patients were somehow endangered by the HIV virus vector. In 2013, a short film circulated online, making the claim that June had cured leukemia in a dying girl named Emily Whitehead by "injecting her with HIV." More recently, a full-length TV documentary described several forms of cancer immunotherapy that utilized altered viruses, either as a gene delivery vector or to attack the tumor cells directly. It reported one trial that enrolled high-grade glioma patients who were given one dose directly to their brain tumors and saw remarkable remissions in 12 percent. Eighteen months after treatment, they showed no signs of recurrent tumors. Moving as they were, the stories of the adults featured in the documentary were eclipsed when Emily Whitehead appeared in the film. Just five years old when she was first diagnosed with leukemia and eight when she received the experimental treatment, she was a compelling figure on the screen, and the story of her rescue from an apparent death sentence was breathtaking.

Emily's story was retold on websites around the world, but, too often, the scientific details, including precise information about how the HIV was defanged and T cells were utilized, were ignored or glossed over. Without careful reading and, in some cases, additional research, it was easy for lay readers to conclude that doctors were giving people active and dangerous versions of the virus that causes AIDS. This caused more than a little confusion for people with cancer, their families, and caregivers. Eventually the official website of the authoritative British organization called Cancer Research UK published an article knocking down these fears. It was titled "No, Doctors Did Not 'Inject HIV into a Dying Girl' to Treat Her Cancer."

With work continuing apace, bringing more people with more different kinds of cancer into viral vector trials, a variation on this concept further challenged scientists' ability to communicate with the public. At Duke University, a team led by Matthias Gromeier used an altered polio virus and a common cold virus to create a hybrid that would be attracted to a protein secreted by cancer cells. (This was work he began while studying with virologist Eckard Wimmer at the State University of New York–Stony Brook.) The group at Duke wanted to use their engineered virus to pierce a chemical cloak that prevents the immune system from recognizing glioma cells and doing their job. In theory, the virus would destroy some of the malignant cells and remove this disguise, which would make them vulnerable to the immune system.

As the Duke team proved in the lab, the hybrid virus would home in on the "scent" of cancer, invade only the malignant cells, and destroy them. To the team's excitement, the hybrid virus also triggered T cells to swing into action and polish off those virus-infected cancer cells that survived. But even though they had confirmed that the idea worked, they would have to prove it was safe to literally drop the virus into the brains of people with glioma. This safety review lasted seven years, and included an intense effort to show that a fat molecule derived from beef, which was used in the treatment, would not cause bovine spongiform encephalopathy (the so-called mad cow disease). The Duke team also had to test the virus on the brains of three dozen monkeys (no serious adverse reactions were observed) before the FDA permitted its use with even one person.

In 2012, a small group of people with glioma became the first human subjects to receive the treatment, which came to be known as PVS-RIPO, for recombinant oncolytic poliovirus. The drug was administered directly into their brains, via tiny holes drilled through the skull and catheters directing the medicine to the tumor site. After the surgery, which caused little trauma, patients did experience the symptoms of infection as the virus went to work. Some patients would become quite ill, with swelling in their brains causing problems with speech and movement.

At the time, median survival for people first diagnosed with glioma who received standard care was a little more than fourteen months. Half of patients died before this date, and half lived longer. Given that PVS-RIPO was an experimental drug, no one knew what to expect. Then tests done on patient number one, a twenty-year-old college student named Stephanie Lipscomb, showed that after a brief period of tumor growth, her cancer had started to recede. Indeed, she responded so well that, in less than two years, that single dose of the virus had wiped out all signs of the tumor in her brain. Other patients saw similar progress, with the imaging of their brains showing that tumors were literally dying, bit by bit, and collapsing.

Because they were conducting a so-called phase I trial, which is intended to test the safety of new therapies, the Duke scientists adjusted the virus dose they administered, hoping to determine the maximum dose that could be given without a severe adverse effect.

Some patients who received high doses developed fatal complications. However, half did well, and two years after the trial, the scientists reported higher rates of survival than what would be expected for patients with the disease. They also determined that the optimal treatment did not require giving patients the most drug they can tolerate, as is often the case with chemotherapy. Instead, they discovered that higher doses not only increased side effects but inhibited the immune response they were trying to provoke. Paradoxical as this finding may seem, it cannot be considered a surprise. The immune system is a complex mechanism, and it's possible that, like a watch, it can be overwound with too much stimulus and simply refuse to work.

In 2017, as I write, Stephanie Lipscomb has earned a nursing degree and is healthy and well. She chose to work in oncology. Two other patients, who otherwise would have surely died, were alive three years after treatment. People around the world are clamoring for the therapy tested at Duke, but more work remains to be done before good protocols could be established for its wide use. The U.S. Food and Drug Administration gave the therapy "breakthrough" status, which meant that it could be studied further and evaluated on an accelerated basis. This regulatory category had been created in response to criticism of the FDA by people who feared that people were suffering and dying as promising therapies were considered in a process that was unnecessarily slow. For their part, FDA officials were doubtless worried about a disaster like thalidomide, a drug used mainly outside the United States for the relief of morning sickness that caused fetal deformities. Nevertheless, fifty years after thalidomide became a global scandal, the agency sought to make exceptions to its painstakingly slow process. When PVS-RIPO got breakthrough status, the group at Duke began work on phase II and phase III trials, which would involve many more patients. However, at of the start of 2017, they were not yet enrolling patients.

In the meantime, Carl June was reporting truly astounding

results from his CAR T cell / HIV vector work. He teamed with a pediatric oncologist scientist, Stephan Grupp, to treat children who fell into the small portion of acute lymphoblastic leukemia (ALL) that doesn't respond to chemotherapy. Of the first thirty-nine children treated, several of whom had undergone bone marrow transplants, thirty-six went into remission. June has seen similar success with CLL and has received substantial new support for his work. (Penn has even opened a new Center for Advanced Cellular Therapeutics.) June's targets include some very-difficult-to-treat diseases, including pancreatic cancer, which is the only form of cancer with a five-year survival rate below 10 percent. (A member of June's research team died of pancreatic cancer in 2010.) He has also begun to work on ovarian cancer. This is another tough one when it comes to therapy. His wife was diagnosed with it in 1996 and died after five years of off-and-on treatment. Given the fact that Carl began his work on cancer immunotherapy many years before these losses, no one can say that his work was the result of his personal experience. But it is also true that no one is untouched by cancer and, sadly, the losses that remind us of why we do this work.

EIGHT

GENE HACKING

With engineered T cells providing some spectacular results for people who were otherwise out of options, new ways to modify cells opened up additional opportunities. Carl June's addition of a chimeric antigen receptor to T cells worked, but had to made individually for each patient. It was the ultimate personalized therapy. But like anything bespoke, it is expensive and hard to make widely available. Companies are doing it, but other innovations are entering the field.

New technologies for editing genes rather than just adding them are now in the clinic. DNA is the written text for all living things. Over the eons, life-forms have developed a wide array of tools for cutting, repairing, and editing genes: a virtual sewing kit for life. The scissors are called nucleases. They can be directed to cut particular parts of the genome. One group of these, called TALENs (transcription activator-like effector nucleases), do so with great precision and, when the cut is repaired, it can be made to do so in a way that inactivates the targeted gene. TALENs have been used to cut out the genes in a T cell that guide its normal function, so that they only respond to the new chimeric antigen receptor that is put into them. That means a CAR T cell could be made that can be given to anyone. It could become an "off the shelf" rather than a customized, patient-specific cell. In 2015, Cellectis scientists used TALENs to create such "universal" T cells that would work in every body. This process could be particularly helpful to get around the problem, presented most often by children with cancer, of patients who don't have enough T cells of their own to use in therapy.

In the summer of 2015, a call from Great Ormond Street Hospital in London (formerly called the Hospital for Sick Children) gave the Cellectis scientists a chance to test their idea. Researchers at GOSH possessed a vial of frozen T cells enhanced by Cellectis, but it was meant for experiments, not treatment. (A scientist at University College London was collaborating with Cellectis.) The doctors in London said they were desperate to save a one-year-old baby named Layla Richards, who, in her short life, had undergone chemotherapy and a bone marrow transplant, which failed to cure her acute lymphoblastic leukemia, which had been diagnosed fourteen weeks after she was born. Even though it had been tested only in mice, British regulations permitted the use of the treatment on an emergency basis if all of those involved gave permission. Her parents and doctors saw it as the only hope. Cellectis executives weighed the risk, which included the damage that failure would do to their reputation and stock price, and agreed to go forward.

Layla received a one-milliliter dose of enhanced T cells, which had been donated by a stranger. Thirty days later, tests turned up no sign of leukemia. Two years later, she was still cancer-free and thriving. It was still too early to use the word *cure*, but as she recovered, Cellectis and its collaborators planned trials that would involve groups of patients. When the media spread word of the success, Cellectis's stock soared while the value of tech companies pursuing personalized forms of cell-based therapies sank. Investors seemed to believe that thanks to gene editing, Cellectis could produce an off-the-shelf treatment that would be far less expensive to make than the type of bespoke cures devised at the University of Pennsylvania. The verdict is still out. Cellectis has since had a major setback when a patient died. Other gene-editing methods are proceeding quickly to clinical testing.

A newer technology is based on the discovery of something called CRISPR, which stands for clustered regularly interspaced short palindromic repeats. These are bits of DNA that repeat inside the genes of bacteria and are separated by short snatches of DNA called spacers. The early work on CRISPR was done mainly by Spanish microbiologist Francisco Mojica, who published a report on them in 1993. He collaborated with Ruud Jansen of Utrecht University on naming CRISPR in 2002. The chemical that seemed to enable this process—a protein called Cas9—was discovered by Alexander Bolotin of the French National Institute for Agricultural Research, who reported his work in May 2005. It was Bolotin who recognized that the CRISPR-Cas9 system functioned like a very precise genome-editing machine, snipping genes and creating openings where viral DNA could be inserted.

It fell to a remarkably focused and intuitive scientist named Eugene Koonin, who immigrated to the United States from Russia in 1991, to recognize that bacteria retained bits of DNA from viruses so that in the future, invaders of the same sort could be recognized and defeated. Most people don't realize that viruses attack bacteria and that this assault happens in and on our bodies in every moment of every day. CRISPR-Cas9 creates what Koonin calls a "mug shot" of a virus, and this imagery is used to establish immunity. In future encounters, bacteria check a virus against the mug shot and, when a match is made, handily defeat it.

The CRISPR-Cas9 dynamic also clarified the remarkable role that viruses have played in evolution. In 2016, David Enard of Stanford University would report that almost one-third of the genetic changes that make humans different from chimpanzees were caused by viruses. Sometimes the change would occur as a result of the immune system's response to an invader, but sometimes it happened spontaneously, without this intermediary step. Bits of virus would combine with bits of DNA to produce something entirely new. His coauthor, Dmitri Petrov, said, "The discovery that this constant battle with viruses has shaped us in every aspect—not just proteins that fight infection but everything—is profound. All organisms have been living with these viruses for billions of years. This work shows that the viruses have affected every part of the cell."

Petrov's enthusiasm was merited, as work done around the globe, much of it inspired by the CRISPR-Cas9 discoveries, energized the fields of genetics and stem cell biology and offered hope to those working on cancer and other diseases driven by genetic abnormalities. Few tales of scientific discovery are more twisting and range as far afield as the story of CRISPR-Cas9. Among the more unexpected players in this drama were food industry researchers in Denmark who were curious about improving yogurt production, and a globe-trotting scientist who was an expert in microbiology, genetics, and biochemistry. The well-traveled scientist, Emmanuelle Charpentier, of Berlin's Max Planck Institute for Infection Biology, worked with Jennifer Doudna of the University of California–Berkeley to discover how to use CRISPR-Cas9 as a genome-editing tool. Charpentier would eventually describe the high point in her CRISPR work, which came when a colleague reached her cell phone. "I stood on the curbside for ages," she would recall, "while we discussed when would be the right time to publish because by then we had actually got the story."

The story culminated in a successful experiment that proved the CRISPR-Cas9 process could reliably edit genes. Doudna would write about how this work affected her personally, recalling how startled she was by the success. This was December 2012. Soon, CRISPR-Cas9 had been used to edit the genes of wheat, fish, human stem cells, and mice. (The mice had benefited from the correction of a gene defect that caused a hereditary disease.) Most startling of all was an experiment that changed the genetic makeup of monkey embryos. Implanted in the uteri of surrogates, the embryos developed into monkeys that carried the new genetic code in most of their cells, including their sperm cells and egg cells, which means they would be able to pass along their genes to future generations.

"Every day brought an influx of papers describing research using Crisper-Cas9," wrote Doudna in 2015. "My inbox was full of requests from researchers seeking advice or collaboration. All this activity could have a direct impact on human life yet most people I knew outside of work—neighbors, extended family members, parents of my son's classmates—remained largely oblivious. I felt as though I was living in two separate worlds."

In her professional world, Doudna would win awards and attract worldwide press attention. However, she and Charpentier would also become embroiled in a patent dispute with other scientists who had made CRISPR breakthroughs. Big institutions stood behind each of the parties, and the dispute seemed destined to go on for years. At one point, an insider who had worked with Doudna and Charpentier's rivals even wrote them to promise bombshell evidence to help their case. He also sought employment. Patent conflicts are not unusual when hugely valuable advances are achieved by scientists, but no one enjoys the process of dealing with lawyers and scrambling to assert a claim. Scientists may be competitive types, but we also tend to eschew conflicts over who did what first. It distracts from the real work of research and discovery, and amid the argument and intrigue, productive relationships are threatened.

Fortunately for those working on cancer and other genetic diseases, CRISPR-Cas9 was available, extremely inexpensive—ninety-nine dollars could get you started in the gene-editing business—and reliable. The magazine *Popular Mechanics* called this work "gene hacking," which suggested that with the barest training almost anyone could get into it. One extremely effective nonprofit organization, Addgene of Cambridge, Massachusetts, collected and preserved variants on the CRISPR-Cas9 technology that performed different tasks. Scores of labs around the world contributed to what became a catalog of these chemicals, which were then supplied to labs worldwide. By 2017, the service had nearly one thousand contributors and had supplied hundreds of thousands of tools to scientists around the world. (This included special proteins that could make genes fluoresce for easy observation.) Addgene treated vectors and fluorescent proteins like open-source code in software engineering, as resources that could be easily accessed for the good of all.

One of the first projects to use the new class of gene technology to develop a potential treatment for human disease was a partnership forged by Columbia University Medical Center and the University of Iowa. They used CRISPR-Cas9 and stem cells to create a potential treatment for one of the main causes of vision loss in adults, a heritable condition called retinitis pigmentosa. The early lab work was promising. Similarly, using CRISPR-Cas9 to fix genes has been tested in animal and shown to work in other disease settings caused by genetic abnormalities like muscular dystrophy. CRISPR-Cas9 can be used to both cut genes to make corrections in abnormal genes and to cut genes to damage them. Some genes are abnormal and cause problems like the oncogenes discussed earlier. Other genes are used for nefarious purposes by infections as is the case with HIV. That virus depends on a gene product that does not seem to be essential for humans. Since correcting a gene is much harder and much less efficient than cutting a gene to kill it, some, including a group I participate in, are planning to use CRISPR-Cas9 to render blood stem cell impervious to HIV infection. The idea of using CRISPR-Cas9 to cut and kill abnormal genes driving cancer, oncogenes, is an appealing one, but is not feasible. The problem is in the ability to accomplish that with sufficient efficiency to compromise all the tumor cells. We just don't have the ability to do that and the remaining, uncut tumor cells would rapidly take over.

Still, cancer was the focus of the first clinical trial using CRISPR-Cas9 to be given a green light to proceed in the U.S. In the summer of 2016, the National Institutes of Health approved the use of T cells edited with CRISPR-Cas9 to treat eighteen people with three different kinds of cancer, including melanoma, sarcoma, and multiple myeloma. The technology would be used to add a single powerful gene to help T cells find malignancies. It would also be used to remove genes that could inhibit the cancer-killing process and make the new T cells vulnerable to a chemical counterattack by the cancer. The University of Pennsylvania will run the trial, but the patients will come from around the country. Funding was supplied by the Parker Foundation and the Parker Institute for Cancer Immunotherapy. The hundreds of millions of dollars spent by the two entities came from Sean Parker, a self-taught computer scientist.

Parker created his institute to great fanfare in the spring of 2016 with the announcement of $250 million in grants to fund work at six universities, including Penn. The money represented about 10 percent of his wealth, which he had derived from his work in the tech industry. Parker got his start at age nineteen with a music file-sharing service called Napster, which outraged record company execs because it permitted free copying of music. He started other companies, served as president of Facebook, and was a billionaire by age thirty. Although his initiative was one of the most ambitious, Parker was just one of many tech entrepreneurs who made big investments in charities, research projects, and development to benefit the world's poor. At the time, he explained that his interest began with a concern about allergies (he has food allergies and asthma), but his investigation of immunotherapies soon led him to encouraging immunotherapies for cancer. He imagined his institute as a way to fund promising ideas without burdening scientists with the usual grant processes. He also thought he could maintain support for research in the face of disappointments that would discourage other funders.

In addition to the money from philanthropists like Parker, funding for immunotherapy research came from foundations, the government, and pharmaceutical firms. For example, Novartis, which makes Gleevec, put $20 million into the Penn Center for Advanced Cellular Therapeutics. These types of commercial investments, as well as many that come from foundations, involve profit-sharing arrangements that nonprofits hope will supply future grants, and corporations expect to contribute to their bottom lines. The money pouring into immunotherapy research indicated the wide agreement on its potential, especially in oncology. Add the dynamic potential created by CRISPR-Cas9 and you get such enormous potential that labs around the world raced to try out new ideas.

Governments, investors, and scientists worldwide understand that biotechnology may hold the greatest promise for mankind of any field of science and that for generations to come, treatments based on genetic and molecular interventions could cure a host of deadly and debilitating illnesses. As I write this, I am attending an international meeting of hematologists where remarkable results of gene therapy to correct hemophilia are being presented. The results are truly breathtaking. People who otherwise had lifelong risks of massive bleeding and a dependence on regular infusions of clotting factors appear to become free of both. It is early days, but it looks as if we are witnessing the transformation of this disease and the lives of the individuals affected by it. What this will mean to the families carrying this genetic abnormality is incalculable. Literally generations of uncertainty and suffering may be relieved. That is what biomedical science is doing and doing now.

Jim Allison looked at big advances in the science and compared them with Sputnik, the first-ever man-made satellite that circled Earth in 1957 and set off the space race. That competition to conquer space pitted the United States against the Soviet Union. But as these two countries notched ever-greater achievements in the pursuit of prestige, they also sparked the development of advanced electronics, computers, specialized materials, and many other new technologies. Indeed, the greatest legacy of the space race was not the image of men on the moon but the scientific and engineering excellence that made space missions possible. Combine those achievements with the spirit and management of such complex endeavors and you see a template for the future of research. Except cancer isn't going to be solved by engineers. Biologists work differently and think differently. Though they too stand on the shoulders of giants who worked before them, the progress of discovery is far less linear and step-wise in biology. The fitful stops, turns, and jumps of biology take determined visionaries who can also tolerate a lot more pondering and a lot less calculating.

The iconoclastic Texan is a good example. Allison had pointed out the importance of immune checkpoints in the 1980s, but it took thirty years for things to play out as he envisioned. A bit eccentric, even for a biologist, Jim is a man who pursues his interest with great enthusiasm. For example, he turned his love for the harmonica into a jam session with Willie Nelson, which in turn led to the creation of a blues band called the Checkpoints. All the members are immunologists and oncologists.

In 1996, Jim published a paper in *Science* that reported on the use of a "checkpoint blockade" to release T cells from a go-slow signal sent by a molecule called CTLA-4. Swimming against the academic mainstream, which largely focused cancer treatments on gene mutations, not immunology, Jim continued this work until it produced a drug that could be tested in trials with patients who had reached the end of conventional treatments for melanoma. In a typical year, doctors diagnose roughly seventy-five thousand new cases of melanoma in the United States, and as many as ten thousand Americans die because it has spread from the initial skin site to other organs. Common sites for this kind of metastasis include other portions of tissue beneath the skin, the lymphatic system, liver, lungs, and brain.

The drug was called ipilimumab, and the work of testing it was taken on by Bristol-Myers Squibb. In 2010, they reported good results, with almost a quarter of patients living more than two years, compared with 14 percent of those who didn't get the drug. In all, 540 people got the drug, and continued to demonstrate far superior outcomes compared with standard approaches. This doesn't mean the drug was found to be a magic bullet. More than 60 percent of people who got it suffered significant side effects as their immune systems targeted their own healthy organs. Seven people died from this effect. However, the risks associated with the new drug were no greater than the risks of traditional chemotherapy, and for most people, the side effects were far less troubling. And of course, many patients hoped to be among those for whom ipilimumab worked remarkably well. One man posted a testimonial online about how, six years after starting the drug, doctors could locate no cancer in his body. He rightly declared that the drug "saved my life!"

Success with Allison's discovery set off an avalanche of other efforts to unleash the immune system against cancer. Work in the 1990s on mouse models of autoimmune disease had led to the discovery by a Harvard colleague, Gordon Freeman, of a molecule that could turn down a T cell's ability to get activated. Despite having the proper signal to become active, the presence of this molecule, PD-L1, kept the T cells relatively quiescent, as if they were exhausted. If PD-L1 was out of the picture, the T cells were vigorous. Antibodies against PD-L1 or its receptor, PD-1, have made an enormous impact on patients' lives and are now approved by the FDA for treatment of some lung cancers, kidney cancer, bladder cancer, head and neck cancer, Hodgkin's lymphoma, and others. Some of these were essentially untreatable by standard cancer chemotherapy. The so-called checkpoint inhibitors are a major step forward. Medicines targeting new or recently defined immune checkpoints are entering the clinic with clinical trials numbered in the dozens. It is not hyperbole to say that these immune-based therapies represent a revolution in cancer care. They have their limitations—patients do relapse or not respond, and complications are not trivial—but the number of years of life given to those previously with a death sentence is awe inspiring. And we are still at the beginning of the so-called immune-oncology field. Immune harnessing to fight cancer is here to stay and it came from basic research that initially did not have cancer as its focus.

A far bigger target of research could be found in a family of genes responsible for regulating cell growth. First discovered in rats with a type of sarcoma (hence the term *Ras* for "rat sarcoma"), these genes drive switches that control a host of activities, including the proliferation of cells and their migration around the body. They also switch off these functions. Trouble arises when mutations disrupt their normally well-regulated activity. About 30 percent of *all* cancers involve Ras mutations, which transform them into oncogenes, which means they cause cancer, particularly pancreatic, lung, colon, and thyroid. Within the Ras family, three main ones—KRas, HRas, and NRas—are the main drivers of cancer.

Ras oncogenes were deemed so significant that the National Cancer Institute funded an independent Ras initiative in 2013, which was intended to end decades of failed efforts to find ways to block Ras gene functions. Many researchers came to believe these oncogenes are undruggable, meaning they couldn't be treated. They have chemical structures that are just not amenable to having a drug dock into it and turn off its function in a stable manner. Unwilling to accept defeat, immunology experts redoubled their efforts on the three big Ras oncogenes. In Bethesda, Maryland, Steven Rosenberg focused on mutations in KRas (named for discoverer W. H. Kirsten), which is implicated in lung, colon, and pancreatic cancers. Indeed, doctors have noticed that these three types of cancer seem to occur in the same patients.

Rosenberg had long studied cancer-fighting immune cells, including T cells, and had been using immunotherapy to treat melanoma since 2002. He developed processes that would allow him to isolate the immune cells that were found in a person's tumor. Reasoning that the immune cells were attracted to the tumor in a failed attempt to kill it, he harvested those cells, grew more of them in a lab, and then returned them to the body where they could pursue their mission. Rosenberg saw long-term remissions in as many as a quarter of his patients. Although melanoma is a serious problem, the KRas cancers affect far more people and an immune-based treatment for them would bring a new era in oncology. Rosenberg began a trial with a small number of people who had been tested to determine that their tumors involved KRas mutation and had reached the end of the line with standard care.

After first rejecting her application in late 2014, Rosenberg enrolled a patient named Celine Ryan in their trial in March 2015. The mother of five children, then forty-nine-year-old Ryan had been treated for colon cancer with all the standard treatments—chemotherapy, surgery, radiation—only to learn she had malignancies in her lungs. Her eligibility for Rosenberg's protocol depended on whether her body was producing the kinds of cells that could defeat her cancer, if only there were enough of them. This would require surgery to remove three of her tumors, which were studied to determine that they did contain the right antitumor immune cells. Rosenberg's group also studied the cancer to discover the cells that produced the right antigens, which are chemicals that attract immune cells.

Having identified both the right immune cells and the antigen-producing cells that would help them go after the cancer, Rosenberg's team created supportive lab environments where the cells could live and multiply. Eventually they cultivated one hundred billion cells, most of which were T cells equipped to go after Celine Ryan's cancer. She underwent surgery to remove some of her tumors, and chemotherapy, which destroyed most of her existing immune cells and made way for the new ones, which were then infused into her bloodstream. All seven of the tumors that remained in Ryan's lungs shrank over the months following the infusion, with six disappearing entirely. The last one seemed to be affected like all the others, shrinking after treatment, but then it stabilized and began to grow. Surgeons removed the part of a lung where it resided, and Celine Ryan was given hope for a substantially longer life.

Rosenberg's trial provided such an encouraging result that Carl June hailed it in an editorial that was published in the same issue of *The New England Journal of Medicine* that included news of the success against KRas. It was titled "Drugging the Undruggable Ras—Immunotherapy to the Rescue?" The question mark at the end of the title pointed to the fact that, as with most trials, Rosenberg's treatment of Celine Ryan raised at least as many questions as it answered. The main ones involved Ryan's own special genetic makeup, which predisposed her to treatment success, and the fact that one of her tumors developed the ability to resist the attack of the T cells.

When the cancer was removed, along with surrounding lung tissue, study showed that its cells no longer presented the antigen that drew the attention of the immune cells. They were, it seems, new, invisible mutants and free to multiply unseen and unmolested. When asked to comment on this development, Drew Pardoll, an immunologist at Johns Hopkins, said, "The tumor always seems to come up with a workaround." Nevertheless, he and just about everyone else in cancer immunology considered Rosenberg's use of immunotherapy against a cancer based on a mutant Ras gene a huge step forward.

Rosenberg's work also represented further support for the idea that cells themselves could be therapy. In the blood field, that is certainly not a new concept as the first transfusions were done centuries ago. Blood cell infusions have been historically viewed as supporting a depleted blood system. An extension of that thinking is blood stem cell transplant, where the cells were repleting stem cells eliminated by therapy. The engineering of immune cells or stem cells represented an important departure from the mere replacement concept. Blood or immune cells could be the definitive treatment itself. They could essentially be a drug.

Drugs are only used after it is understood where they go in the body and how long they last. That has been extremely difficult to do for cells. To see if we could learn more about how transplanted blood stem cells behaved we teamed up with a photon physicist who is a colleague within the Harvard Stem Cell Institute.

An extremely inventive scientist, Charles Lin has built custom instruments that use lasers to peer into tissues at the cellular level. Since we still had many unanswered questions about how bone marrow cells act and interact, we worked with him to use a phosphorescent tag derived from glowing jellyfish to paint bone marrow stem cells taken from mice. Here it helps to know a bit of physiology. Like all humans, adult mice produce blood stem cells in the bone marrow of the vertebrae, sternum, and pelvis. These structures are a little bit hard to penetrate with Lin's lasers, but the skull, which is shielded only by a thin layer of skin, also produces these marrow stem cells.

Lots of marrow transplant research is done with mice, so it was a matter of routine for Lin, and us as his collaborators, to perform one with cells tagged to be seen by Lin's lasers. He then trained them on the right spot, and we saw, in real time, where the transplant took up residence in the marrow. What we saw were stem cells that were red in color migrating to microvessels in the bone marrow where they were attracted by a certain protein. I know this may sound a little abstract, but in fact, it's the kind of thing that gets hematologists quite revved up. Finally, we were able to see at the level of individual cells the events that previously were just imagined as the likely events in a stem cell transplant. We were even more excited when we went back, seventy days later, and saw that those cells had divided. They were functioning as if they always lived there and, in fact, this defined on a functional level a home or "niche" for blood stem cells in a transplant. Why did we care? Because it meant that we could better understand a process that we knew was lifesaving. If we could understand it better, we could design rational ways to try and make it work better, be more effective for patients.

Photon physics is hardly the only unexpected scientific specialty aiding our stem cell and oncology research. Another key collaboration we're exploiting involves a lab group devoted to informatics, which means tracking and analyzing so-called big data. In broad terms, big data refers to huge blocks of information that can be analyzed by various programs to detect patterns or associations. Historically, the human brain housed the best system for managing multiple inputs, but over time, the brain's limitations became quite evident. The specialization seen in science and medicine during the eighteenth and nineteenth centuries can be seen as signs that the volume of information being produced by research was outstripping our capacity to absorb it and make sense of it. This specialization increased steadily to the point where, by the 1970s, physicians routinely complained of not being able to keep up with journal articles even if they practiced in a limited subspecialty. Bad as this problem was for clinical practitioners, who worried about providing the best care, it may have been worse for researchers, who could labor in one corner of science for many years and lose touch with the context of the problems they sought to solve.

Repeated experience with ideas that seemed promising in a lab dish, or a mouse, or a few patients but failed to become reliable therapies for human beings teaches us that biology is incredibly complex. The chemical processes that produce life in all its forms, including mutated forms, depend not only on molecular interactions but on events within organ systems and the body as a whole. Add outside forces such as viruses and radiation and the role that chance can play in billions of daily cellular events, and the whole thing can seem beyond any individual's ability to comprehend. This is why we often consult with colleagues who process the data streaming to us from all over the world and others who apply mathematics to cancer science on the theory that we do have the computing power to investigate problems with algorithms.

At a lab affiliated with Harvard and the Dana-Farber Cancer Institute, a group led by computational biologist Franziska Michor studies cancer and cancer treatments, trying to figure out how the disease develops, often in a way that seems to echo evolution, and how it continues to evolve in response to treatment. Michor is working on many of the cancers that first interested me, including leukemia, and hopes to define just how malignancies evolve to become resistant to treatment. She is also determining schedules and dosing, for both chemotherapy and radiation, that would provide the maximum benefit without prompting resistance.

Michor, who came to the United States from Austria, first became interested in her area of science when she read a paper written by Peter Nowell, who codiscovered the Philadelphia chromosome. In what Nowell described as a kind of "thought experiment," Nowell speculated that multiple mutations must take place before cancer gains a toehold in the body. "Over time more and more mutations accumulate," notes Michor, "and eventually the tumor is expressed." Nowell's paper also predicted personalized cancer treatments of the sort devised by Steven Rosenberg with his patients' own immune cells.

Work that followed Nowell's paper turned it from a hypothesis into a theory that has been supported time and again. This science confirmed that one of the tradeoffs made by animals that become multicellular in order to occupy certain environmental niches— the giraffe's long neck is an example—is that as cells differentiate into many different types performing many different functions, the chance that something will go wrong increases. Oftentimes, evolution confers positive traits. Elephants, for example, have forty copies of the famous p53 gene, which confers protection from cancer. Humans generally have two copies. Elephants almost never develop malignancies.

Another good-luck story of evolution and cancer involves the sharp-toothed marsupial known as the Tasmanian devil, which suffered a catastrophic epidemic of cancer, seemingly spread by bites that transmitted cancer cells, that threatened it with extinction. Devils have a short natural life span—five years on average—and scientists who studied the die-off noted rapid evolution in the animal's genome, with cancer resistance increasing. The helpful genes were always present in some individuals, but in six generations, they became more common, and the population loss, which had passed 70 percent, appeared to level off. As of early 2017, it looked like the poor little devils would make it.

Viewed as a whole, the human immune system could be recognized as a significant genetic response to threats from disease, including cancer. It is largely dependent on stem cells that are kept in safe corners of the body where they do their work. Our blood stem cells, for example, migrate from the liver of the fetus to a "niche" composed of two sections inside the bone. This niche is found mainly in the hollow places of flat bones—hips, skull, ribs, shoulder blades, and the like—where the bone marrow is enriched by blood vessels and capillaries. Thanks to evolution, every animal other than fish that possesses blood and a skeleton, from birds to primates, relies on this type of system. Bone, which is made of crystallized calcium and other minerals as well as fibrous collagen, is a fortress that makes the niche less vulnerable than the liver when it comes to genetic disruption from radiation and other insults.

NINE

FROM GORY TO GLORY

To be involved in medical research, a seat belt is sometimes required. The flow of new information coming in from closely allied and distant fields creates its own turbulence. But perhaps the most jarring is the forward-moving research edge colliding with the black hole of our ignorance. Sometimes that collision comes when a great discovery of a prior age is seen through the lens of today.

For example, sometimes a person's immune system will stray beyond its boundaries and start attacking the body's own cells. This so-called autoimmunity is what causes type 1 diabetes, multiple sclerosis, and a host of other ailments, including blood diseases. Blood stem cells, red cells, or platelets needed for blood clotting are not uncommon targets. The result can be life threatening. so for ages doctors have sought ways to treat these conditions. A century ago, it was found that infusing animal serum worked. It could raise the blood counts. I teach a course to Harvard freshman called "Blood: From Gory to Glory." It is about how we constantly re-know things we think we already understand. Blood has been known as the stuff of life since historic time began and yet we constantly are learning new things about it, use old principles to make it better and sometimes scratch our heads at how unbelievably primitive "modern" medical science can be. I took the twelve freshman in my seminar to meet a young woman in the process of getting treatment for her low blood counts. At one of the greatest institutions of medical science in the world, Massachusetts General Hospital, she was getting what could only be considered a primitive therapy: an infusion of horse serum. It worked, but surely we could do better (and, in fact, new approaches have emerged in the intervening three years or so). For the students it was a clear indication of how the forward thinking of one era can seem like magical primitive thinking to another, and how new thinking was constantly needed to improve our condition.

The ancient Greeks opened veins and drained blood from the sick because they thought many illnesses were caused by an imbalance of the "humors," which also include bile and phlegm. Bloodletting remained part of medicine for more than a thousand years. After he suffered a seizure, England's King Charles II was subjected to so much bloodletting by his doctors that he lost one quarter of all his blood. His treatment also involved enemas, emetics, and quinine. Of course he died. The same fate met George Washington, who, when he suffered an extreme throat infection, ordered a servant to open a vein before his doctor arrived to continue the procedure. Belief in this therapy persisted until the second half of the 1800s, when Louis Pasteur and other pioneers of modern medicine began to discredit it.

Lacking the ability to intervene with the body, except to manipulate fluids, physicians turned to bloodletting because it seemed rational in the pseudoscience of the day. The ancient Greeks constructed a logical order of things in nature as comprised of earth, air, fire, or water. That four-part rationality was applied to the seasons of nature and of life and to what gave us life in the four humors: blood, black bile, yellow bile, and phlegm. Each was given significance in our personalities and in our health, particularly by Hippocrates, the great proponent of rationality in medicine whose "Oath" is still recited by doctors receiving their medical degrees today. When health failed, it was regarded as an imbalance in the humors and the response was to purge or bleed. Remnants of this seemingly rational, but highly unscientific reasoning continues today with "cleansing enemas." Physicians commonly used the application of leeches or simple bloodletting well into the twentieth century in part goaded by the imbalance theory, but also because it allowed them to do something dramatic in the face of suffering.

Blood being central to life is something no one could dispute. Old medical practice leveraged that instinctive knowledge and in so doing also indirectly claimed connection to higher powers. Blood is a part of virtually every mythology and every religion, particularly religious ritual. Blood sacrifice was a critical component of ancient Mesoamerican practices as a means to feed the gods so their gift of a good harvest would continue: blood was a kind of restorative fuel. In ancient Middle Eastern traditions, it was often used in sacrifice. The word origin of *sacrifice* is to "make sacred," a way of connecting us to what is holy. In South Asian traditions it represented the fearsome power of the gods, as in the terrifying Hindu goddess, Kali. The ancient Greek myths perhaps synthesized the duality of blood's power to take and to give life in the story of Asclepius, the son of Apollo and a mortal mother. He was taught by the centaur, Chiron, in the healing arts and was said to be given by Athena two vials of blood: one from the right side of the head of Medusa that gave eternal life, and one from the left side that gave instant death. Blood was the basis of both and yet Zeus, angered at the notion that Asclepius could use blood to change the order of things, struck him down with a thunderbolt. No matter what power may appear to be in the hands of healers, it is the fate the gods impose that ultimately wins out.

The duality of blood embodied in the myth of Asclepius is mirrored in the stick he is often depicted as carrying. It is entwined by a snake—a fearful creature, but one that also has great regenerative power; it sheds its skin and creates it anew. That combination of horror and regeneration is associated with blood in a more modern tale, Dracula

The tale of Dracula, first published in 1897 by the Irishman, Bram Stoker, borrows from much older Eastern European tales of vampires. But while Stoker's nocturnal, pale-faced monster might be considered elegant and magnetically appealing, the traditional vampires that inspired him were hideous, ruddy-faced corpses that became animated and pursued their prey day and night.

Experts in myth say that every monster we invent is a reflection of some basic human fear—most often our fear of death—and that in confronting these creatures in stories we gain some mastery over existential realities. In the case of Dracula and other bloodsucking creatures we can also see that on a conscious and even subconscious level blood is our well-being, both physical and psychological. As Dracula takes the blood of innocents, he converts the victims into creatures of evil, building on the fearful notion that blood can create a contagion. Central to the story is that blood rejuvenates Dracula, not just giving him life but making him younger and more vigorous. This is a theme that permeates all the vampire myths and has gruesomely played out in some historic circumstances. The Countess Elizabeth Bathory of Hungary murdered hundreds of young women in the sixteenth century to bathe in their blood so as to retain her youthful looks. Despite the clear madness of such magical thinking, there is some scientific basis to the idea that in the blood there is youth.

Recent animal studies tested whether the changes with age were transferrable by blood. Mice were connected by a skin flap so they exchanged blood over time. Connecting a young mouse to an old one remarkably made the older animal heal better. The blood allowed for rejuvenation, but what in the blood caused this has been difficult to define. A single chemical in the blood may not be sufficient, but candidate molecules are now being tested with some benefit in animals. The fearsome elements of the vampire myth may yet prove to give us hope for healthier aging.

Not long ago, a team led by Harvard geneticist Stephen Elledge announced it had developed a reliable test that would discover, in a single drop of blood, every virus a person had ever contracted. The new technology, which had been tried with patients all over the world, can detect more than one thousand variants of the roughly two hundred species known to infect human beings. In these trials, few people showed evidence of having been stricken with more than a dozen types of viruses, most of which were linked to gastrointestinal illnesses or the common cold. However, signs of other pathogens, like Epstein-Barr, human papillomavirus, or hepatitis, would alert both patients to their increased risk for later disease, including various cancers.

The blood system begins with the marrow, which I consider a kind of foundry where elements are forged into various cell products. The capacity of this foundry is awesome. It depends, in a primary way, on the ten to twenty thousand blood stem cells we each possess. These make about two hundred billion new red cells per day. But as they say in TV infomercials, "Wait, there's more!" In addition to these red blood cells, we also make four hundred billion platelets and about ten billion of the immune system cells called white blood cells. Altogether, this production exceeds the population of stars in the Milky Way, every day.

The activity of the bone marrow is stunning both in its volume but also in its importance to our survival. And all this is accomplished by a part of the anatomy that Aristotle believed was a waste depository and which Hippocrates thought provided nutrients for the bones. Eighteen hundred years would pass before Ernst Neumann squeezed the bones of both rabbits and human beings and discovered—in what was called bone "sap"—red blood cells. Neumann reported his discovery in 1868. In that same year, his colleague Giulio Bizzozero proposed that the marrow produced white blood cells. Bizzozero's theory was correct. He also correctly theorized that the marrow was the site of blood cell destruction. This idea was confirmed in 2017.

In going two for two, Bizzozero's batting average was astounding given the changing fashions of thought over long stretches of time. Most big discoveries are amended and enlarged by later work, and in many cases, the pioneers in one generation become reactionary naysayers in the next. A century after the Europeans discovered the productive capacity of the marrow, and fifty years after Josef Pappenheim proposed there was a blood stem cell, the Canadians Ernest McCulloch and James Till published their experimental evidence on blood stem cells and advanced the ideas that they were the sole creators of the blood and immune system. When a British scientist named Raymond Schofield suggested in 1978 that things were much more complicated than the matter of stem cells birthing offspring, McCulloch reacted with skepticism that veered into antagonism.

As a giant in the field, McCulloch carried the weight of his achievements into the debate, and Schofield felt quite overwhelmed by the controversy that arose. Schofield had recognized that the stem cells were affected by a variety of inputs from what he called the "niche" they occupied and that these inputs determined much of what the bone marrow foundry created. The power of communication, which occurred in the niche, was the big notion that Schofield advanced. A proud and somewhat acerbic man, McCulloch considered Schofield's work not a contribution to his own but an affront. Schofield eventually wearied of the argument and decided to retire from science at age sixty. He bought a farm in an isolated corner of Wales and happily raised sheep and cattle. With time, however, his ideas about the way marrow works gained wide support, and his science inspired a generation of scientists, including me.

In 2008, decades after Schofield retired from what he would call "the science business," I began research for a paper to help mark the fiftieth anniversary of the American Society of Hematology. I was asked to write because my lab had proven Schofield right: we mammals do have stem cell niches. I thought Schofield had been overlooked and should be honored in the record and, if possible, given an award to acknowledge his achievement. Unfortunately, my efforts to track him down went for naught. Then, in 2014, I received an email from him. He reported that he was alive and well and was keeping up with hematology, albeit from a distance. One thing led to another, and I found myself making an appointment to visit him during a planned trip to the U.K. We agreed to meet in the city of Cardiff. Before I left, I bought a small silver Revere-style bowl and had it inscribed for him.

The meeting place Schofield suggested was a cavernous pub called the Prince of Wales, which sat between the Chippy, which was a fish-and-chips place, and a bookmaker's shop called Coral. The Prince of Wales was close to the central station, where Ray arrived by bus from Aberaeron, which was a town of 1,400, most of whom spoke Welsh, located one hundred miles to the north on the Irish Sea. At age eighty-eight, he was a spry, energetic, and talkative fellow. When we settled into our seats, he told me that in a previous incarnation, the pub had been a legitimate theater—Laurence Olivier, Richard Burton, and Rex Harrison had appeared on its stage—and, later, a cinema specializing in X-rated fare. We would laugh quite a bit in the time we spent together.

Schofield's humor suggested the playful, creative spirit that makes for first-rate science.

He also recalled a life story that defied the idea that a straight line is always the best pathway to success. Schofield said he dropped out of school at age sixteen and found work as a technician in a pathology laboratory. Excited by what went on around him, he studied mainly on his own to earn a doctorate. Most of his career was spent at the Paterson Institute for Cancer Research near Manchester, England, which was founded to study the health effects of radiation and ways to protect people or treat them after exposure during an accident or nuclear war. Schofield's more creative methods included using beetles to clean the bones of deceased animals and planting stem cells beneath the membrane that covers the kidney (in animals), where they could be nourished by a blood supply and grow. In another experiment, he used radiation to kill the marrow stem cells in a young mouse and then used some harvested from an old mouse to repopulate the marrow. When the new supply of stem cells functioned normally, he waited for the recipient to age and then repeated the process. The stem cells remained productive as they were moved from mouse to mouse to mouse, which showed the power of these special cells.

Although some of his techniques were rudimentary, Ray built a truly sophisticated understanding of how the blood and immune systems develop and function. He also rebelled against the reductionist thinking that many scientists are trained to follow. Around the world, many students of science and medicine are encouraged to embrace a commonsense philosophy referred to as Occam's razor. Occam was a fourteenth-century thinker who favored an intense kind of reasoning that shaved away at superfluous factors to produce the simplest answer to a question. It was based on the Aristotelian notion that favored theories with the fewest variables over those that suggested intricate processes—and even divine intervention—as answers to scientific questions.

In a general sense, the razor worked. The wind is a far better response to the question, "How did those clouds get here?" than an answer that invokes the gods and the labor of spouting whales. However, many problems, especially in biology, defy such a reductionist approach and require, instead, the inclination to delight in complexity. The grandeur of biology can be seen by comparing the ordinary butterfly to the most complex robots fashioned by human hands and minds. The robots can perform tasks in specified environments but eventually require human interventions for refueling and maintenance. Butterflies emerge from caterpillars, respond to myriad changes in the environment, feed themselves, and even reproduce

without any help at all. Consider the roach, and the success of vastly
complicated organisms like human beings, and it's plain to see that
Occam's razor doesn't always cut it.

One sure way to get around reductionism involves learning to
take some delight in discovering a new facet of a problem and loving the way that the answer to one question may lead you to five
more. Ray possessed this kind of enthusiasm, and it didn't seem
much diminished, even though so many years had passed since his
retirement. He had continued to read avidly in both scientific journals and the popular press, and he had stored up plenty of theories
and ideas for experiments. When he told me about his life in science, I could hear that his spirit had been as important to his success as his intellect. On a trip to Moscow, when the Cold War still
raged, he formed relationships with Soviet scientists who suggested
new ways to explore problems. The irony of getting tips from people
working for the regime that posed the atomic threat that inspired
the creation of Ray's lab in the first place was not lost on anyone.

In the end, science, like every other human endeavor, may come
down to relationships that add to individual creativity. It may sound
a bit sentimental in light of the fact that advances depend on devotion to provable fact, but Schofield's example illustrated the place
that friendship and support but also unfair criticism and isolation
can play in the process. In my view, Schofield had been denied the
recognition he deserved. As we finished lunch, I looked in my bag
for the bowl I had brought and presented it to him. Although the
gift didn't carry with it the acclaim of a professional organization or
a prize committee, it acknowledged Ray's true contribution. A tear
came to his eye as he read the inscription, which said, "To him who
gave stem cells a home." Minutes later, we walked to the bus station, and he climbed aboard for the journey back to his village.

Ray stayed in touch via email after our time in Cardiff and offered well-informed observations about where stem cell science and
society seemed headed. In one email, he seemed as enthusiastic as

the most idealistic undergrad as he described his regular efforts to comprehend the ways evolution led, by natural selection, from unicellular organisms to "simple animals and plants, let alone humans." In another, he complained of the "scientific" (his punctuation) information the popular press feeds the public "about the so-called stem cell 'therapists' who seem to think that if they put stem cells" into the body, they cure any illness or injury. As Schofield noted, the world was fairly buzzing with reports on stem cell therapies that supposedly helped people with everything from autism to sagging skin. Hundreds of stem cell clinics had opened across the United States, many of which took advantage of a quirk in the law that allows patients to have their own cells removed from their bodies, processed, and put back in for any purpose at all. (One orthopedic clinic in New Jersey offers to do this to people who respond to their advertisement at a discounted price of $2,000 per joint.) Similar openings in regulations permitted the marketing and sale of stem cell cosmetics and creams, even though there was no evidence that the special ingredients were effective.

The science of blood, including the work done with blood stem cells, continues to evolve. I am especially intrigued by the progress being made toward the goal of understanding how the variety of these cells protects us from disease, including cancer, but also lose some of this capacity over time. The best way to think of this involves imagining a chess board before the start of a game when each player has a full complement of pieces. This is the immune system at the height of its powers, which exists as we enter adulthood. Some of the cells in this array are quite powerful, like the queen, and can meet a great many threats. Others are pawns that can basically carry out a single mission.

As the body engages with various events like the common radiation exposure from the sun, chemicals, or inflammation, certain stem cells break down and stop producing. Like a chess player who gradually loses pieces, the body is left with a lesser variety of stem cells with which it can create responses to nascent cancer or infections. This process, like the endgame of chess and not simply the passage of time, may explain why older people are more susceptible to diseases as disparate as pneumonia and cancer in most of its forms. Interestingly, the total number of stem cells in the body remains relatively constant, but we see a decrease in the variety needed to maintain health. Understanding the system as a sort of community of cells that is more diverse and powerful at some points in life could lead us to therapies that strengthen the system to fight more diseases over a greater portion of the life span.

Understanding the cells that provide us with resilience or susceptibility to disease is one thing; modifying the stem cells we have to protect us is another. Both are themes of active, early-stage research. What is closer to application is the use of cells to rebuild damaged tissues. Indeed, some stem cell approaches are moving forward on rebuilding whole organs. The idea of doing so immediately comes to mind simply by looking under a microscope at stem cells that have human heart muscle cells, grown in a laboratory, beating with telltale rhythm. Experiments generating cardiac cells mainly use induced pluripotent stem cells (iPSCs), of the sort developed by Shinya Yamanaka from skin cells. They can be encouraged to form cardiac cells and will start beating. They can then be taken from the culture plate and used to populate a heart "scaffold." The scaffold is derived from an animal heart where the cells of the heart have been dissolved by detergents. What remains is a fine web mesh of proteins exactly outlining the fine structures within the heart and its blood vessels. This 3-D matrix appears to convey important information as the cells that are applied organize and take on the features of a mature heart.

The excitement that attended stem cell work that created human heart muscle was informed by the prevalence of heart disease and the limits of our current therapies. Heart failure, as a group of conditions is generally known, can be treated partially with lifestyle

changes, drugs, implantable devices, surgeries, and transplanted organs. At any given time, more than four thousand Americans are on
waiting lists for heart transplants, but in most years, fewer than
twenty-five hundred procedures are performed due to the small
number of healthy hearts made available when people die. Overall,
about nine people waiting for organ transplants die every day. If labs
could take skin cells from individuals, turn them into iPSCs, and
then create usable organ cells, they might be used to treat a wide
number of diseases.

The ultimate dream of scientists who addressed the problem of
organ failure involved manufacturing entire genetically specific
hearts, kidneys, lungs, and other organs that would spare many
patients the wait on the transplant list. In 2016, a thoracic surgeon,
Harald Ott, reported on a project that involved using human hearts
that were not suitable for transplant to create scaffolds. His team created scaffolds out of the left ventricles and then seeded them with five
hundred million reprogrammed human skin cells. They placed individual scaffolds in chambers, where they were bathed in nutrients
that allowed the cells to develop. The chambers, called automatic bioreactors, also stimulated the scaffolds and cells with intermittent pressure to simulate the functioning of a real heart. Fourteen days later,
they used an electrical current to stimulate the cells, which started to
beat like mature tissue. Imagine the team's excitement as they saw the
organs that they had created and suspended in the bioreactors flexing.

Photos of the partial heart, suspended in the clear plastic bioreactor
and illuminated by bright lights, look like nothing less than a small
human heart. Construction of a full-size, functional heart and testing its durable function will take years and overcoming engineering
and biologic problems. However, Ott's success has made it much
easier to imagine the leap from lab to patient. Ott's lab, which was
allied with both the Harvard Stem Cell Institute and the Center for

Regenerative medicine at Massachusetts General Hospital, was also working on creating lungs, kidneys, and tracheas. In a step that could be regarded as a halfway point in the effort to produce transplantable organs, Ott and others produced three-dimensional representations of organs—they are called organoids—that mimic many functions of organs as varied as the tongue and the thymus. Scientists in the Netherlands have used organoids grown from people with cystic fibrosis to test how their bodies might respond to certain drugs. The process eliminated the time, expense, and discomfort of trying medications as therapies and waiting to see if they worked.

Other stem cell projects did not require constructing either organoids or organs built on scaffolds. In 2014, Harvard Stem Cell Institute cofounder and my close friend, Doug Melton, reported that he had used stem cells to create pancreatic cells—called beta cells—that could produce insulin. He transplanted these functioning cells into diabetic mice where they cured the disease. Melton and his group were able to produce these cells in the millions, which would be required if they were to be used as a treatment.

In nature, beta cells function with exquisite perfection, maintaining insulin levels in a way that is impossible to match with blood monitoring and injections. However, the early animal tests determined that the implanted cells stopped functioning because the immune system identifies the implants as unwanted invaders and eventually destroy them. This action, a mistaken immune response that degrades normal insulin production, is the cause of type 1 diabetes, which is usually diagnosed in children and young adults.

One creative workaround for the immune response problem called for encapsulating new cells in a substance that would protect them from immune system attacks while letting in key cell nutrients and letting out the insulin that the beta cells produce. Melton's team worked with a bioengineering group led by Robert Langer of the Massachusetts Institute of Technology to test nearly eight hundred substances. They discovered one that seemed to act as a cloak of invisibility for the cells, which meant the immune system wouldn't attack them. Beta cells were packed into little spheres of this gelatin and the package was tested in animals. It worked for six months. Melton thought the system could be tweaked to last a year or longer. If the problems of cell production and packaging are solved, it is possible to imagine a time when people with diabetes will get cells to replace the continual testing and insulin injections used by millions of people.

The Melton lab and others are also looking at type 2 diabetes, which is linked to obesity and marked by a breakdown in the body's ability to use insulin. A huge advance was made in this area of science when iPSCs were induced to turn into human brown fat cells. Brown fat, unlike regular white fat cells, burn energy rather than store it. They could lead to people getting thinner and more in metabolic balance.

The other advantage of iPSCs is that they offer human cell models of disease rather than depending on mice or cancer cell lines that have been passed in culture for years the way Henrietta Lacks's (HeLa) cells are. Too often a treatment that helps a diseased mouse does nothing for human beings. Some of these disappointments may be avoided by having cells from individuals with the disease providing iPSC that can then be made into the cells that participate in the disease. Neurological diseases can be extremely complex, but some of them have particular cells that appear to be central to the process. Parkinson's disease and amyotrophic lateral sclerosis (ALS) represent two such diseases and are a point of focus for many laboratories using stem cells. Replacing the damaged cells with those grown from iPSCs is a dream that will at least be tested as laboratories in New York ramp up to do just that. Other options for the use of the cells is to test how they behave compared with cells from people without the disease and to try and identify medicines that may improve their behavior. It sounds like fishing and it is, but at least it's fishing for a drug using the right hook (human cells) and bait (abnormal function).

Brain cells for modeling or treating disease using iPSCs is promising and paralleled by developments in studying brain stem cells in the brain itself. The very idea that humans possess brain stem cells was rarely even considered prior to the late 1980s. Back then scientists knew that neural networks developed early in life and believed that that once they were established no new cells were created. In 1989, a neuroscientist named Sally Temple reported the discovery of stem cells in mouse brains. Next came the discovery of similar cells in the human brain. Out of this early work grew a new understanding of the brain and nervous system as dynamic and, perhaps, capable of self-repair.

For generations, physicians have noted that people who suffer in injury that causes partial paralysis may recover some function as inflammation recedes, but rarely regain all that was lost. This observation was in keeping with the long-standing belief that neurons were fixed in number and function beyond adolescence. Based on observing behaviors, though, the famed nineteenth-century psychologist William James argued that the brain was more than a machine which, once built, never changes. Evidence of a growth-and-repair process called neuroplasticity accumulated as experiments showed that the brain could adapt to injuries or deficits. One of the most remarkable reports on this process was published by neuroscientist Paul Bach-y-Rita in 1969. Bach-y-Rita, whose work was inspired by his father, who had suffered a stroke, designed a machine that used a scanning camera and that sent signals to tiny vibrating devices attached to a chair. Blind subjects who trained with the machine developed the ability to decipher words and recognize pictures as if they were viewing them. The experiment suggested that the adult brain could develop a new network.

Proof of neuroplasticity poured out of laboratories beginning in the 1990s. Some of the most persuasive work used imaging technology to document changes in the brains of medical students engaged in what experimenters called "extensive learning." These events reflect dynamism that is likely due to the forming and re-modeling of connections between neurons. The cells do have an arbor of cell extensions that connect over long distances with other neurons' extensions, forming a network. The network changes but that does not necessarily mean the cell numbers change. Just because we have stem cells in the brain does not mean that they are active in making new cells in adults. But it is now clear that we can, in fact, make new neurons. It was discovered by a brilliant use of information derived from military events. Aboveground testing of nuclear weapons in Russia created clouds of radioactive carbon that wafted over northern Europe. Jonas Frisén, a neurologist and stem cell biologist in Sweden, realized that people born when the cloud was around would have levels of radioactive carbon far higher than people born before or after. If the carbon was used to make the molecules in cells, then measuring the amount of radioactive carbon in cells would determine if the cell were made when the person was being born or later. If the cells had less carbon they would likely be descendants of the original cells. Frisén measured the carbon in human brains. Most of the neurons all had the same amount and were like the model predicted. But some in places predicted by the model, did not. They had less and suggested that we do have brain stem cells that make some new brain cells. Now the issue is how to get them to make more, and particularly to make more when people need them after a brain injury. One thing that appears to encourage the formation of new neurons is exercise. Whether medicines can be found that do the same is an ongoing quest.

Making more brain cells of particular types is an important goal, but for them to function properly their connections to other neurons is key. It is the web of interactions that allows the processing of information we call thinking. It is also the maintenance of connections that is critical for memory. Enhancing those interactions with stem cells is not something we can currently imagine doing even though few health problems evoke more fear and anxiety than

Alzheimer's and other forms of dementia. The experience, which includes memory loss, cognitive decline, personality changes, and physical symptoms, can be devastating to people with these diseases who feel as if they are literally fading out of their own lives. Family and friends bear a similar burden. For every one person with Alzheimer's, roughly three people are involved in unpaid caregiving, which is both physically and emotionally demanding. The cost associated with the medical services needed by people with dementia exceeds $230 billion annually. Increases in life span, primarily due to improved health care, have contributed to a rapid increase in the number of people living with this disease. At the current rate of diagnosis the number of Americans with Alzheimer's will grow from about five million today to fourteen million in 2050. The call to action is undeniable, but this aspect of aging is not going to yield to a cell replacement the way Parkinson's might.

Loss of cell function that we associate with aging was generally thought as inevitable. But the studies connecting the circulation of young and old animals suggest that there might be something in young blood that can change that inevitability. Also, it is now clear from studies we and others have done that there are genes that cause at least some of what we call aging. Inhibiting those genes improves how cells and the tissues they inhabit perform with age. Why we have genes destined to compromise our function seems to defy what evolution should accomplish. But some of these genes keep us from getting cancer. Thus, evolution probably chose wisely. However, it does suggest that deterioration with aging is not a fixed attribute. It also may allow us to think about aging and longevity as different. Aging is the decline of function, but longevity is determined by collapse of the entire system. The maximum possible human life span is estimated to be about one hundred and twenty-five, but only extremely rare people will live beyond one hundred and fifteen. Barring an unexpected breakthrough, science and medicine are more concerned about providing healthier aging than adding signifi-

cantly more years at the end of life. Indeed, many of us share concerns about the desirability of adding decades onto the life span.
Would delayed mortality cause us to regard life as less precious, since
we would possess more of it? What about the impact of life extension
on the natural environment and human communities? If the old stop
making way for the young, will we exhaust the Earth's carrying
capacity?

Political scientist Francis Fukuyama, who once declared prema-
turely the "end of history," gazes upon the science of longevity and
sees big problems. Fukuyama points out that ultra-longevity would
be so expensive that only the wealthiest or most powerful people
could afford it. A dictator could purchase extensions on his reign.
With this outcome in mind, he says that "extending the average
human life span is a great example of something that is individually
desirable by almost everyone but collectively not a good thing." I
think he is right.

The leading edge of the science devoted to maximizing healthy
aging, regenerative medicine deals with the challenges of translating
discoveries in stem cells, bioengineering, genetics, and other disciplines into therapeutic interventions. More progress has been made
in regenerative medicine than most laypeople recognize. Some of the
big advances involve technologies beyond biology. Robotics labs are
already producing light, silent, battery-powered exoskeletons and
joints that allow paraplegics to walk. (More modest devices restore
movement to a single joint.) Even more dramatic than the exoskeletons are the technologies enabling paralyzed people with a condition called complete locked-in syndrome (CLIS) to communicate.

Although it can be caused in several different ways, CLIS is
tragically common in cases of advanced amyotrophic lateral sclerosis. In this condition, people are even unable to blink their eyes in response to questions. For decades, scientists have tried to help patients
communicate via electroencephalograph machines, which measure
brain activity. When brain waves were studied, these experiments

never produced "yes" or "no" replies above the rate of chance. In 2016 scientists in Switzerland worked with four CLIS patients who were connected to sensors that detected the blood flow that corresponds with neural activity. Accurate answers to questions such as "Is your husband's name Joachim?" exceeded the chance-response rate.

CLIS is a terrifying condition to observe and it is easy to assume that it produces despair in people who live in its confinement. However, the lead scientists in the Swiss-based study told the press that replies from study subjects showed they often existed in a positive state of mind. "What we observed was, as long as they received satisfactory care at home, they found their quality of life acceptable," said Niels Birbaumer. "It is for this reason, if we could make this technique widely clinically available, it would have a huge impact on the day-to-day life of people with complete locked-in syndrome."

Birbaumer's work is just one example of efforts to bridge the mind-machine connection. Much of it is inspired by trying to relieve the suffering of those with brain disorders, but it has a more fantastical side. Some in the world of high technology envision that machine learning, done now in ways that are affecting our lives and will replace many current human jobs, has the capacity to mimic human thought. In its most extreme, some think it can recreate consciousness sufficiently so that we could essentially "download" our brains. Ebay cofounder Peter Thiel and Oracle's Larry Ellison seek to create what's called "life extension" using computers.

Ellison, who has said "death makes me angry" and "death has never made any sense to me," has put hundreds of millions of dollars into research on how we might forestall the end of life. This now-ended program was a superb way to gather scientists and fund their best ideas on overcoming age's effects. I was fortunate to be one of those, though I confess my ability to significantly improve aging is yet to be realized.

The work of others is impressive in both connecting computer technology to humans and in using manufacturing technology and applying it to biology. On the computer side, there is increasingly common news about hardware allowing the brain to direct action even when normal nerve connections have failed. Brain control of artificial limbs has been fashioned to operate in ways that seem quite human. A prosthetic hand can pick up a sheet of paper without crumpling it. A software driven leg takes a steady step.

In cell biology the progress is even more impressive. Functioning, laboratory-produced bladders have been placed successfully in people with congenital defects. Eye surgeons in Japan have found some success in repairing damaged human retinas with stem cells coaxed to become the tissue that supports sensory neurons. Cartilage made from samples taken from human trial subjects has been used to repair knees. New tissue and organ "printing" technology has been used to assemble living cells into bone, muscle, and even an artificial ear. When a printed muscle was implanted in a mouse, blood vessels and nerves engaged it to keep it alive. The machines used to create these tissues are similar to the 3-D printers that have developed to make objects out of metal, plastics, and other materials. Although the software required to run them is complex, the hardware is not. One creative scientist at the Scripps Clinic in La Jolla, California made his own machine out of an old ink-jet printer and managed to use it to manufacture animal tissue.

Engineered organs represent just one possibility for renewing the body. Another can be glimpsed in the animal world, where zebrafish regrow lost tails and starfish create new limbs. Human beings can regenerate liver tissue, blood, and skin, but our bodies do not reactivate the programs by which stem cells make new tissues to nearly the same level that zebrafish and starfish accomplish routinely. Why do humans lack this ability? One reason may be that we are better engineered to repair, not replace. We scar. At Harvard, my colleague Leonard Zon and others have rooms filled with rows of fish tanks that are populated with zebrafish. The quest is to study how zebrafish can remake a damaged heart or kidney while we cannot. These fish have now gone from good tools to the study the genetics of how repair is governed, to testing for drugs that might improve regeneration. Zon may not discover ways for humans to regenerate lost fingers, but he has used the fish to discover a drug that increases blood stem cell regeneration and is being tested in blood stem cell transplantation.

Sometimes the promise of regenerative medicine can make it seem like human beings will soon be treated like machines—motor vehicles come to mind—and that the future of care will involve removing worn-out parts and installing new ones. The analogy is a limited one, but it's not completely inaccurate. We have long been replacing worn-out parts with better one with transplants. If bioengineering frees us from the constraints of using organs taken from the deceased and permits the production of custom ones, we should embrace the technology. And I would like to take the machine analogy one step further. It is increasingly apparent that we all accumulate genetically abnormal blood stem cells over time. It is also apparent that this imposes increased risk of heart disease and death. Many diseases once thought to be those of a specific organ now implicate the blood. Therefore, I can imagine a future when commonplace periodic replenishments of blood stem cells may in an effort to prevent deterioration. Perhaps it will allow our bodies to function better longer and suffer fewer breakdowns. Think of it as an oil change.

This big news came from a five-year, $30-million endeavor called Blueprint, which engaged researchers at forty-two European universities and sought to discover how genetic changes in bone marrow cells affect the blood cells that they produce. The target of interest here was what is called the epigenome, which is comprised of all the chemicals that turn genes on and off. The epigenome helps cells differentiate into different tissues and then helps drive their activity. Heredity determines much of the epigenome, but it can also be affected by environmental influences like diet and exposure to chemicals. The epigenome may also be changed by infection and even stress. This process, which once would have been regarded as an impossibility by many scientists, gives support to the notion of a connection between our experience of life and our physical state. Blueprint drew on the records of 170,000 people and identified thousands of epigenetic changes that altered the characteristics of blood cells. This data was then compared with health records.

For more than a decade a small study in Canada has tested immune system restoration via bone marrow stem cell transplant as a treatment for MS. About 70 percent of the twenty-four enrolled patients, who were suffering extreme symptoms when they underwent transplantation, showed marked improvement in their symptoms. Forty percent experienced either increased muscle strength, improved vision, or better balance. Some have had no progression in this otherwise progressive disease for years. The greatest recovery saw one woman go from retirement at a nursing home to a fully active life, including downhill skiing. Brain scans showed that inflammatory processes had been halted, and the rate of brain atrophy was slowed to the normal range.

Bone marrow transplant is currently a high-risk procedure. One of the patients in the Canadian study died from complications. For this reason, it has not become a standard of care for people with MS. However, the therapeutic benefits seen in the trial are almost impossible to deny, and the results illuminate where new science could change lives. My lab has tried to take the specificity of antibodies to create an approach to transplantation that reduces the "collateral damage" seen with current methods. We have shown that it is extraordinarily effective with little toxicity in animals. We tested it in animals with sickle cell anemia. If we could reproduce the same results in humans with that disease, it could dramatically change the outlook for those who have that disease. We also have developed a method for rapidly getting stem cells from the bone marrow into the blood, where they can be collected in the blood bank. That could make being a stem cell donor much simpler and, we think, safer. It also yields stem cells that seem to be overachievers. These highly effective stem cells would be ideal for doing gene therapy or gene-editing manipulations. My lab could never scale these up to test and develop them as medicines. We are a discovery shop. To do so, we have had to team with inspired venture capitalists to create a company, Magenta Therapeutics, that is rapidly moving these forward toward clinical testing. One of my greatest joys is that it is doing so under the leadership of a former postdoctoral fellow from my lab, Jason Gardner. Jason and I worked together over twenty years ago and I have long admired his passionate commitment and energetic approach to move things forward for patients. Importantly, he also gives complete confidence in his moral instincts. He has created a company culture that reflects values we share, focus on patients, partners with doctors taking care of them, and builds platforms of excellent science that are a foundation for therapies. Together we hope Magenta will transform stem cell transplant to make it so safe, so well tolerated that the oil change concept may become a reality, and the use of gene therapy for blood disorders will become commonplace.

Having lab work move from discovery to application is the dream for virtually all the scientists with whom I work. I have the good fortune of other recent work moving in that direction. It involves a lengthy project in which we decided to test whether our understanding of normal stem cell biology could give us novel insight into cancer. One of the young geniuses who came to train in my lab came up with the method to do just that. David Sykes is a physician-scientist in the group who reasoned that leukemic cells likely fail to shut off genes that must turn off for a stem cell to move through the steps of maturation necessary to make a functioning blood cell. He found such a gene and created a system that allowed us to test hundreds of thousands of chemicals to find any that might overcome the blockade in differentiation that cancer imposes. He found just a handful and then discovered that most of them targeted the same unexpected enzyme (an enzyme is a protein that modifies its neighbors and so is usually involved in turning things on or off in cells). That enzyme is one previously targeted by a drug company for other indications. It was safe but wasn't active as tested so it was abandoned. We wanted to resurrect it so we could quickly get it to people to see if we could improve their leukemia. We had strong motivation because a rare subset of myeloid leukemias (AML), in which drugs could be used to overcome a differentiation blockade, had shown remarkable results. This type of leukemia (acute promyelocytic leukemia) was the worst form to get and I recall taking care of patients who died miserable deaths from this rapidly lethal disease when I was in training. It didn't respond to standard cancer drugs that are basically cell poisons. When drugs were found that induced differentiation (one was an acne drug), it flipped the situation entirely and now 98 percent of patients are cured without ever receiving a standard cancer chemotherapy drug. We wanted to do the same for the rest of the leukemias and thought we might have identified a drug that could do it. Safe enough for acne, strong enough for leukemia was our goal.

When doing research, partners are needed because the path is long and the resources needed are enormous. We eventually teamed up with colleagues at the Broad Institute and with Bayer Pharmaceuticals. We had all agreed that our greatest goal was to find something that could help people with leukemia. We soon learned that meant different things to different parties. If we took the old drug and revitalized it, it would be faster to patients, but less lucrative since the patent was expired. David and I were confident that we could get the drug, and we did all we could to convince our partners that we could do this together and find a creative business model so that all could be rewarded. We just did not think it right to waste time waiting for new, previously untested drugs when we could re-employ an old, well-understood and well-tolerated one. People would die in the interim. For over eighteen months, we repeatedly made our case and were met with silence or worse, even by our academic colleagues. We parted ways. Patients first, as long as money really came first, was not the way we wanted to live. Fortunately, we found some inspired funders and a passionate CEO and are making the drug and finalizing the clinical study as I write. Also, the paper announcing our findings also inspired four other companies to move forward and we hope that at least one will find the right medicine to flip the outcome for patients with leukemia. That is the dream and all that went into it will fade away if it can be realized. If so, we hope it will pave the way for thinking about other cancers in similar ways: as rogues that have gotten stuck in development. Rather than bludgeoning them to death, maybe we can find drugs that encourage their arrested development, allowing them to mature to the point where they no longer invade and destroy, but quietly reside as good neighbors.

As of 2017, it seems clear that we are advancing cell biology at a pace that will dramatically improve our approaches to malignancies and diseases that have long defied science and medicine. The changes are happening now. There were twenty-five new drugs in 2015 in my field and twenty this year. I have finally hung up my stethoscope because of it. I seemed to always be catching up on new medicines to simply keep up. The residents and medical students I taught needed to know vast amounts of information on these emerging therapies and when I was on call, I spent hour upon hour poring over journals to make sure I was ready to handle any emergency that might arise. I always knew I had the backup of superb physicians at the MGH. One, David Kuter, who is head of hematology at Mass General, was always available to discuss particularly gnarly cases with me. (I would find is reassuring, were I a patient, to know that doctors do this.) But, I felt a little like the ballplayer who has reached the end of his athletic career and has begun to fear that he's not carrying his weight for the team. I called Kuter and said, "I need to talk to you about stepping away from the clinic." He answered, "What took so long?" He knew before I did—or at least before I could accept the fact that I might not be a clinical doctor.

The decision wasn't easy. The greatest rewards in my professional life have involved caring for patients who, every day, reminded me of what truly matters in life. But I didn't want to put patients at risk for selfish reasons. I dropped clinical care, but will never drop being a doctor at heart. I am now a lab director, a department chair, an institute coleader, and a professor. I have to be a manager of diverse teams, but the skills of clinical medicine transfer well.

An attentive bedside manner, which includes confidence and optimism, is essential if I'm to give young scientists the support as well as the structure they require. The same is true for the financial partners that make science possible. Governments and big pharmaceutical firms supply much of the funding to keep America's labs running. However, every year private philanthropies, some of which are managed by individuals and families, also donate tens of billions of dollars to medical science. Many of our consistent donors have personal experiences with cancer, diabetes, and other diseases and they give in order to help spare future generations. Others, who have larger sums to give, are looking for a big breakthrough to give them the sense that they have done something substantial, for all of humanity, with their fortunes.

Partnering with individuals of such means can be extremely exciting. No one accumulates an immense fortune without possessing real intelligence, and some of these philanthropists can ask extremely challenging and interesting questions. People want to have some confidence that their investment, even if it's a charitable donation, has some chance of yielding a big return like, say, a new drug or a durable discovery. Some will even shop around for just the right institute or individual, as if they are studying the racing form to pick the winning thoroughbred. Meeting with these folks is not for the faint of heart, but just as we evaluate research proposals to find the ones with the best promise, philanthropists must get answers to their questions before they choose between a seemingly endless number of worthy proposals. The Harvard name (you could even call it a brand) might get us in the door, but no one will write a check on the basis of that alone. With this in mind, I worked to develop my ability to make the science understandable and discovered I enjoy it.

I have also come to enjoy even the difficult aspects of managing scientists, which often means helping brilliant young people stay on track in the face of technical and personal challenges. Everyone who comes to our labs is hoping, in the end, to develop medicines that cure. The best people for this work are fiercely independent and feel a powerful drive to achieve. The problem is that fiercely independent people sometimes struggle to take advice, even when it's in their best interest. In one recent case I spent a year counseling a truly brilliant person who cannot see he has reached a scientific dead end. In every conversation my advice has been met with a proposal to test one more compound, and then another. The trouble is that each test can take months to complete. Before you know it, a gifted mind has wasted a year chasing a chemical ghost. My task in these situations, which arise quite often, is to serve as mentor, parent, boss, and coach. In this instance a new teammate, added at my suggestion, has helped set the project on a new, Plan B course. In the process the original scientist is developing a bit more emotional intelligence.

This may be the moment to note that even with all the technical resources at our disposal, from instruments to artificial intelligence, science still needs the human touch. The best example may be in the hard-to-quantify but nevertheless significant force of intuition. What most of us experience as hunches can turn out to be signals from the brain, which is observing developments and making connections at a rate faster than we can comprehend. That nagging feeling about a hypothesis or an experiment can be an emotional prod, deployed by the subconscious. Studies of the brain done with FMRI (functional magnetic resonance imaging) machines have located parts of the brain that fire when intuition is sparked. The best theories suggest that the feelings produced in these moments of inspiration represent the brain's effort to snap the conscious mind to attention to something that engages its computing capacity at its highest levels. This process was understood by Albert Einstein to represent the "leap in consciousness" that is more valuable to the process of discovery than the intellect.

Although it's not medicine, modern biology is a passionate pursuit that engages as much of you as you can give and requires an expansive and generous style. The idea of the isolated scientist alone with his or her thoughts and experiments has been eclipsed by the model demonstrated to me decades ago by Adel Mahmoud, who was as good with people as he was with ideas. I see this quality in many of the younger scientists affiliated with the stem cell institute. In addition to their scientific brilliance they are resilient and effective at leading team talents. However, there is plenty of room for improvement. Some of our young scientists have to be drawn out, encouraged to think big, and prodded along the path. Others must be mentored in the art of letting go. We have to kill projects, which is fine because there's value in checking off the answer to any question, even if it's disappointing.

Fortunately, there is always the next idea. And in time you will see your work added to others to create a better and longer life for many. This is the result I hoped to realize when I first recognized the power of blood and bone. It seems to be coming faster every day.

POSTSCRIPT: SCIENCE IN THE FUTURE TENSE

In every generation, science and medicine are challenged to make genuine progress in a way that truly serves humanity. Success in medical science depends on a hierarchy of interests that starts with the physical and emotional suffering of individuals and their families who deserve compassionate care. Step higher and you encounter ways that communities can be served through sanitation, safe food supplies, immunizations, and other prevention strategies. Science should make all the baseline efforts of care and prevention better, and more effective, while limiting unintended negative outcomes.

Unfortunately, the frontier quality of some research can make it impossible to see that a new medicine or technology comes with risks. Radiation used for the diagnosis and treatment of some diseases was not known to cause malignancies until they had already occurred. More commonly, as you've read in these pages, promising therapies turn out to be less useful than initially imagined. However, these disappointments should not discourage us entirely. In oncology, for example, some treatments that disappoint after appearing to be breakthroughs still work for just a small number of patients with specific genetic mutations. Patients who are diagnosed with the same general kind of cancer but fall outside this subgroup may feel devastated by this twist of fate. But those who occupy the thrilling sweet spot are certain that all the effort to develop the therapy was more than justified.

In the biological age, when genomic sequencing is becoming routine, we have reached a point where most cancers can be screened for mutations. This practice is now routine at major medical centers and is making its way to community hospitals and oncology clinics nationwide. Similar screening is now possible for a variety of diseases and has improved both diagnosis and treatment in dramatic ways. For example, in a recent positing on a popular website called The Mighty, a young woman who had lived for two decades with a diagnosis of cerebral palsy recounted how genetic screening determined she had a different disorder—dopa-responsive dystonia—that could be treated with a single medication. She took the pills and began to walk unassisted, a day later.

Dramatic success stories are not the norm, but they become more possible with inexpensive gene sequencing and as we get better at processing huge amounts of data. The information I'm talking about is collected every day, in billions of bits, as people move through the health care system, track their fitness on wearable devices, manage their diabetes with finger-stick tests, and complete electronic health diaries.

As of 2017, far too little of this data is being scooped up, organized, and used in an effective way. However, efforts are being made to correct this problem. In 2015 the government launched the Precision Medicine Initiative Cohort Program, which will enroll one million people in a program that will collect biological samples for genetic testing and medical histories. Individuals will, of course, be notified if something is discovered in their samples. However, the main purpose of the project will be to provide research fodder for scientists studying a huge range of health issues. Organizers believe they will discover relationships between environment and various conditions, and, perhaps, identify diseases that appear connected.

They also expect the project will establish the basis for trials of targeted drugs by creating groups of people with relevant genomes and helping scientists locate and work with them

Experts who collect and manage billions of pieces of information refer to it, generally, as Big Data. Big Data, and, to be more precise, the ability to process Big Data, causes excitement because it allows us to act with more knowledge and less guesswork. Genetic testing can determine which people will respond to a special drug and which will not. This is what it meant by the term "precision medicine." Many tech companies are moving into this field with huge investments. IBM's "Watson," which is an advanced artificial-intelligence technology, has been adapted to provide information about treatment options to breast cancer patients who submit their genetic information.

An aid and not a replacement for doctors, Watson was found to closely match so-called tumor board recommendations when tested by a big health care system in Bangalore. IBM is also using Watson to check medical imaging results and other test results to uncover diseases that have been overlooked. Beyond oncology, IBM is looking at using Watson to read imaging and consult medical records to find patients who may have early-stage heart disease or be vulnerable to stroke and certain types of eye disease or neurological conditions. Intel is working on a project called All in One Day, which will give cancer patients both a genetic profile of their malignancies and a plan of treatment within twenty-four hours of their diagnosis. The target price for the service is $1,000. Today this process can take weeks or even months, and costs much more.

For high-level science, the next step in Big Data could involve liberating information to serve more purposes. Right now, academic scientists, private laboratories, pharmaceutical companies, and others feel enormous pressure to protect the information they collect in order to maximize the reward for all their hard work. To some extent the incentives to keep this work secret make sense. Who would invest all the time and money required by science if someone else can come along and capture the benefits? However, if there's one thing that was learned from the human genome project it was that people working together, in an open-source way, can push science along very rapidly. The key to encouraging this pace will lie in maintaining the kind of incentives that drive people to create while opening up avenues of collaboration.

In medicine, the challenge of information overload will grow greater every year. Managing may well involve technologies that allow us to monitor patience remotely, leaving much of the routine work to some form of artificial intelligence. I'm not saying that doctor robots will be taking over, although we will become more reliant on some forms of computing. Instead, we will depend on sophisticated algorithms, which will improve on their own as data grows. This technology will tell us how people respond to medications taken in different doses, at different points in their illness, and under varying conditions of stress. Inputs on diet and exercise could change our understanding of how drugs are metabolized.

The great potential available to us with a rapidly expanding knowledge base and biologically precise therapies, many of which will leverage the power of the immune system, suggest a future rich in possibilities. The promise also calls upon us to embrace the guidance available, not in technology or biology, but in the humanities. Using what we are discovering is going to require an ethic that takes into consideration the value of each human being and the recognition that we all deserve care and cures. Recent research has turned up the fact that in America, one's health can depend on where you live, right down to a particular neighborhood in a city or town. A recent decline in the life expectancy of middle-class whites in America, driven mainly by stress-related issues—substance abuse, mental health crises—tells us that it's not enough to develop treatments to target organic illnesses. We must attend to the human spirit along with the body and this requires respect for the human experience.

Science in the service of society will give us medicine that is also just. My experience in both communities—those of caregiving and research—give me hope in this regard. Almost no one takes up either without the desire to see suffering reduced and health increased across communities, nations, and the globe. This improvement, in all our lives, is the future we will realize. And it is coming fast.

ACKNOWLEDGMENTS

It has been a privilege to work with Michael D'Antonio. Michael's friendship, patience, and storytelling prowess have converted our conversations about medical science into this book that I hope will convey the purpose-driven creativity that is that process. Michael endured much with indomitable good cheer throughout. His enormous skills as writer and researcher are superseded only by his humanity; I am forever indebted to him and his friendship is much cherished.

A book is the product of every influence in an author's life, and this is especially true for the people who provide love, friendship, inspiration, and guidance. Kathryn Scadden, the love of my life and my partner in every sense of the word, can be felt in every compassionate passage of this text. Margaret Scadden, Elizabeth Scadden, and Ned Scadden are all here in their distinctively inspiring and deeply virtuous ways: they make every day richer and worthy.

From an early age, I was instructed in matters of humanity and curiosity-driven pursuits by my parents, grandparents, sisters, friends, neighbors and classmates. My sisters encouraged me and while I never had brothers, four people became my brothers in all but blood: Tim Reynolds, Keith Mendelson, Bruce Walker, and Doug Melton. I am a better human because of them.

I am indebted to those who sparked my love of learning and gave me confidence that curiosity could turn to useful action. First and foremost are my parents, my teachers like George Walthoff, my family doctor, Salvatore Baldino, my professors at Bucknell like Michael Payne, John Murphy, and James Carens, my classmate and friend John Richard, my inspirations in medical school Adel Mahmoud, Charles Carpenter, Richard Graham, and George Bernier, and those extraordinary physicians who shaped my medical career like E. Franklin Bunn, David Rosenthal, Marshall Wolf, Eugene Braunwald, George Canellos, Robert Mayer, Robert Schwartz, Jerome Groopman, James Cunningham, John Potts, Kurt Isselbacher, and especially, Bruce Chabner.

It is impossible to pursue science without the material and emotional support of individuals and institutions. I am forever grateful to Gerald and Darlene Jordan for the honor of a Harvard Chair in their name, to John Hess, Wilber and Janet James, Craig and Tracey Huff, Susan and Michael Hazard, and the many donors who have given stem cell science at Harvard and MGH the opportunity to deliver benefit for patients. The leaders of the institutions I have been fortunate to be a part of make an often unsung, but enormous impact on the lives they shape and foster. I thank them and MGH, Harvard, BWH, Case Western Reserve and Bucknell for what they have given me.

Those who been my students or post-doctoral fellows have been an intellectual family whom I treasure and whose success is an ever-expanding source of joy. It has been a privilege to work with them. They include: Barbara Fuller, DVM, Anna Berardi, Ph.D., David Feder, M.D., Andrew Freedman, M.D., Ph.D., Lucia Columbyova, M.D., Michael Franken, M.D., Hongmei Shen, Ph.D., Tao Cheng, M.D., Nadia Carlesso, M.D., Ph.D., Antonio Daga, M.D., Ph.D., Tajiro Ishiyama, M.D., Jason Gardner, Ph.D., Byeong-Chel Lee, Ph.D., Christian Brander, Ph.D., Mark Poznansky, M.D., Ph.D., Richard Evans, M.D., Nobuyuki Miura, M.D., Ph.D., Neil

Rodrigues, Ph.D., John Patrick Whelan, M.D., Ph.D., Zhengyu Wang, Ph.D., Paula O'Connor, M.D., Leonor Sarmento, Ph.D., Kenneth Cohen, M.D., Sebastian Stier, M.D., Gregor Adams, Ph.D., Yorikio Saito, M.D., Henry Dong, M.D., Ph.D., Zbigniew Szczepiorkowski, M.D., Ph.D., Robin Mayfield, M.D., Anna Gallazi, M.D., Dipti Patel, M.D., Randolf Forkert, M.D., Paul Robertson, MRCP, Eyal Attar, M.D., Dojun Gohara, Ph.D., Todd Suscovich, Ph.D., Keith Orford, M.D., Ph.D., Dorothy Sipkins, M.D., Ph.D., Chou-Wen Lin, Ph.D., Tong Chen, M.D., Richard Haspel, M.D., Ph.D., Heather Fleming, Ph.D., Viktor Janzen, M.D., Jonas Larsson, M.D., Ph.D., Louise Purton, Ph.D., Siddhartha Mukherjee, M.D., Ph.D., Nathaniel Jeanson, Ph.D., Brian Garrison, Ph.D., Shangqin Guo, Ph.D., Cristina LoCelso, Ph.D., Stephanie Xie, Ph.D., Marc Raaijmakers, M.D., Ph.D., Andre Catic, M.D., Ph.D., Daniela Krause, M.D., Ph.D., Borja Saez, Ph.D., Dongsu Park, Ph.D., Vionnie Yu, Ph.D., Siyi Zhang, Ph.D., Rushdia Yousuf, M.D., Lev Silberstein, M.D., Ph.D., Stephen Sykes, Ph.D., Stephania Lymperi, Ph.D., Gerd Bungartz, Ph.D., Francesca Ferraro, M.D., Ph.D., Jorg Dietrich, M.D., Ph.D., Ying-Hua Wang, Ph.D., Andrew Lane, M.D., Ph.D., David Sykes, M.D., Ph.D., Francois Mercier, M.D., Christine Ragu, Ph.D., Youmna Kfoury, Ph.D., Dongjun Lee, Ph.D., Jonathan Hoggatt, Ph.D., Rahul Palchaudhuri, Ph.D., Julien Cobert, M.D., Ninib Baryawno, Ph.D., Nicolas Severe, Ph.D., Demetrios Kalatzidis, Ph.D., Toshihoko Oki, M.D., Ph.D., Karin Gustafsson, Ph.D., Nisarg Shah, Ph.D., Amir Schjanovich, Ph.D., Nick Van Gastel, Ph.D., Yiping Wang, Ph.D., Azeem Sharda, MS, Cheuk-Him Man, Ph.D., Catherine Rhee, Ph.D., Xiao-Jing Yan, M.D., Ph.D., Adrian Berg, B.S., Phillip Chea, B.S., and Ting Zhao, Ph.D.

It is not possible to thank enough the people who have been partners in making laboratory science and clinical care mesh without daily chaos. My assistant, Lisa Tramontozzi, has been heroic and ever cheerful in keeping the wheels turning. Those before her, including Ellen Kornell and Chris Pasker, also have my special thanks. The Center for Regenerative Medicine at MGH could not exist without the tireless effort, commitment and indefatigable good humor of Dave Machon. Brock Reeve has been a beacon of strength and creative drive for the Harvard Stem Cell Institute. Catherine Link, Willy Lensch, Ph.D. and now Heather Rooke, Ph.D. managed the Department of Stem Cell and Regenerative Biology at Harvard University with exceptional skill and personal touch. I am indebted to them and those they lead for their dedication and friendship.

Finally, colleagues and patients are the greatest source of inspiration and wisdom for anyone in medical research. I cannot name them all nor adequately express how I value their spirited engagement with our shared mission to improve health. Collectively, they are the true wellspring of ideas and motivation. My work in clinical cancer research was made possible by a team that was unparalleled in commitment to giving patients the best possible care. They are Jocelyn Bresnahan, R.N., Walter Howard, P.A., and Kathleen Shea. I would be remiss to not thank one patient in particular, Linda Allen, who has shown how joyful living and serendipity can mean everything, even in Cancerland.

BIBLIOGRAPHY

INTRODUCTION

Bero, Lisa A. "Tobacco Industry Manipulation of Research." *Public Health Reports* 120, no. 2 (2005): 200–208.

Hartmaier, Ryan J., Jehad Charo, David Fabrizio, Michael E. Goldberg, Lee A. Albacker, William Pao, and Juliann Chmielecki. "Genomic Analysis of 63,220 Tumors Reveals Insights into Tumor Uniqueness and Targeted Cancer Immunotherapy Strategies." *Genome Medicine* 9, no. 1 (2017): 16.

Mukherjee, Siddhartha. *The Emperor of All Maladies: A Biography of Cancer.* New York: Scribner, 2011.

Nightingale, Stuart L. "Laetrile: The Regulatory Challenge of an Unproven Remedy." *Public Health Reports* 99, no. 4 (1984): 333–338.

Public Papers of the Presidents of the United States, Richard Nixon, 1971: Containing the Public Messages, Speeches, and Statements of the President. Washington, D.C.: General Services Administration, 1999. 406–410.

Sinkovics, J. G., R. J. Pienta, J. M. Trujillo, and M. J. Ahearn. "An Immunological Explanation for the Starry Sky Histological Pattern of a Malignant Lymphoma." *Journal of Infectious Diseases* 120, no. 2 (1969): 250–254.

CHAPTER 1: DAWN OF THE BIOLOGICAL AGE

Campisi, J. "Aging, Cellular Senescence, and Cancer." *Annual Review of Physiology* 75 (2013): 685–705. http://doi.org/10.1146/annurev-physiol-030212-183653.

"Cancer May Be Infectious." *Life*, July 22, 1962.

Chedd, Graham. "Threat to U.S. Genetic Engineering." *New Scientist*, July 1, 1978, 14.

De Chadarevian, Soraya. "Sequences, Conformation, Information: Biochemists and Molecular Biologists in the 1950s." *Journal of the History of Biology* 29, no. 3 (1996): 361–386.

Edelson, Edward. *Francis Crick and James Watson: And the Building Blocks of Life.* New York: Oxford University Press, 1998.

Falkow, S. "The Lessons of Asilomar and the H5N1 'Affair.'" *mBio* 3, no. 5 (2012): e00354-12. doi:10.1128/mBio.00354-12.

Goodell, Rae S. "Public Involvement in the DNA Controversy: The Case of Cambridge, Massachusetts." *Science, Technology, & Human Values* 4, no. 27 (1979): 36–43.

Jones, James. *Bad Blood: The Tuskegee Syphilis Experiment*. New and expanded edition. New York: Free Press, 1993.

McCall, Matt. "The Secret Lives of Cadavers: How Lifeless Bodies Become Life-Saving Tools." *National Geographic*, July 29, 2016.

McLaughlin-Drubin, Margaret E., and Karl Munger. "Viruses Associated with Human Cancer." *Biochimica et Biophysica Acta* 1782, no. 3 (2008): 127–150. doi:10.1016/j.bbadis.2007.12.005.

von Boehmer, Harald. "Thoracic Thymus, Exclusive No Longer." *Science* 312, no. 5771 (2006): 206–207.

Weisz, George. "The Emergence of Medical Specialization in the Nineteenth Century." *Bulletin of the History of Medicine* 77 (2003): 536–575.

Wiernik, Peter H., John M. Goldman, Janice P. Dutcher, and Robert A. Kyle, eds. *Neoplastic Diseases of the Blood*. New York: Springer, 2013. 825.

CHAPTER 2: SEEING CANCER

Aptowicz, Cristin O'Keefe. "The Dawn of Modern Anesthesia." *Atlantic*, September 4, 2014.

Gill, P. S., et al. "Paclitaxel is safe and effective in the treatment of advanced AIDS-related Kaposi's sarcoma." *Journal of Clinical Oncology* 17, no. 6 (1999): 1876–1883.

Grimes, Jack, et al. "The Roles of Water, Sanitation, and Hygiene in Reducing Schistosomiasis: A Review." *Parasites & Vectors* 8 (2015): 156.

Hollingham, Richard. *Blood and Guts: A History of Surgery*. New York: St. Martin's Griffin, 2009.

Imber, Gerald. *Genius on the Edge: The Bizarre Double Life of Dr. William Stewart Halsted*. New York: Kaplan Publishing, 2010.

Sakorafas, G. H. "Breast Cancer Surgery—Historical Evolution, Current Status and Future Perspectives." *Acta Oncologica* 40, no. 1 (2001): 5–18.

Strain, Daniel. "Crushing Cancer's Defenses: Vaccine Approval Offers Hope While Other Armies Muster." *Science News* 179, no. 10 (2011): 20–23. www.jstor.org/stable/41332337.

Teng, Michele W. L., et al. "From Mice to Humans: Developments in Cancer Immunoediting." *Journal of Clinical Investigation* 125, no. 9 (2015): 3338–3346.

Tilney, Nicholas L. *Invasion of the Body: Revolutions in Surgery*. Cambridge, MA: Harvard University Press, 2011.

Villa, Nancy Y., et al. "Therapeutics for Graft-versus-Host Disease: From Conventional Therapies to Novel Virotherapeutic Strategies." *Viruses* 8, no. 3 (2016): 85.

CHAPTER 3: CANCERLAND

Ward, R. M. "The Criminal Corpse, Anatomists and the Criminal Law: Parliamentary Attempts to Extend the Dissection of Offenders in Late Eighteenth-Century England." *Journal of British Studies* 54, no. 1 (2015): 63–87. doi:10.1017/jbr.2014.167.

"A Failure Led to Drug Against AIDS." *New York Times*. September 20, 1986. http://www.nytimes.com/1986/09/20/us/a-failure-led-to-drug-against -aids.html.

Albritton, Lorraine, Lena Tseng, David Scadden, and James M. Cunningham. "A Putative Murine Ecotropic Retrovirus Receptor Gene Encodes a Multiple Membrane-Spanning Protein and Confers Susceptibility to Virus Infection." *Cell* 57, no. 4 (1989): 659–666. doi:10.1016/0092-8674(89)90134-7.

Chapple, A., et al. "Stigma, Shame, and Blame Experienced by Patients with Lung Cancer: Qualitative Study." *British Medical Journal* 328, no. 7454 (2004): 1470–1473. http://www.jstor.org/stable/41708038.

de la Morena, M. T., and R. A. Gatti. "A History of Bone Marrow Transplantation." *Hematology/Oncology Clinics of North America* 25, no. 1 (2011): 1–15. doi:10.1016/j.hoc.2010.11.001.

Engel, Jonathan. *The Epidemic: A Global History of AIDS*. Washington, D.C.: Smithsonian Press, 2006.

Goodman, Jordan, and Vivien Walsh. *The Story of Taxol*. Cambridge, UK: Cambridge University Press, 2001.

Greenberg, Daniel S. *Science for Sale*. Chicago: University of Chicago Press, 2008. 73–80.

"GSS General Social Survey." NORC at the University of Chicago. http://gss .norc.org.

Hamburg, N. "Emil 'Tom' Frei III." *British Medical Journal* 347, no. 7920 (2013): 26.

Holland, James F., and Emil Frei III, eds. *Cancer Medicine*. Philadelphia: Lea & Febiger, 1973.

Kolata, Gina, and Kurt Eichenwald. "Hope for Sale: A Special Report; Business Thrives on Unproven Care, Leaving Science Behind." *New York Times*, October 3, 1999. http://www.nytimes.com/1999/10/03/us/hope-for -sale-special-report-business-thrives-unproven-care-leaving-science .html.

Kuhn, Thomas. *The Structure of Scientific Revolutions*. Chicago: University of Chicago Press, 1962.

"Medicines from Nature." Harvard T. H. Chan School of Public Health. http:// www.chgeharvard.org/topic/medicines-nature.

Newman, D. J., and G. M. Cragg. "Natural Products as Sources of New Drugs over the 30 Years from 1981 to 2010." *Journal of Natural Products* 75, no. 3 (2012): 311–335.

Pavlů, Jiří, Richard M. Szydlo, John M. Goldman, and Jane F. Apperley. "Three Decades of Transplantation for Chronic Myeloid Leukemia: What

Have We Learned?" *Blood* 117 (2011): 755–763. https://doi.org/10.1182/blood-2010-08-301341.

Rettig, Richard A., et al. *False Hope: Bone Marrow Transplantation for Breast Cancer.* New York: Oxford University Press, 2007. 28–29.

Roush, W. "Dana-Farber Death Sends a Warning to Research Hospitals." *Science* 269, no. 5222 (1995): 295–296.

Scadden, D. T., Fuller, R., and J. M. Canningham. "Human cells infected with retrovirus vectors acquire an endogenous murine provirus." *Journal of Virology* 64, no. 1 (1990): 407–427.

Sibbald, B. "Death but One Unintended Consequence of Gene-Therapy Trial." *Canadian Medical Association Journal* 164, no. 11 (2001): 1612.

"Technology Transfer: NIH–Private Sector Partnership in the Development of Taxol." Washington, D.C.: Government Accounting Office, June 2003.

Yu, Nancy, Zachary Helms, and Peter Bach. "R&D Costs for Pharmaceutical Companies Do Not Explain Elevated U.S. Drug Prices." *Health Affairs*, March 7, 2017.

CHAPTER 4: CHEMICALS IN CONVERSATION

Berardi, A. C., Wang, A., Levine, J. D., Lopez, P., and D. T. Scadden. "Functional isolation and characterization of human hematopoietic stem cells." *Science* 267, no. 5194 (1995): 104–108.

Berman, Mark, and Elliot Lander. *The Stem Cell Revolution.* Bloomington, IN: AuthorHouse, 2015.

Bonnicksen, Andrea L. *In Vitro Fertilization: Building Policy from Laboratories to Legislatures.* New York: Columbia University Press, 1989.

Collins, Nick. "Sir John Gurdon, Nobel Prize Winner, Was 'Too Stupid' for Science at School." *Telegraph*, October 8, 2012. http://www.telegraph.co.uk/news/science/science-news/9594351/Sir-John-Gurdon-Nobel-Prize-winner-was-too-stupid-for-science-at-school.html.

Davis, Rebecca, and Joe Palca. "A Scientist's Dream Fulfilled: Harnessing the Immune System to Fight Cancer." NPR. June 9, 2016. http://www.npr.org/sections/health-shots/2016/06/09/480435066/a-scientists-dream-fulfilled-harnessing-the-immune-system-to-fight-cancer.

Dick, J. "Breast Cancer Stem Cells Revealed." *Proceedings of the National Academy of Sciences of the United States of America* 100, no. 7 (2003): 3547–3549.

Grady, Denise. "They Got Breast Implants, Then a Rare Cancer." *New York Times*, May 15, 2017.

Jacobsen, Eric. "Anaplastic Large-Cell Lymphoma, T-/Null-Cell Type." *Oncologist* 11, no. 7 (2006): 837–840. http://theoncologist.alphamedpress.org/content/11/7/831.full.

McElheny, Victor K. *Drawing the Map of Life: Inside the Human Genome Project.* New York: Basic Books, 2010.

Shen, H., et al. "CXCR4-desensitization is associated with tissue localization of hematopoietic progenitor cells." *Journal of Immunology*, 166, no. 8 (2001): 5027–5033.

Venter, J. Craig. "Taking Genomics into the Environment." *BioScience* 56, no. 3 (2006): 197–201. doi:10.1641/0006-3568(2006)056[0197:jcvtgi]2.0 .co;2.

Wade, Nicholas. "Genome Analysis Shows Humans Survive on Low Number of Genes." *New York Times*, February 11, 2001.

Yanai, Itai, and Martin Lercher. *The Society of Genes*. Cambridge, MA: Harvard University Press, 2016.

CHAPTER 5: STEM CELLS AND A RENEWABLE YOU

Carnes, Bruce A., and S. Jay Olshansky. *The Quest for Immortality: Science at the Frontiers of Aging*. New York: W. W. Norton, 2002.

Druker, B. J. "Janet Rowley (1925–2013)." *Nature* 505, no. 7484 (2014): 484.

Grens, Kerry. "Amy Wagers: Setting the Record Straight." *Scientist*, January 1, 2008. http://www.the-scientist.com/?articles.view/articleNo/25891/title /Amy-Wagers—Setting-the-record-straight/.

Lawler, A. "Steering Harvard toward Collaborative Science." *Science* 321, no. 5886 (2008): 190–192.

Lin, H., M. Otsu, and H. Nakauchi. "Stem Cell Therapy: An Exercise in Patience and Prudence." *Philosophical Transactions of the Royal Society B: Biological Sciences* 368, no. 1609 (2013): 1–14.

Maehr, R., S. Chen, M. Snitow, T. Ludwig, L. Yagasaki, R. Goland, R. Leibel, and D. Melton. "Generation of Pluripotent Stem Cells from Patients with Type 1 Diabetes." *Proceedings of the National Academy of Sciences of the United States of America* 106, no. 37 (2009): 15768–15773.

Marx, J. "Cancer Fighter's Modus Operandi Revealed." *Science* 289, no. 5486 (2000): 1857–1859.

Melton, D., and H. Lodish. "Stem Cell Challenges in Biology and Public Policy." *Bulletin of the American Academy of Arts and Sciences* 60, no. 4 (2007): 6–12.

Sinatra, Roberta, Dashun Wang, Pierre Deville, Chaoming Song, and Albert-László Barabási. "Quantifying the Evolution of Individual Scientific Impact." *Science* 354, no. 6312 (2016). http://science.sciencemag.org/content /354/6312/aaf5239.

Travis, J. "Gleevec, Chapter Two: New Leukemia Drug Aims to Overcome Resistance." *Science* 305, no. 5682 (2004): 319–321.

CHAPTER 6: SNUPPY THE HOUND AND iPSCs

Brooke, James. "Without Apology, Leaping Ahead in Cloning." *New York Times*, May 31, 2005. http://www.nytimes.com/2005/05/31/science/without -apology-leaping-ahead-in-cloning.html.

Cutler, D. "Are We Finally Winning the War on Cancer?" *Journal of Economic Perspectives* 22, no. 4 (2008): 3–26.

Haber, Daniel A., et al. "An Internal Deletion within an 11p13 Zinc Finger Gene Contributes to the Development of Wilms' Tumor." *Cell* 61, no. 7 (1990): 1257–1269.

Holden, C., D. Normile, and C. Mann. "Asia Jockeys for Stem Cell Lead." *Science* 307, no. 5710 (2005): 660–664.

Keidan, J. "Medicine and the Media: Sucked into the Herceptin Maelstrom." *British Medical Journal* 334, no. 7583 (2007): 18.

Normile, D. "Shinya Yamanaka: Modest Researcher, Results to Brag About." *Science* 319, no. 5863 (2008): 562.

CHAPTER 7: PROVOKING A RESPONSE

Bhat, R., and C. Watzl. "Serial Killing of Tumor Cells by Human Natural Killer Cells—Enhancement by Therapeutic Antibodies." *PLOS ONE* 2, no. 3 (2007): e326. doi:10.1371/journal.pone.0000326.

Cohen, J. "Building an HIV-Proof Immune System." *Science* 317, no. 5838 (2007): 612–614.

Radic, M. "Armed and Accurate: Engineering Cytotoxic T Cells for Eradication of Leukemia." *BMC Biotechnology* 12 (2012): 6. doi:10.1186/1472-6750-12-6.

Sedwick, C. "Craig Thompson: The Method to Cancer's Madness." *Journal of Cell Biology* 191, no. 4 (2010): 696–697.

"Vaccines: Calling the Shots." PBS video, 53:10. http://www.pbs.org/wgbh/nova/body/vaccines-calling-shots.html.

Wailoo, Keith, Julie Livingston, Steven Epstein, and Robert Aronowitz, eds. *Three Shots at Prevention: The HPV Vaccine and the Politics of Medicine's Simple Solutions.* Baltimore, M.D.: Johns Hopkins University Press, 2010.

CHAPTER 8: GENE HACKING

Bennett, Jay. "11 Crazy Gene-Hacking Things We Can Do with CRISPR." *Popular Mechanics*, January 26, 2016. http://www.popularmechanics.com/science/a19067/11-crazy-things-we-can-do-with-crispr-cas9/.

"Cancer Stat Facts: Melanoma of the Skin." National Cancer Institute. https://seer.cancer.gov/statfacts/html/melan.html.

Fineran, P., M. Gerritzen, M. Suárez-Diez, T. Künne, J. Boekhorst, S. van Hijum, R. Staals, and S. Brouns. "Degenerate Target Sites Mediate Rapid Primed CRISPR Adaptation." *Proceedings of the National Academy of Sciences of the United States of America* 111, no. 16 (2014): 5772.

Horvath, P., and R. Barrangou. "CRISPR/Cas, the Immune System of Bacteria and Archaea." *Science* 327, no. 5962 (2010): 167–170.

June, Carl H. "Drugging the Undruggable Ras—Immunotherapy to the Rescue?" *New England Journal of Medicine* 375 (2016): 2286–2289. doi:10.1056/NEJMe1612215.

Lou, Dianne I., et al. "An Intrinsically Disordered Region of the DNA Repair Protein Nbs1 Is a Species-Specific Barrier to Herpes Simplex Virus 1 in Primates." *Cell Host & Microbe* 20, no. 2 (2016): 178–188.

"6 Year Survivor on Ipilimumab/Yervoy." Melanoma Research Foundation. March 28, 2011. https://www.melanoma.org/find-support/patient-community/mpip-melanoma-patients-information-page/6-year-survivor-ipilimumab-yervoy.

Staahl, Brett T., et al. "Efficient Genome Editing in the Mouse Brain by Local Delivery of Engineered Cas9 Ribonucleoprotein Complexes." *Nature Biotechnology* 35, no. 5 (2017): 431–434. doi:10.1038/nbt.3806.

Walkington, L., P. Lorigan, and S. Danson. "Advances in the Treatment of Late Stage Melanoma: Immunotherapies and Targeted Treatments: The Future of Cancer Therapy." *British Medical Journal* 346, no. 7898 (2013): 10.

"World First Use of Gene-Edited Immune Cells to Treat 'Incurable' Leukaemia." Great Ormond Street Hospital for Children. November 5, 2015. http://www.gosh.nhs.uk/news/latest-press-releases/2015-press-release-archive/world-first-use-gene-edited-immune-cells-treat-incurable-leukaemia.

CHAPTER 9: FROM GORY TO GLORY

Atkins, Harold L. "Immunoablation and Autologous Haemopoietic Stem-Cell Transplantation for Aggressive Multiple Sclerosis: A Multicentre Single-Group Phase 2 Trial." *Lancet* 388, no. 10044 (2016): 576–585.

Bailey, Ronald. "Transhumanism: The Most Dangerous Idea? Why Striving to Be More Than Human Is Human." Reason.com. August 25, 2004. http://reason.com/archives/2004/08/25/transhumanism-the-most-dangero.

Bombar, D., R. W. Paerl, and L. Riemann. "Marine Non-Cyanobacterial Diazotrophs: Moving beyond Molecular Detection." *Trends in Microbiology* 24, no. 11 (2016). http://dx.doi.org/10.1016/j.tim.2016.07.002.

Calvi, L. M., et al. "Osteoblastic cells regulate the hematopoietic stem cell niche." *Nature* 425, no. 6960 (2003): 841–846.

Cha, Ariana Eunjung. "The Human Upgrade." *Washington Post*, April 14, 2015. http://www.washingtonpost.com/sf/national/2015/04/04/tech-titans-latest-project-defy-death/.

Gilpin, S. E., et al. "Bioengineering Lungs for Transplantation." *Thoracic Surgery Clinics* 26, no. 2 (2016): 163–171. doi:10.1016/j.thorsurg.2015.12.004.

Greenstone, Gerry. "The History of Bloodletting." *BC Medical Journal* 52, no. 1 (2010): 12–14.

Koch, Christof. "Intuition May Reveal Where Expertise Resides in the Brain." *Scientific American*, May 1, 2015. https://www.scientificamerican.com/article/intuition-may-reveal-where-expertise-resides-in-the-brain/.

Marx, Vivien. "Where Stem Cells Call Home." *Nature Methods* 10 (2013): 111–115. doi:10.1038/nmeth.2336.

Palchaudhuri, R., et al. "Non-genotoxic conditioning for hematopoietic stem cell transplantation using a hematopoietic-cell-specific internalizing immunotoxin." *Nature Biotechnology* 37, no. 7 (2016): 738–745.

Phoenix, T. N., and S. Temple. "Spred1, a Negative Regulator of Ras-MAPK-ERK, Is Enriched in CNS Germinal Zones, Dampens NSC Proliferation, and Maintains Ventricular Zone Structure." *Genes & Development* 24, no. 1 (2010): 45–56.

Ribatti, D., and E. Crivellato. "Giulio Bizzozero and the Discovery of Platelets." *Leukemia Research* 31, no. 10 (2007): 1339–1341. doi:10.1016/j.leukres.2007.02.008.

Robbins, Hannah. "Progress against Acute Myeloid Leukemia." *Harvard Gazette*, September 15, 2016. http://news.harvard.edu/gazette/story/2016/09/progress-against-acute-myeloid-leukemia/.

Seppa, N. "Kidney Rebuilt Using Fresh Cells." *Science News* 183, no. 10 (2013): 14.

Villanueva, M. Teresa. "Pushing Differentiation." *Nature Reviews Cancer* 16, no. 678 (2016). doi:10.1038/nrc.2016.110.

White, Mary C., Dawn M. Holman, Jennifer E. Boehm, Lucy A. Peipins, Melissa Grossman, and S. Jane Henley. "Age and Cancer Risk: A Potentially Modifiable Relationship." *American Journal of Preventive Medicine* 46, no. 3S1 (2014): S7–15. doi:10.1016/j.amepre.2013.10.029.

INDEX